Event Policy

As the event management field expands, there has been an emergence of a distinctive 'event' policy field of study and a need for more advanced texts that look at this subject with a multidisciplinary research and theoretical orientation.

Event Policy: from theory to strategy is the first text to embrace this new direction in the field of event management. Its main aim is to locate the phenomena of events (and festivity) within a theoretical and strategic framework, and in doing so demonstrate the links between the development of events in policy-making and the theoretical exploration of the role of events as policy. Building on a strong, coherent framework, the book explores the conceptual terrain in which events and festivities are located, evaluates the range of theoretical perspectives pertinent to the study of event policy, appraises the socio-economic and socio-cultural implications of event-led policies internationally and draws together the main event policy issues for the future. It utilises a good range of international cases, from Dubai, Singapore, New Orleans and Glasgow, to help demonstrate the relationships between theory and strategy, and includes useful features to help students understand the subject and deepen their knowledge of the event policy terrain.

This groundbreaking volume will be essential reading for students, researchers and academics of events and other related disciplines.

Malcolm Foley is Vice Principal and Executive Dean at the University of the West of Scotland.

David McGillivray is a Reader in Events and Culture within the School of Creative and Cultural Industries at the University of the West of Scotland.

Gayle McPherson is a Professor of Events and Cultural Policy within the School of Creative and Cultural Industries at the University of the West of Scotland.

D0273629

Event Policy

From theory to strategy

**Malcolm Foley, David McGillivray
and Gayle McPherson**

Routledge
Taylor & Francis Group

LONDON AND NEW YORK

First published 2012
by Routledge
2 Park Square, Milton Park, Abingdon, Oxon OX14 4RN

Simultaneously published in the USA and Canada
by Routledge
711 Third Avenue, New York, NY 10017

Routledge is an imprint of the Taylor & Francis Group, an informa business

British Library Cataloguing in Publication Data
A catalogue record for this book is available
from the British Library

Library of Congress Cataloging-in-Publication Data
Foley, Malcolm.
  Event policy / Malcolm Foley, David McGillivray and Gayle
  McPherson.
  p. cm.
  Includes bibliographical references and index.
  1. Special events—Planning. 2. Special events—Management.
  I. McGillivray, David. II. McPherson, Gayle. III. Title.
  GT3405.F65 2011
  394.2—dc22   2011005286

ISBN: 978–0–415–54832–8 (hbk)
ISBN: 978–0–415–54833–5 (pbk)
ISBN: 978–0–203–80642–5 (ebk)

Typeset in Times New Roman
by Florence Production Ltd, Stoodleigh, Devon

Contents

List of illustrations   vii
Foreword   viii
Preface   ix
Acknowledgements   x

1 Event policy: an emerging field of study   1

PART I
Event policy rationales   19

2 Events and festivity: from ritual to regeneration   21
3 Trends in events and festivities: the policy panacea   32
4 Evaluating event outcomes: a legitimation crisis   49

PART II
Event policy formations   63

5 The politics of events in an age of accumulation   65
6 Consuming events: from bread and circuses to brand   76
7 Events and social capital: linking and empowering communities   89
8 Events as cultural capital: animating the urban   102

PART III
Event policy implementations   115

9 Glasgow 2014: demonstrating capacity and competence   117
10 Destination Dubai: event policy in an Arab state   130

11 Mardi Gras, New Orleans: policy intervention in an historical event   141

12 Singapore: a mixed economy of events   152

13 Conclusions   163

Bibliography   179
Index   192

Illustrations

Figures

3.1	Global shifts in tourist arrivals	38
3.2	The World Tourist Organization's '2020 Vision'	40
3.3	International tourism arrivals in Europe	41
3.4	International tourism expenditure in Germany around 2006	42
3.5	International tourist arrivals in the Middle East	43
3.6	International tourist arrivals in the Asia-Pacific	44
4.1	The balanced scorecard approach to evaluating events	57
13.1	Event policy typology	170
13.2	Event policy 'pull'	171

Tables

1.1	Event Management Stages of Complexity	7
13.1	Event dimensions	173

Boxes

2.1	Chingay Parade and Thaipusam Festival, Singapore	27
3.1	South Africa World Cup	47
4.1	The balanced scorecard approach	57
5.1	Place marketing events: Glasgow City Marketing Bureau	70
6.1	Destination Melbourne: the world's event capital	85
7.1	Molson Indy Vancouver	96
8.1	Notting Hill Carnival	111

Foreword

Firstly, I'd like to say how delighted I am to see a book like this being published at a time when competition to bid for, win and, deliver major sporting, cultural and business events has never been more intense. EventScotland was established in 2003 with the aim of strengthening and promoting Scotland's events industry. EventScotland does this by attracting, generating and sustaining a portfolio of world class events in Scotland, which help this small nation to compete successfully in an increasingly international market place and keep it aligned with its strategy 'Scotland The Perfect Stage'. This book is truly international in its outlook and content. It poses the right questions to policy makers – both governmental and non-governmental – and it encourages us all to strike the right balance between public support and private sponsorship of major events. As the Chief Operating Officer of EventScotland I am always mindful of the political, economic, social and cultural dimensions of events and the need to adopt impeccable standards of accountability, transparency and citizen involvement in each an every element of our own and partners' work.

Perhaps most importantly, this *Event Policy* title makes a clear statement to academics, governments and event owners that events are about policy; about competing claims to the allocation of scarce resources; about the balance between public subsidy (and ownership) and private capital investment. As someone involved in developing the rationale for events, forming policies to underpin them and ensuring effective implementation this text is presented in an exemplary manner. Students, academics, policy makers and practitioners will find the content both engaging and thought provoking.

Paul Bush, OBE

Preface

This book has been a long time in the making. From the initial development of a Leisure Management degree course at Glasgow Caledonian University in 1993, we always had it in mind to produce a text that offered a critical appraisal of the policy processes that pertain to leisure environments. That the eventual text is focused entirely on one leisure environment – events – illustrates the direction the study of leisure has taken in the ensuing eighteen years. The leisure sector can be segmented into the realms of sport, recreation, tourism, entertainment, hospitality and the like, but it is the events sector that has undergone the most spectacular growth over the last decade. This book is the culmination of our career-long collaboration that produced a plethora of other publications but had yet to produce a co-authored book. *Event Policy: from theory to strategy* addresses that omission and, hopefully, starts the ball rolling on the publication of a series of critical commentaries on the event management field.

Malcolm Foley, David McGillivray
and Gayle McPherson

Acknowledgements

Invaluable assistance in the completion of this book has been provided by the following people to whom we are greatly indebted: Matt Frew, Jenny Flinn, Daniel Turner, Aaron McIntosh, Robert Kielty, Andy Murray, Clare Mackay, Lynn Black, Sabina Siebert and Irene Brown. For their assistance in providing access for case study enquiries we would like to thank colleagues in Singapore, New Orleans, Glasgow and Dubai – there are too many to mention by name here. Our thanks also go to those who commissioned and assisted in the production of this work at Routledge, particularly Emma Travis, Faye Leerink and Michael Jones. Finally, we thank our partners and children, Claire, Aaron, Ethan, Michael, James and Daniel for allowing us to use some of their precious family time to complete this book.

1 Event policy

An emerging field of study

Introduction

Events are of local, national and international importance. They are important signifiers of personal, community, national and globalised identity. They represent opportunities for celebration and commiseration, for rejoicing and for resisting. They are political and politicised, ritualistic and regenerative. They come in both commercial and charitable forms, contributing to the logic of capitalism while simultaneously acting as vehicles for contesting it. They not only are written into history but can also be utilised to alter it. They are planned and unplanned, small and large, sporting and cultural, hallmark and special. Events touch everyone in one way or another, yet understandings of their impacts and outcomes remain underdeveloped. A lot is known about how they can be organised more efficiently and effectively, how they can be marketed, how they can be managed safely and how appropriate venues can be selected for their delivery. Much less is known about how ownership of events might be evaluated, about who should resource them, about choosing among competing claims for support, about which other public investments should be curtailed at their expense, about how they can best be used to assuage social and economic problems, and so on. These are questions of policy – of choices about how public funds should be allocated to address an identified problem, whether that is political, economic, social or environmental. This book asks these difficult questions and attempts to provide guidance upon how they might be answered effectively.

The growing significance of events

Whereas the *study* of events and festivities is a relatively recent phenomenon dating back a decade or two, their celebration has been long recorded. This chapter considers the development of the academic consideration of events in some detail. Before that task is undertaken it is prudent to illustrate their growing contemporary significance across a number of levels, from global to national to local, in order to provide both a context and a counterpoint for the rise in interest of 'the academy'. At a global level, the significance of events is almost beyond dispute. Few people on the planet were unaware of the 2008 Olympic Games in Beijing, China. Billions of the world's population tuned in to the 2010 FIFA World Cup Finals in South Africa. Over a decade ago Maurice Roche coined the term mega-event (Roche, 2000) to reflect events that were of short duration but produced long-term impacts; events that contained dramatic effect, changed whole economies and transformed national and international ideas of cultural citizenship, consumerism and collective identity. Alongside such wide-ranging powers to affect, these events were also said to generate mass popular appeal, culminating in increased inbound tourism to the host destination in both the short and long term. Perhaps most crucially, Roche argued that these were 'public' events whose impacts reverberated throughout the world. Since Roche committed his thoughts to paper a decade ago, the significance of mega-events has, if anything, grown. The competition to host peripatetic, 'footloose' (Getz, 2007) or 'ambulant' (Gold and Gold, 2008) events is more intense than ever, with some of the world's greatest cities competing with one another to secure, or maintain, their position as global leaders (Shoval, 2002). The 2012 Olympic Games in London, UK, the millennium event (recognised as one of the best ever) in Sydney and other events in recent years in Tokyo, New York, Paris, Madrid and Moscow mark these destinations as current, or future, Olympic candidate cities. The act of bidding for an Olympic Games requires a decade or more of planning, and the ensuing legacies, whether positive or negative, can last much longer.

Mega-events have been credited with the potential to change perceptions of host cities and nations, generate significant economic value, catalyse physical and social regeneration, reposition a destination and provide opportunities for the celebration of local and national identities. The 2008 Beijing Olympics is a useful exemplar of these professed benefits. A cursory glance at the media coverage before, during and after the event reinforces the success of the People's Republic of China in driving an image against a backdrop of political protest over China's relationship with Tibet and international outcry with respect to its record on human rights and environmental degradation:

- 'Beijing Olympics Set to Improve West's View of China'
- 'Beijing Olympics Will Strengthen Investors Perceptions of China'
- 'Global Media Coverage of Olympics Avoids Politics'
- 'With Olympics Over, China's Self-Confidence Soars'
- 'China's Winning Olympic Spirit'
- 'Magnificent Olympics Earned China Global Respect'
- 'China's Public Relations Success'
- 'The Opening Ceremony: What the media said'
- 'A Victory for China'

Not only did China appear to win the public relations (PR) wars, but the Beijing Olympics also produced remarkable television audience viewing figures. Reuters estimates that between 63 per cent (393 million) and 69 per cent

(842 million) of the Chinese population tuned in to the opening ceremony alone. The official website for the Olympic Games claimed that nearly 4 billion people worldwide tuned in. The scale of interest in broadcasting the event was illustrated by the USA's NBC network paying $450 million for exclusive rights and securing 34.2 million viewers, the most viewed and highest rated non-US Summer Olympics opening ceremony ever. In terms of overall viewing figures for the Games, the Nielsen Company claims that over 4.4 billion viewers tuned in during the first ten days alone. *China Daily* claims that 96 per cent of the population of China watched the games at some point. The opening and closing ceremonies, opportunities to showcase the host nation on a global scale, were universally acknowledged as spectacular events that provided the host government with a valuable communications vehicle. As Tom Shales of the *Washington Post* put it:

> Eye-poppers gave way to jaw-droppers, stunners were followed by dazzlers, and if the absence of a big emotional catharsis was a little disappointing, the Opening Ceremonies of the 2008 Summer Olympics from Beijing still added up to one of the most visually beautiful evenings of television ever seen.

While the extent of long-term change attributed to mega-events remains open to debate, it is widely acknowledged that events on the scale of the Summer Olympic Games can transform entire nations and act as a catalyst for change, both internally and externally. Commentaries on the Beijing Olympics suggest that perceptions of China improved as a result of its hosting of the Games. The nation's competence in delivering an awe-inspiring Games – architecturally, organisationally, culturally and in sporting terms – produced a narrative that spoke of its 'coming out' and its forward march into modernity. China's confidence about itself and the merits of its one-party system – dubbed socialism with Chinese characteristics – were reinforced in hosting the 29th Summer Olympic Games. Political and economic commentators were unanimous in their view that China's position in the world order had been strengthened by the manner in which the Games had been delivered and the tacit support that visiting world leaders gave to the event (both the US President and the British Prime Minister were in attendance, among others). The power of the Olympic Games was illustrated in the way that pre-Games doubts over internal dissent, human rights and pollution were wiped from the media agenda in favour of glowing praise for spectacle, hospitality, friendship, harmony, supermodern architecture, culture and heritage. China's 'soft power' (Nye, 2004) offensive produced an Olympic Games that were both a sporting and political success.

The world's other foremost mega-event, the FIFA Soccer World Cup, also has significant global appeal and has been utilised by host nations for the last seventy years to achieve wider political, economic, social and cultural objectives. The South Africa 2010 World Cup was built on a developmental agenda

(Bob and Swart, 2009), addressing issues of poverty, inequality, crime, race and infrastructural capacity in the country. Its predecessor, the Germany 2006 World Cup, was also heralded as a great success, not only in terms of media audience figures and the number of inbound visitors to Germany, but also in terms of the perceptual dimension. Again, a cursory glance at media reports demonstrates the significance of the event for national and international stakeholders alike:

- 'Trying to Be German as the World Watches'
- 'National Patriotism in Black, Red and Gold'
- 'League of Nations Allows Germans to Fly Flag with Pride'
- 'We Want to Be Loved by You . . .'
- 'Klinsmann Keen to Show Germany's New Identity – On and Off the Field'
- 'World Cup Kicks off New German Patriotism'
- 'Changing German Identity Revealed at World Cup'
- 'Germany's Fairytale Comes True'
- 'Bringing Germany's Turks into the Family'

Here, a mega-event initiated an international review of German national identity and, perhaps even more importantly, it enabled an internal conversation about history, identity, new and old, pride and hope, to take place. This event had a national importance that reached beyond the global rewards that every mega-event craves. At its heart was the concept of identity. The German hosts deliberately sought to alter perceptions of their nation through the vehicle of the World Cup. They did this by developing an outward-facing strategy that had at its heart the slogan 'A Time to Make Friends'. This visionary ideal governed the organisation of the tournament itself while talking directly to the German public about the impressions of nation being portrayed. These impressions were built on the concepts of tolerance, diversity, friendship, openness, good humour, joy and unity. Strategically, the identity problems that the German people had struggled with between 1945 and the fall of the Berlin Wall were placed at the forefront of people's minds. The World Cup became a stage on which to display a 'new' Germany – a nation at ease with itself, accepting of difference, liberated from its past and demonstrating a playful engagement with its (previously tarnished) national symbols. This was as much a process of internal reunification as an external one. The German population in its diverse totality – young and old, rich and poor, immigrant and indigenous, east and west – finally felt sufficiently confident to participate in patriotic expression (e.g. flag waving) on a global stage via the mechanism of a mega-event. Such expressions of identity via state-endorsed public spectacle had previously held associations with a period of oppression, aggression and brutality. While there is a need for caution over the sustainability of these regenerative effects, there can be little doubt that few other media provide the sort of catalyst for change, or opportunities to mobilise support, that these mega-events represent. That said, while these two examples illustrate the global–national significance of sporting events, this should not undermine the importance of national and local events in addressing policy objectives.

As one example of the national-to-local reach of events, the Liverpool European Capital of Culture (ECoC) in 2008 is worthy of some discussion. The ECoC title is awarded annually following two rounds of competition. First, the national candidate city is selected from within the host nation. Second, a specially convened cultural commission awards the ECoC title to the national candidate that best meets the criteria set out by the European Union (EU). The Liverpool 08 ECoC case is interesting both because of its successful bid process and for the subsequent approach to delivery adopted. First, with respect to the original bid process, Liverpool was an unexpected victor in both the national (UK) and European 'rounds' of competition. Suffering from significant economic and social deprivation brought to the fore by de-industrialisation, the narrative of Liverpool in the British media had, in preceding decades, invariably been negative – a narrative of crime, social inequality and negative cultural stereotypes. Even the original bid committee had acknowledged that they were underdogs when compared with their respective British and European competitors. Nevertheless, Liverpool's strategy to emphasise the economic, social and cultural regenerative transformations that the ECoC title could bring to the city placed it in a unique position in comparison with other candidate cities. Liverpool made the case for *becoming* a city of culture rather than for *being* one. It stressed the need to secure the ECoC title as a catalyst for regeneration rather than as a showcase for cultural excellence *per se*. For the awarding committee this represented a persuasive argument and Liverpool was (surprisingly) awarded the title in 2005.

Having won the ECoC title on a manifesto for change, Liverpool 08 embedded this vision via its delivery in ways that demonstrate the growing significance of events as a mechanism to achieve wider social, cultural and economic policy objectives. First, the organisers struck a delicate balance between policies for the democratisation of culture and those promoting cultural democracy. While the ECoC title represents a platform for cities to showcase their nationally and internationally recognised cultural assets to a wider audience (the democratisation of culture), in Liverpool 08 the title was also used to mobilise resources to facilitate community arts and cultural projects that supported and celebrated 'local' forms of cultural expression (cultural democracy). Liverpool 08 was deemed a success for the way in which it engaged locally with the culturally 'uninitiated' while generating positive media exposure nationally and internationally for its 'signature' cultural events, exhibitions and artworks. Part of this success was owing to the way in which it evaluated itself and projected a unique identity to a wide range of stakeholders. Its trailblazing research programme, *Impacts 08 – The Liverpool Model*, was unique, acting as an independent voice recording the successes and failings of the year from which 'impacts' were measured. Chapter 4 of this volume addresses the growing importance of evaluating event outcomes and the need for more longitudinal, action-based research such as that epitomised by the Impacts 08 programme. Liverpool 08 had national, European and, perhaps, international pretensions with respect to putting the city on the cultural map, but, like the 2006 World Cup in Germany, it was its role in opening up new possibilities that made it meaningful in the longer term. It generated discussion of a new narrative for Liverpool, one liberated from engrained negative regional and national stereotypes. The Creative Communities Manager with the Liverpool Company sums up the feeling well when reflecting back on the successes of the ECoC year:

> I think culture has reached people on many different levels . . . You can see the difference in the people just by walking around the city. Everyone has a new found pride in the city. We have been able to dispel stereotypes that have been attached to Scousers [a negative colloquialism for residents of the city] in recent years.
>
> (*Liverpool Echo*, 3 December 2008)

Above and beyond the feelings of civic pride generated by the ECoC year of celebrations, the event also posted some 'hard' outcomes from this culture-led regeneration programme. Impacts 08 reported (Impacts 08, 2010) that the ECoC had a significant positive effect on visitor figures to Liverpool, with an increase in first-time visitors to the city and in those influenced to visit by the Liverpool ECoC. Furthermore, the city benefited from an increase in the number of references to Liverpool's cultural system in the lead up to and duration of the ECoC and the positive tone of the coverage of the year's activities. In the context of this book, what this selection of coverage from the ECoC event demonstrates is that by following an event-led strategy, Liverpool made significant strides forward in addressing its economic and social issues as well as its sense of itself as a city.

As powerful symbolic and material entities, events are now commonly used to address a series of political, social, economic and cultural 'problems'. However, they also generate debate, dissent, protest and disagreement. The chapter now moves on to navigate a path through these travails, offering insights into how researchers, practitioners and policy makers have dealt with, and might better address, the challenges of translating theory into strategy in their own particular contexts. Before this task is undertaken, it is necessary to locate the origins, and subsequent development, of events analysis.

Analysing events: a genealogy

Elsewhere, we have provided a brief overview of the emergence of a distinct field of study that can be termed event policy (Foley, McGillivray and McPherson, 2009). The focus here is on providing a genealogy of the analysis of events as a means of locating this book's main aim within the wider canon of leisure and tourism-related knowledge. The term genealogy is used as it relates to the notion of lineage or descent as the intention is to 'locate' the underpinning disciplinary influences that have contributed to the emergence of an identifiable 'study of events' while simultaneously acting as an impediment to the establishment, and current status, of the field.

Getz (2007) has made the case for three levels of event education (event design and production, event management and event studies). While there is merit in this model, for the purposes of this text, two of his levels have been collapsed and an intermediate level has been introduced to indicate that the event management field of study has broadly evolved through three stages of complexity, detailed in Table 1.1.

Rehearsing the arguments made recently, the first stage of complexity in the study of event management works at a 'purely instrumental level' and, 'reflecting on practical experience, it reaches general conclusions about what works organisationally and it essentially produces a "how to" approach' (Foley *et al.*, 2009). It is concerned with the generation of micro-level conclusions and their relevance for the operational dimension of the emerging events 'industries'. Invariably, it draws on related fields of business studies and management (especially operations management, consumer behaviour, marketing, logistics and finance) and the cognate 'contextual' fields of hospitality, tourism and leisure. It may also incorporate aspects of design and production (see Berridge, 2006). In the study of event *management* there is a crowd of published materials, commencing in the 1990s and early 2000s with the work of Hall (1992), Graham, Goldblatt and Delpy (1995), Getz (1997), Bowdin, Allen, O'Toole, Harris and McDonnell (1999), Mossberg (2000),

Table 1.1 Event Management Stages of Complexity

Stage	*Characteristics*
Event management (including production and design)	Instrumental Practical experience Operational/logistical Creative/technological Micro-level concerns Abundant literature
Event policy (Foley *et al.*, 2009)	Macro-level contextualisation Policy angle evident Social, cultural and economic effects (or impacts) of events considered Paucity of specialised literature
Event studies (Getz, 2007)	Considers wider socio-historical context for events Macro-level concerns Informed by a range of academic disciplines Emerging literature

Source: Adapted from Foley *et al.* (2009).

Shone and Parry (2001), Van der Wagen (2002) and Goldblatt (2004), and gathering pace over the ensuing decade as event management reached an established academic position. The development of the field spawned, and has subsequently been sustained by, the exponential growth in the availability of Higher Education courses in this area. The pre-eminent authors in the event management field often refocused their interests from cognate subjects, including tourism management (and to a lesser extent, tourism studies), leisure management and hospitality management. Before them sat the blank canvas of an academic and educational field open to be shaped with wide ranging possibilities and potentialities. These early authors mapped the sector to create a series of events typologies. Event planning models were developed and toolkits for use in delivering successful events were published. This field was (and still is) an applied one, focused on a relatively limited knowledge base (e.g. business and management) and concerned largely with the development of an area of professional practice (Getz, 2007).

However, the emphasis on the micro-level in the 1990s and early 2000s worked, ironically, to undermine the claims of the subject area with respect to its pretensions to become a recognised field of study with its own onto-logical, epistemological and methodological commitments. The field had few identifiable *analyses* to draw on other than the ubiquitous, and largely norma-tive, management base. Here, context was everything; conceptual appreciation was conspicuous by its absence. This representation of event management mimics directly what Henry (1990) said of the history of leisure management, in that 'links between the predominantly prescriptive concerns of leisure man-agement (theories about how to "improve" managerial practice), and the analytic concerns of leisure theory (how best to understand and explain leisure and other related socio-political phenomena) have not normally been made explicit' (p. xii).

That said, even from the early days of event management, some researchers were already concerned with the formulation of their questions from a policy angle. They attempted to contextualise events within a conceptual entity that is the wider macro-level environment. In the second stage of complexity (see Table 1.1) – the event policy stage – researchers consider the '*policy* angle and inquiries are made into the socio-economic (and socio-cultural) effects of an events-led policy' (Foley *et al.*, 2009). Attention in this stage is also paid to what constitutes an effective use of events and, occasionally, to what the goals of event policy might be. Drawing on public policy, social policy and cultural policy perspectives, this sphere of activity extends the reach of event management from the micro to the macro and also challenges the norma-tive, management-dominated direction of the field. It acknowledges that decisions on management actions, 'take place within, and are often directly influenced by, the context of political values, attitudes and decisions' (Coalter, 1990: 149). It addresses the effects of events and draws attention to the ideological preoccupations that govern decision-making and the allocation of scarce resources across local, national and now transnational boundaries.

This might, for example, include the division of responsibility for events across the commercial, voluntary and public sectors, the role of local government vis-à-vis its national counterpart, the relative merits of income maximisation or catering for disadvantage and the ideological positions that exert greatest influence in the policy-making process in different regions of the world. There is a need to widen understandings of the alternative systems of governance and cultures present across the globe because significant events are as likely to take place in the Middle East as in Manchester or Montreal. Thus, in the event policy stage, the conceptual is introduced alongside the contextual but there remains a paucity of material related to a specific *event* policy analysis.

In the third stage of complexity, *event studies*, events are conceptualised in a broader socio-historical context. This problematic situates events from the perspective of social, cultural and economic reproduction. Maurice Roche's (2000) text, *Mega-events and modernity*, was indicative of the emergence of a studies approach to planned events. This text drew on a multi-perspective analytical framework to assess the value and meaning of World Fairs and Expos, the Summer Olympic Games, and the soccer World Cups for their immediate localities, for nations and for the emergence of global cultural citizenship. More recently, Getz (2007) has employed the moniker of event studies to represent the maturation phase in the development of the field of study. It maps out the academic disciplinary influences on the events subject and fuses these to produce a distinctive ontological, epistemological and methodological guide for researchers and students alike. This field draws on a diverse set of social science disciplines, including political economy, political science, urban geography, sociology, anthropology, social policy, history, tourism planning and leisure studies. The initiation of an event studies paradigm mirrors the experience of the study of leisure from the 1960s. Leisure Studies drew on a wide range of social–scientific theoretical perspectives to generate critically informed analyses of the sphere of free-time activity. Having defined what leisure 'was' and measured its extent, researchers then moved their attention onto what it 'meant' to people, how some people participated and others did not (access) and the ideological role it played in economic and social reproduction (social control). As an increasingly important sub-field of leisure, the study of events has followed a similar trajectory. Crucially, both event management and event policy draw upon knowledge and theory from the event studies field.

In this book, the concentration will be on appraising the socio-economic and socio-cultural implications of events-led policies locally, nationally and internationally. To that end, the practical experience of events operatives is not of primary interest (here), nor is an in-depth evaluation of the field of management studies – that is covered well elsewhere. Instead, this book takes as its starting point that 'events have policy implications that cannot be ignored and that they are not the sole domain of event producers and managers' (Getz, 2007: 3). The concern here is with the significance of events-led policy and strategy for local and central governments and other voluntary and private sector actors (e.g. NGOs). The topic is approached with theoretical preoccupations influenced by facets of event studies, integrated to produce a critical event policy perspective (see Chapter 13, 'Conclusions'). Understanding event policy within a critical perspective requires attention to the political, economic, social and cultural backdrop against which events are created and consumed. For example, in Chapter 5, insights are drawn from the fields of political economy and political science to analyse the role of event policy in the wider context of capitalist accumulation and reproduction. This analysis posits that events are a valuable tool in intense inter-urban competition and investigates the role of 'power' in framing the interests and decision-making processes at local and central government levels. From urban geography (Chapter 6), analytical tools are developed to question the role of events in the division of urban space, especially in the context of 'gentrification' debates (see MacLeod, 2002) and the potential spatial injustices that might result from a commitment to events-led entrepreneurial governance.

Sociological influences are analysed to assess the importance of events with respect to social capital and the relative social costs and benefits of events for their proposed beneficiaries (Chapter 7). Sociological and cultural studies inform the discussion of events and cultural citizenship (Chapter 8). Each of these foundation disciplines has an influence, whether explicit or implicit, on how policy makers in the real world go about making decisions on the allocation of scarce resources and the relative costs and benefits of their actions thereafter.

The contemporary need for an event policy perspective

In developing the idea of an event policy text it was important to ask the question, 'why event policy and why now?' The preceding discussion has addressed some of the main reasons, based on the maturing field of the study of planned events, but before moving on to outline the structure of the book and describe its main pedagogical features, it is necessary to further reinforce some of the environmental factors that necessitate the production of this text at this time.

The publication of Getz's (2007) text, *Event studies*, represented a breakthrough in the serious study of planned events as it sought to explore the disciplinary origins of the field. Others had already achieved this in tourism and leisure (e.g. Tribe, 2004; Henry, 1990), but the youthful field of events had been synonymous with a rather fragmented, haphazard, opportunistic and random approach to study, despite experiencing a proliferation of research activity with 'events' in the title. However, being the first to introduce the notion of an area of enquiry entitled event *studies* (forty years after the development of a *leisure studies* tradition) brought with it the daunting challenge of mapping out the foundational theories underpinning the field in a single, solitary text. With a veritable avalanche of materials vying for space in this text, only one chapter of the book was given over to the peculiarities of policy as a subset of event studies, and this was by no means presented as central to the main thrust of the overall argument. As a result, Getz's text did not fully address the totality of policy-related considerations that demand contemporary discussion. Moreover, while Getz provided an impressive breadth of coverage in mapping out the confines of event studies, the absence of analytical *depth* weakens the case for the book to be used as a main text in the teaching of event policy beyond an introductory level. Since the publication of Getz's text four years ago, a number of chapters and journal articles have appeared in the events-related canon (including those from the authors of this book – see recommended reading and bibliography), but again, many of these suffer from the same accusation of a lack of analytical depth. A feature of the proliferation of events-related texts over the last few years has been the exponential growth in the number of edited collections. While these texts represent a valuable addition to the event-management and related literature base, they tend to lack conceptual coherence and explore 'issues' as opposed to developing a coherent theoretical preoccupation. These texts often mention policy-related discussions but they are rarely *about* policy. Yeoman, Robertson, Ali-Knight, Drummond and McMahon-Beattie's (2004) text *Festivals and events management: an international arts and culture perspective* contains a chapter or two concerned with policy preoccupations, but this is not the central premise of the text. In a similar vein, two further edited collections published over the past two years, Ali-Knight, Robertson, Fyall and Larkin's (2008) *International perspectives of festivals and events: paradigms of analysis* and Musgrave and Raj's (2009) *Event management and sustainability* both fail to deliver a comprehensive, coherent, and theoretically informed study of the event policy phenomenon.

In contrast, *Event policy: from theory to strategy* is developed and differentiated from the texts above owing to its

- specific focus on policy;
- coherence (i.e. not an edited collection);
- depth (i.e. not a 'how to do it' manual);
- scope (i.e. events are placed in a global and local context beyond the narrow fields of hospitality or leisure management); and
- approach (i.e. the phenomena of events and festivity are definitively located within a theoretical and strategic framework).

In academic terms this text is timely and a range of audiences will benefit from its focus on translating theoretical constructs into strategic actions. Developments in academe across the world further emphasise the importance of this text. In the UK, the publication of the revised Hospitality, Tourism, Leisure and Sport subject benchmarks for Higher Education in late 2007 provides a guide to the enhanced status of events within the sector. In the revised benchmarks, events secured its position as a new stream, and the disaggregation of what events 'means' in an academic context calls further for the inclusion of event policy as a legitimate subject area. These benchmarks, which are shaping the future curriculum of new event management and related degree programmes in the UK, state that graduates in event management should be able to 'utilize and understand the impact of, rationales, sources and assumptions embedded in policy' (QAA, 2008). This change necessitated the adaptation of degree curricula in England and Wales to further embed policy considerations in the minds of approval (or validation) panels and external industry stakeholders.

Moreover, the exponential growth in events as a subject area over the last decade (Universities and Colleges Admissions System currently lists 412 events-related courses at colleges and universities throughout the UK alone) in the UK and beyond has been a catalyst for a number of strategic developments that have sought to promote a greater understanding of the knowledge base for events education and have produced an increased recognition of events as a legitimate subject internationally. Initiatives such as the development of the International EMBOK (Event Management Body of Knowledge) (Silvers, Bowdin, O'Toole and Nelson, 2006) seek to define, research and understand the parameters of events and the knowledge, understanding and skills required in order to succeed in this environment. An appreciation of event policy theory and strategy is essential in achieving this aim. Moreover, the establishment of a subject body, the Association for Event Management Education (AEME), in 2004 further emphasised a desire on the part of educators and practitioners alike to add credibility to the notion of event management as a profession. To secure this designation, subjects require an agreed (and accepted) knowledge base (e.g. HE courses, accreditation, subject benchmarks), barriers to entry (e.g. qualifications), an influential professional body (e.g. AEME), codes of conduct (e.g. the Health and Safety 'Purple Guide') and the authority to speak on the subject – equating to legitimacy (e.g. AEME). While in the UK context progress has been made with respect to an agreed knowledge base, some barriers to entry and codes of conduct, there remains a significant degree of contestation over the absence of a unified professional body with legitimacy to lobby governments and represent the diverse interests prevalent across the sector. Furthermore, the sub-field of event policy is perhaps even more fragmented than at the operational level, with quarrels over the extent to which generic public policy analyses can be applied unproblematically to the field of events against the merits of a specialised event policy approach.

Beyond UK borders, the content of this book attests to the transferability of policy approaches in many territories across the globe. The analyses contained in this text are relevant to students in the US, Australia, Europe, Asia, the emerging Emirate states and in other countries where academic research and HE content have followed the growth of an events and festivities industrial sector. That this is necessary is illustrated in returning to the case of the 2008 Summer Olympic Games in Beijing. As the event itself recedes from the media gaze, its legacy in the People's Republic of China is a rising number of thirty HE courses in event management.

Guiding research questions and the structure of the book

Having provided an argument for the development of the event policy field, it is timely to reiterate the specific aims and objectives of this particular text. This is best achieved by drawing attention to the research questions that give direction to the remainder of the book:

- What is the rationale for events and festivities being 'used' as a mechanism for the achievement of wider social outcomes, and how does this differ in different geographical territories?
- Which ideologies and discourses underpin the rationale for, and subsequent formation of, policy with respect to events and festivity across alternative geographical territories?
- What role do events play in new forms of urban governance and inter-urban competition, and what effect does this have on local and central government strategies, across the world?
- How are ideas of consumption, commerce and entrepreneurialism accommodated alongside notions of citizenship, community and culture with respect to the intention and outcomes of event policy?
- What roles do stakeholders play in influencing policy decisions, and what power relations are in operation that act to include and exclude some interests over others?
- Who gets to be counted as a stakeholder?
- How do we know whether policy interventions in the realm of events are effective in achieving the desired outcomes?

To adequately address the research questions discussed above, the book is divided into three distinct parts. Part 1 focuses on 'Event policy rationales'. Here, over the course of three chapters, the underpinning factors that have led to the formalisation of a field of event policy are analysed. Chapter 2, 'Events and festivity: from ritual to regeneration', provides an archaeology of the underlying functions and forms of events and festivity and their influences upon subsequent developments and uses. It opens by considering the origins of events and festivals as ritualistic practices and markers of identity tied closely to ideas of community and the locality. It proceeds to consider how popular pastimes, festivals and fairs were subject to increasing regulation in the eighteenth and nineteenth centuries as the class-driven improvement ethos of the rational recreation movement subjected those considered unruly to its gaze. Finally, the changing role of events and festivals in the late-twentieth century as vehicles for economic and (more infrequently) social regeneration of urban environments – and the implications of this shift in policy for the 'authenticity' of these events – is considered. Building on this discussion, Chapter 3, 'Trends in events and festivities: the policy panacea', focuses exclusively on the contemporary trends in events and festivities that have contributed to their current status as an important vehicle for the attainment of wider public policy objectives. It reviews issues around the volume, value and scope of the field of events and festivals in local, national and international terms, drawing on the recent research into the economic contribution of events and festivals while taking cognisance of the wider social and public policy roles played by these phenomena in achieving a myriad of policy outcomes. In reviewing trends, the impacts of small-scale festivals and events, through hallmark and special events, to the mega spectacles of global sporting events are considered. In illustrating a wider context for the contribution of events and festivals to economies, communities, and individuals, this chapter legitimates the serious study of events and their associated policy drivers in the early twenty-first century. The final chapter in Part 1, 'Evaluating event outcomes: a legitimation crisis', addresses the growing importance of event evaluation processes in legitimating the policy interventions made by local and national actors alike. It evaluates how monitoring and evaluation has become closely linked with policy development at a strategic level and reflects critically on the politics of evaluation – on the way in which the predominance of economic impact evaluation is slowly giving way to a wider toolkit approach based on the public policy need to 'include' a plethora of stakeholders in an events-led strategy.

Having outlined the main rationales for event policy in Part 1, Part 2 on 'Event policy formations' focuses more closely on the conceptual dimension of event policy and how certain 'knowledge claims' influence the types of policy formation that have been developed with respect to the uses of events. Chapter 5, 'The politics of events' in an age of accumulation, focuses on the way in which urban events policies are being created and shaped to transform or restructure public space on the premise of continually attracting and winning major events to the urban environment. Drawing on the notion of a global neoliberalised order emerging, this chapter contends that hallmark, special or mega-events, along with associated culture-led regeneration processes, are part of the refashioning of urban governance in the context of the neoliberalised state and its roll-back of managerial welfare programmes. It argues that a key feature of this refashioning is that the principal risks are borne by a highly active entrepreneurial (local) state, with the involvement of the private sector being conditional upon the support of the public purse as a safety net. The chapter concludes by arguing that the governance structures formed to permit entre-preneurial activity to flourish can, at the same time, reduce levels of public participation and ownership of the policy-making process.

Chapter 6, 'Consuming events: from bread and circuses to brand', starts from the critique of regimes of accumulation given in Chapter 5 to evaluate the role of events and festivals in legitimating a mode of consumption as the defining rationale for events-led policy investment. In this chapter it is argued that, when used as part of wider destination branding strategies, 'manufactured' events are often supported in favour of indigenous community events that fail to portray the desired aesthetic or represent the ubiquitous cosmopolitan ethos being sought. There is a problematic emanating from the local state's commitment to branded events designed to attract affluent mobile capital. While these may satisfy the lifestyle aspirations of the sought-after tourist audiences, they may also exacerbate the exclusionary processes that blight the urban nightscape of post-industrial cities.

In contrast, Chapter 7, 'Events and social capital: linking and empowering communities', addresses the weaknesses of the entrepreneurial event policy drive. As international competition to host global events intensifies, national and local political action is influenced as the institutional foundations for 'winning' events are resourced to the detriment of other means of delivering on public policy objectives. This chapter contests the notion that at the global and national level, greater integration is secured between the popular spectacular element of events and local community representation and empowerment. Instead, in the presence of continuing spatial injustices, social polarities and disenfranchised groups, attention must be drawn to the (un-)sustainability of an event policy based on an entrepreneurial (economic) logic. The chapter ends with the argument that cities need to pursue a much deeper commitment to ongoing legacy planning around their events so that policy makers can maximise social utility, not only during the celebratory phase of event winning and delivery, but for the longer term. Only then can events secure the long-lasting effects about which their patrons proselytise on a regular basis.

The final chapter of Part 2, 'Events as cultural capital: animating the urban', takes as it focus the increasingly symbiotic relationship between events and festivals and culture-led regeneration in urban environments. However, this chapter proposes that as the economic discourse becomes ever more synonymous with events-led cultural policy in the developed (and increasingly the developing) world, there is a need to offer a critique of the implications of this drive. As culture becomes viewed as a *product* open to commercial exploitation (commodification) rather than as a *process* or *way of life*, so the forms of cultural expression chosen to lead this regeneration do not necessarily reflect the cultural experiences of the host audience and are overly instrumentalist (and economic) in intention. The chapter concludes by reflecting on the use of cultural events and festivals as a means of generating some historical or 'local' significance and cautions policy makers that in trying to create authenticity and uniqueness, alienating effects and outcomes are possible.

In Part 3, 'Event policy implementations', the book focuses on the implementation of event policy globally. Each chapter addresses an implementation issue illustrated through a worked case study. Chapter 9, 'Glasgow 2014: demonstrating capacity and competence', uses the context of Glasgow's successful bid for the 2014 Commonwealth Games to demonstrate how political actors from across the public, private and third sectors came together to secure public support, or legitimation, for their investment in a hallmark sporting event. The chapter provides a critical analysis of the successful bid process and the early stages of event implementation to indicate how the competing economic, political, social and cultural objectives were managed so that aspects of commerce, consumption, community and citizenship were integrated into the fabric of the event.

Chapter 10, 'Destination Dubai: event policy in an Arab state', takes the context of Dubai as its focus to explore an alternative discourse of event policy – a discourse that is built upon the use of events (particularly, but not only, sporting events) as an economic generator and image enhancer in an Arab state without pretensions to liberal democratic politics but with intentions to become one of the world's most popular tourist destinations. The chapter outlines the development of Dubai from a small Emirate to its current position as the region's dominant commercial centre with an economy that is increasingly service-, business- and tourism-orientated. It then reflects on its sports-event tourism policy successes, as Dubai is positioned as a destination that has sought to utilise major sporting events as a way of developing tourism and commerce in the region, with the goal of gaining image and importance at the international level. Significant investments have been poured into the Emirate in the staging and sponsorship of the world's leading sports events and the building of sporting infrastructures. As global competition to host major sports events increases apace, the importance of the patronage of a wealthy ruling family, as well as the presence of a significant transitory working population, provides an interesting alternative policy terrain to that experienced by those operating in liberal democratic nations.

Chapter 11, 'Mardi Gras, New Orleans: policy intervention in an historical event', focuses on the implementation of event policy in the US around an event that is ambiguous, amorphous and 'owned' by stakeholders outside the official public policy domain. Mardi Gras is an historical hallmark event on which the city of New Orleans is heavily dependent, both economically and socially. In the wake of the devastation wrought by Hurricane Katrina in 2006 this significance has intensified as the populations who have produced the festivity and the communities in which it has been sited have been atomised. As local state officials attempt to manage Mardi Gras to achieve wider social and public policy outcomes, they face resistance from a powerful lobby of embedded social organisations, the Krewes, who run the Mardi Gras celebrations. As the premodern meets modernity, the contestation created provides some valuable insights into the dilemmas of event policy implementation and ownership associated with an historical event.

The final chapter in Part 3, 'Singapore: a mixed economy of events', addresses events implementation evidenced in the situation of the city-state of Singapore, South East Asia. Singapore has followed an approach to the delivery of its events that relies heavily on de-contextualised commercial events, but which is also supported by significant public investment (e.g. Singapore F1 Grand Prix) and, due to its ethnic mix, is also identifiable with its highly contextualised range of 'indigenous' festivals, which are reflective of organic, community events. This case study provides a counter-point to the UK and US contexts as the democratic socialism of Singapore politics with an unassailable one-party domination of the political process translates into a policy process that supports those events that reinforce shared national values (National Day), a consumerism logic (Singapore Grand Prix) and multi-ethnic diversity (Chingay Parade).

Finally, the book closes with 'Conclusions' in Chapter 13, which reviews the implications for academic study of the sub-field of event policy alongside the nature of the knowledge transfer relationship between academe and practice. This leads to a critique of existing policy perspectives within the context of the leisure and tourism sectors. Last, a summative, final section will draw together the main theoretical and policy issues into an agenda for professional, institutional and organisational reflection among those studying, working and researching in the sector.

Pedagogical features

The inclusion of a number of pedagogical features is designed to make this an accessible text for both students and practitioners. Each of the subsequent chapters follows a common structure and is written in an accessible style. Short, internationally focused illustrative 'cases' are boxed and embedded in Chapters 2–8 to help illustrate the theoretical arguments being made. These are complemented by critical review questions at the conclusion of each chapter. These aids are intended to help the reader apply theory to practice and to encourage reflection on completion of each chapter. Further reading recommendations are also located at the end of each chapter. These are based on the authors' judgement of the most pertinent literature sources that will help extend the reader's knowledge. For those interested in delving deeper into the subject matter of each chapter, the extensive reference section at the end of the book will provide a greater challenge.

Critical review questions

- What are the principal differences between event policy and event management?
- What developments over the last two decades have enhanced the status of event management as a profession?
- Explain why it is important to consider event policy perspectives across international territories.

Recommended reading

Foley, M., McGillivray, D. and McPherson, G. (2009) 'Policy, politics and events: a match made in heaven?', in Musgrave, J. and Raj, R. (eds) *Event management and sustainability*, Wallingford, CABI.

Getz, D. (2007) *Event studies: theory, research and policy for planned events*, Oxford: Elsevier.

Hall, C.M. and Rusher, K. (2004) 'Politics, public policy and the destination', in Yeoman, I., Robertson, M., Ali-Knight, J., Drummond, S. and McMahon-Beattie, U. (eds) *Festivals and events management: an international arts and culture perspective*, pp. 217–231, Oxford: Elsevier.

Resources for event policy

Festival Management and Events Tourism (now titled *Event Management)*: This journal was launched in North America in 1993 and continues to be a source of valuable policy-related materials for students studying event management.

Leisure Studies: From the late 1990s onwards, this UK journal has contained a number of event policy-related articles as event management academics find a niche within the wider leisure studies community.

Managing Leisure: A UK journal preoccupied with management and practice, but which also contains a number of event policy-related articles.

The Journal of Policy Research in Tourism, Leisure & Events: A UK journal that takes as its critical focus a variety of policy debates relating to the tourism, leisure and events sectors. These policy debates encompass economic, social, cultural, political and environmental perspectives.

Part I
Event policy rationales

2 Events and festivity

From ritual to regeneration

Introduction

Before concentrating more fully on the contemporary status of event policy, it is necessary to subject the term 'event' and its history to some scrutiny. This chapter provides an historical overview of events and festivity and their subsequent developments and uses. First, the origins of events and festivals as ritualistic practices and markers tied closely to ideas of time, space, community and the locality are considered. Consideration is then given to the ways in which popular pastimes, including festivals and fairs, were subject to increasing regulation in the eighteenth and nineteenth centuries as the middle class improvement ethos of the rational recreation movement subjected the unruly classes to their gaze. Finally, the chapter charts the changing role of events and festivals in the late twentieth century as vehicles for economic and (more infrequently) social regeneration of urban environments – and the implications of this shift in policy for a range of stakeholder interests.

Events: temporal and spatial dimensions

In the process of becoming a field of study and gaining enhanced recognition within both academic and professional communities, the word 'event' has undergone something of a metamorphosis. Social anthropologists argue that events have been around for as long as can be remembered, but they were not always referred to using the umbrella term generated by the event management academics of the present. Instead of the unifying label 'events', those writing in the foundational disciplines used the terms celebrations, holidays, fairs, festivals, rituals, ceremonies, processions and parades to describe what are now frequently collapsed under the banner of events. Over the last two decades, in parallel with the emergence of a distinct field of study, there has been an astounding increase in attempts to define, categorise and classify events. This process of categorisation has also been revisionist in its intention – events of the past have been re-evaluated and incorporated as part of the growing knowledge base about events, drawing comparisons, continuities and discontinuities with their ancestors. For example, the Roman 'circuses' (Veyne,

1990) have been categorised as events with their own form and function, spatial and temporal dynamic, and are frequently compared with contemporary mega-spectacles (Kellner, 2003) like the Olympic Games (Waitt, 2001).

No matter how events are defined, there are some obvious analytical continuities that are worth drawing attention to here. 'Place' and 'time' represent important dimensions for understanding the history of events (Getz, 2007). Whatever their previous label, events are one-off occurrences that normally have a defined start and finish (temporal dimension) – although, as the function of events has altered, their short-term nature is being revised (e.g. year-long cultural festivals such as the European Capital of Culture). Nonetheless, in the agrarian, pre-industrial period, events were inseparable from the rhythms of the calendar, occurring on a cyclical basis (e.g. feasts, fairs, rituals, holidays). The relationship between work and leisure in this period was, invariably, organic, and more parochial rural social systems existed. The events of the day were ritualistic celebrations of the impending harvest, of the arrival of summer, or of the passing of time. In this sense, events played an important collective social role, linking communities (e.g. farmers) together in important symbolic celebrations and commemorations. As some of the foremost historians of pre-industrial leisure have suggested, the focus was on communality and collectivity (Malcolmson, 1973; Bailey, 1979; Cunningham, 1980). There existed an abundance of fairs and festivals, invested with significant localised *meanings* and, in the main, free of external governance. These events were depicted as disorganised spaces of desire, chaos and abandon – very different from the structured, ordered, controlled and self-disciplined spaces commonplace in Western urban public space (Edensor, 1998).

However, in assessing the changing nature of events it is important to note that time itself is a contested concept with its own history. Durkheim's (1912) discussion of the 'sacred' and the 'profane' is relevant here, as religious observance (the sacred) has been the driving force for the longevity of a number of well-known events (e.g. Christmas, Easter, Ramadan), and yet these sacred events are also increasingly subjected to the criticism that their original meanings have been lost in favour of the consumption of the profane (e.g. mass commercialisation). The meaning of time in the pre-industrial period was very different from that experienced during the Industrial Revolution of the eighteenth and nineteenth centuries. For example, in the eighteenth century, Britain experienced rapid unplanned urbanisation and the onset of the Industrial Revolution, producing significant changes to both the temporal and spatial dimensions of events. With the emergence of the factory system, the clock entered the lexicon and time was fixed into distinct segments for work and for non-work (or free time). In the process, the temporal significance of events was altered fundamentally. Rather than a reflection on the passing of time and the celebration of long-held traditions and customs, events became more important as controlled escape routes (Cohen and Taylor, 1976) from the stresses and strains of industrial life. As Malcolmson (1973) has noted, popular activities, including festivals, fairs and wakes, were suppressed by the recently legitimated public authorities of the nineteenth century out of concern for public order and to ensure adherence to the new work discipline required by the owners of production. As Coalter (1990: 5) stresses, these early examples of state intervention in events, albeit piecemeal and enabling, were concerned with managing the 'temporal parameters' of leisure, reordering organic traditions into defined spaces and times.

Of course, these developments were by no means replicated across the globe where engagement with industrial capitalism differed markedly. In different parts of the world, the clock time associated with industrial capitalism has only recently arrived (or, in some cases, has yet to arrive). Take the example of India's religious and cultural festivals. In the march towards modernity, long-standing festivals and events now face extinction as they fight to preserve deeply engrained values in the face of the rapid expansion of the industrial (clock-based) economy. As the wider world coalesces around the rhythms of the clock, communities in every corner of the earth face the dilemma of retaining a sense of shared heritage while governed by an accelerated (Virilio, 2000) and interdependent world demanding an efficient delivery of products and services.

The preceding discussion attests to the temporal dimension of events, but they are also, crucially, located in space. It is common in the early twenty-first century to talk of flexible space, of event venues fulfilling temporary, multi-purpose functions. Events have the potential to transform, temporarily, the spaces they occupy, but there are also longer-lasting spatial implications that emerge from the hosting of events. In the Roman period, coliseums were specially designed for events, whether politically motivated or for pleasure (Veyne, 1990). Hobsbawm (1983a), whose writings on 'invented traditions' will be further developed later in this chapter, also suggests that as ceremonies, parades and gatherings grew in the nineteenth and twentieth centuries, they were accompanied by the construction of specially designed spaces to accommodate them. These spaces included those for the emerging institutionalised sport culture (e.g. Olympics) of the late twentieth century as well as the 'development of formal spaces for mass ritual which was to be systematically fostered by Fascist regimes' (Hobsbawm, 1983b: 305).

Events have colonised public space for centuries, illustrated most clearly in the spectacle of carnival across Europe, parts of America and South America (Gilmore, 1998). Carnivals often meander through the streetscape of towns and cities, engaging with everyday space in a unique way. In more recent years, academic commentators have analysed the increasingly rationalised and governed spectacle that carnival has become (Gotham, 2005a), further emphasising the temporary meanings associated with the colonisation of spaces across time. Moreover, writing of the distinctions evident between what he calls 'Western streets' and the 'Indian street', Edensor (1998) argues that the historical period that includes the industrialisation process and development of the modern state in the West has produced a marked reconstitution of spatial dimensions. For him, the outcomes of political, economic, social and technological changes are that the colonial Western globalising discourse imposes structure on anti-structure, creating sterility and eradicating 'social, sensual and rhythmic diversity in urban space' (p. 213). This rhythmic diversity can be associated with the organic solidarity and disordered events of the pre-industrial period. In place of the relatively unplanned, episodic and amorphous fairs and festivals comes the *disciplined spontaneity* wrought by modern planning, turning 'symbolic spaces into functional spaces for maximising consumption and facilitating transit' (Edensor, 1998: 213). Reflecting on the changing function of events, the introduction of market logic to urban space is a significant precursor to the contemporary focus on urban regeneration and economic development (see Chapters 5 and 6 for more detailed discussion).

While there may be an element of romanticising the past, it is nonetheless clear that the nature of those spaces used for collective gatherings in preceding historical epochs has altered markedly. From the mid-nineteenth century onwards, across Europe and the US, the state intervened in free-time activity, marking those spaces deemed appropriate for collective leisure pastimes. Built on the back of public policy concerns to improve sanitation, health and to embed the idea of free, non-work time, the outcome was the growth of public open spaces for citizens. This was married to the desire to establish a greater sense of social integration, social control and community bonding deemed necessary as an antidote to the apparent atomisation of industrial society. Re-establishing Tönnies' (2001) *Gemeinschaft* (focus on kinship) relations in a time of intensified *Gesellschaft* (impersonal and contractual) social relations was supported by the Rational Recreation movement, armed with an improving, educating and liberating set of ideas to enhance the 'moral welfare' (Coalter, 1990: 6) of the working classes.

Spatially, out of this policy drive came the provision of museums and libraries, the establishment of Sunday schools, Mechanics Institutes, Working Men's Clubs and the Muscular Christianity movement, in the UK. These institutions themselves became important venues for events and festivals and fulfilled a normalising and disciplining role. The origins of brass bands and other parading organisations can be traced to this time. In the late nineteenth century, a mass generation of traditions took place, pre-war, across Europe. These developments took two forms: those that were politically motivated, organised by states or movements (e.g. national holidays); and those organised by social groups (e.g. May Day). The state intervened with the creation of new official holidays, ceremonies and national symbols at this time to engage the public imagination and secure 'popular resonance' (Hobsbawm, 1983b: 264) for its activities. The state tried to take a more interventionist role in the policy and provision of leisure in the late nineteenth and early twentieth centuries, and also had to devise ways to secure the consent and co-operation of its subjects. 'Official' public ceremonies (events) were crucial in legitimating state and political power in Europe (e.g. Bastille Day 1880) but also in the US (e.g. Fourth of July and Thanksgiving Day), built around official and unofficial elements alongside popular festivities celebrating and commemorating the idea of the 'nation'. These events expressed both the state's pomp and power and its citizens' pleasure. When tied in to World Fairs and Expositions and, latterly, Olympic Games, it is clear that the state also showcased its progress, prosperity and political influence through events. These mega-events (Roche, 2000) left a physical legacy that was often utilised thereafter for other forms of festivity – especially sporting events, as sport was institutionalised at the end of the nineteenth century.

Returning to place and space, events have also played an important role in putting destinations on the world map for centuries – think of the intrinsic link between the (ancient) Olympics and Greece – and this function has intensified in the last twenty years as cities compete to be recognised globally in a time of inter-urban competition for inward investment, tourism and people. Hall's (1992) identification of *hallmark* events as providing the host with significant recognition due to its tradition, attractiveness, quality or publicity is tied closely to place-making and the spatial dimension of events. It is almost impossible to think of the Wimbledon tennis tournament without imagining its location. Similarly, the Rio Carnival could not take place in any other city without losing its hallmark status. One final example of the importance of events in defining a space in the long term is the 1936 Berlin Summer Olympics. Seventy-five years later, the Olympic Stadium continues to represent more than a mere architectural structure. It carries with it discourses of power, Nazism, fascism, remembrance and commemoration. This venue has a social significance that has outlasted its original purpose.

Event categorisation and classification: changing forms and functions

It is difficult to talk of the temporal and spatial dimensions of events without reflecting on the principal forms and functions they have taken historically. The form and function of events determines when and where they take place (e.g. remembrance events) and their intended outcomes. Over time, events have come in many different forms and performed a range of functions. First, addressing form, it is now recognised that events 'look' different and are segmented into distinct typologies. For example, there are cultural, political, arts-based, sporting, business, educational and private events. The way events are conceived, programmed (their content) and delivered differentiates them in terms of form. Historically, the range of event forms was more restricted than it is today. Sporting events, for example, were less institutionalised, as modern sport emerged only in the nineteenth century. Festivals and other celebrations containing themes and symbolism were commonplace in the pre-industrial period, but even these events have multiplied in form over the last century (e.g. arts, food and drink, literature and science festivals) and their functions have also been transformed.

The intended outcomes of events have also been subject to significant change, including how the introduction of clock time was accompanied by a transformation in the use of events from collective celebration to a release valve. In the present day, events play a multitude of functions, some demonstrating continuity with the past (e.g. celebration, commemoration, community cohesion and control) and some intimating a new role (e.g. image enhancement, economic regeneration or development, media expansion, and social cause promotion). A crucial distinction that needs to be drawn between pre-industrial, industrial and post-industrial events is their increasingly planned nature. There exists a shift from events that were ritualistic in nature, fixed in time and space and deriving their importance from that stability, longevity and continuity, to events conceived and exploited for regenerative (economic) imperatives that venerate the new, the transitory, the contrived, the nomadic and moveable nature of celebrations to secure a plethora of social, political and economic externalities. Many events are now spatially and temporally de-contextualised, infinitely portable to new locations and times in the name of securing planned outcomes. They are, like other areas of cultural life, administratively planned.

A good example, which illustrates the transportable nature of events and their varying functions, comes from carnival (see Chapter 11 for a more detailed analysis of Mardi Gras, New Orleans). Carnivals have existed for centuries and were, historically, defined by their rituals, symbols, localised 'meanings' and inversion of established hierarchies (Gilmore, 1998; Gotham, 2002). However, with the onset of post-industrialism and the associated global economic restructuring that accompanied it, cities and nations sought out alternative ways of generating economic return. Leisure, tourism and entertainment were viewed as panaceas, permitting cities to attract visitors to consume their various attractions, many of which were long-established festivals and events. However, as a result, the functions played by these events came under scrutiny. In the 1980s Carnival in New Orleans took on the mantle of economic salvation for the city's fragile economy. Its focus, at least for the city authorities, is now about economic return, marketability and media spectacle. It represents a perfect illustration of a move from *ritual* to *regeneration* in the rationale for and meaning of events and festivals. Box 2.1 also illustrates the dilemma facing cities as they decide whether to 'exploit' their indigenous cultural assets for economic gain.

It is also possible to relate the changing function (and form) of events to the biggest extravaganzas of this historical epoch – mega-events (Roche, 2000). Roche argues that these events (world fairs and expositions, Summer Olympics and, more recently, the soccer World Cup), with their origins as nineteenth-century invented traditions (Hobsbawm, 1983a), were originally about the promotion of international public culture, cultural citizenship and supranational values (e.g. universal human rights). For example, hosts were awarded the honour of staging the Summer Olympics every four years and their role was to ensure that the ethos of the Olympic Movement, laid out in the Olympic Charter, was protected and promoted in the way the Games were organised. Rich with symbolism (e.g. the Olympic Rings, the Olympic Flame, the Olympic Anthem, the Torch Relay and the Emblem), the event owner, the

---

Box 2.1 Chingay Parade and Thaipusam Festival, Singapore

Chingay Parade, at Chinese New Year, is one of Singapore's most popular festivities, attracting a significant number of participants (and viewers) annually, focused on the South East Asian city-state. This event is an example of the dominance of cultural economic discourses as the global is actively courted by the local for economic gain through tourism. The Chingay Parade has been used to 'position' and 'market' Singapore as an attractive international destination. However, this is not to suggest that the local is excluded in this quest for global tourism. Instead, Singapore attempts to 'preserve' local events oriented towards its indigenous communities and 'hidden' from the tourist gaze. A number of local ethnic festivals represent the heterogeneous cultural, social and religious identities. Thaipusam is a one-day festival involving a thanksgiving procession undertaken by Hindu devotees. By remaining relatively 'invisible' to the global circuit of tourism, the Thaipusam Festival provides an example of 'home' and 'locality' being protected from global influences. However, like Chingay Parade, the rich symbolism and ritualistic dimensions of Thaipusam is attractive to those responsible for the prosecution and delivery of policies for tourism in Singapore.

Further reading: Foley, M., McPherson, G. and Matheson, C. (2006) 'Glocalisation and Singaporean festivals', *International Journal of Event Management Research*, 2 (1): 1–16.

International Olympic Committee (IOC), ensured that *meaning* prevailed over *money*. However, from the Rome Olympics of 1960 onwards, the emphasis, on behalf of the 'host' at least, moved to economic and physical regeneration – what Gold and Gold (2008) call the start of the 'regeneration games' period. Similarly, the IOC has, over the last few decades, followed a strategy of commercialising its ritualistic 'asset', exploiting media rights and sponsor partnerships to generate significant revenues for the organisation.

Event externalities: the politics of planned events

Before concluding this chapter with further reflection on the posited shift from ritual to regeneration, it is necessary to provide one more feature that underpins the change in function, form, time and space that has impacted the events experienced today. Having outlined the nature and shape of pre-industrial events, it is important to draw attention to the fundamental social, economic and political transformations that have contributed to the contemporary fixation on planned events created (or recreated) to produce instrumental, means–end externalities, which often have little to do with celebration, experience, spontaneity or freedom. Whereas in the eighteenth and most of the nineteenth centuries popular festivities were suppressed and regulated, state interventions were not meaningful or systematised until the early twentieth century, in the UK at least. Until this point, interventions were reluctant, concerned with providing for socially beneficial behaviour only when private preferences were distorted. Only in the late nineteenth and early twentieth century did a wider public policy for leisure (including events) come to fruition in the UK (Coalter, 1990). At this time the state was inclined to intervene, either through subsidy, direct provision or regulation, to alleviate urban deprivation, to enhance physical health, to contribute to moral welfare, to secure social integration and to foster self-improvement. Within this public policy process, events and festivity could, realistically, only make a contribution to the objective of social integration and community and, more tangentially, to physical health and urban deprivation. Active leisure forms were the preferred free-time activity promoted to achieve these policy ends.

With the principle of state funding for recreation established in the early to mid-twentieth century in the UK, recognition of the value of leisure as a right of citizenship became enshrined – although this right was not strong nor was it available for the majority of the population. Nevertheless, the establishment of the Welfare State in 1949 set in motion a golden period for leisure in the UK, culminating in the 1975 White Paper on Sport and Recreation, which recognised recreation as 'part of the general fabric of the social services', as recreational welfare (Coalter, 1990) saw value in leisure for its own sake as a right of citizenship. This breakthrough, however, again was based on a restricted view of leisure as representing active sport and recreational activities. Other than viewing national holidays and large sporting events as a means of promoting civic and national pride, the absence of a distinct event policy is illustrative of the political, social and economic situation of the time. However, the change in government in the UK in the late 1970s (a New Right Conservative administration led by Margaret Thatcher), the subsequent introduction of market-led economic reforms and a tightening of public expenditure led to a shift in public policy for leisure from recreational welfare to recreation *as* welfare. In this new policy environment, the rationale for investment in leisure services was made on the basis of accruable externalities – including the achievement of civic pride, health improvement, reductions in crime and economic return. This 'harder pragmatism' (Coalter, 1990: 16) had the effect of diluting the right of citizenship accorded to leisure in the preceding decade. Moreover, as the commercial leisure sector expanded rapidly, worldwide, new mass consumer markets were cultivated, and lifestyle aspirations increased. Free market capitalism and anti- (or at least reluctant) collectivist positions dominated, and the local state role in the allocation and distribution of scarce resources was reduced. As market logic infused central and local government, so urban policies coalesced around North American-inspired strategies of *city boosterism*, embraced by city leaders as a way for former industrial and manufacturing cities to find a new economic base through culture, leisure, major events and tourism (Hassan, Mean and Tims, 2007).

While the specific origins and outcomes of this policy shift will be discussed in more depth in Chapters 5 and 6, at this stage it is sufficient to note that this policy initiated a step change in how cities across the Western world in particular assessed the value of events in terms of their cultural, social, economic and political externalities. In the 1980s and early 1990s the civic boosters created fantasy cities (Hannigan, 1998), investing in iconic architecture, festival marketplaces, cultural quarters, convention and exhibition centres (Law, 2002), alongside a renewed focus on the value of sporting and cultural events. The function and form, temporal and spatial dimensions of events supported by city leaders also changed fundamentally. Unique features of existing festivals and events were marketed to attract the global tourist, and cities started to compete to host peripatetic sporting and cultural events – often with little or no resonance with the host city. Externalities reigned – events were worth growing or creating if they could contribute to economic development, cultural vibrancy, quality of life, image making or even health (e.g. sporting events). If they were not, then public investment (whether in the form of direct delivery or subsidy) was unlikely.

However, urban geographers and policy commentators have been critical of the implications of the 'consumption as salvation' discourse. On one level they bemoan the fact that, while boosterism was undoubtedly successful at the outset (see Barcelona as a good example of the use of a Summer Olympic Games as a cultural regenerator), it suffers from diminishing returns as other destinations follow the same strategy. In event terms, many cities across the globe suffer from the threat of diminishing uniqueness – the ubiquity of festivals for food and drink, comedy, music, arts, gay pride and, of course, sport means that 'distinctiveness gets reduced to a formula' (Hassan *et al.*, 2007: 35). Compare this to the pre-industrial period, where locality (and distinctiveness) was marked by the nature of the celebration, who organised it and who attended it. While there remain many examples of predominantly 'local' festivities across the world, in intense inter-urban competition, cities share formats and bid for events not because of some intimate connection or 'roots' to the locality but out of an economic necessity to draw media coverage and mobile capital in the form of tourism. (See Chapter 3 for an analysis of key trends.)

The challenge for proponents of events as meaningful social entities is that spaces dripping with meaning are, in the name of regeneration (normally economic) turned into 'functional spaces for maximising consumption' (Edensor, 1998: 213). Sennett (1994), Auge (1995) and Mitchell (1995) have

all offered a critique of the way urban planning has created 'dead', 'pseudo' or 'strongly classified' spaces. Each shares a concern that city spaces are, under consumerist logic, surveyed, monitored and normalised to debar uncontrolled social interaction – apparently the very antithesis of traditional festivity. This is, of course, linked clearly to the outcomes of public policy as the discourses of income maximisation lie uncomfortably with those of equity of opportunity and assuaging the ills of social disadvantage and marginalisation (MacLeod, 2002). Promising celebration, freedom and spontaneous interaction with other citizens, it is possible to argue that the commodified landscape of events, manufactured and controlled in time and space, form and function, 'directs desire into the cul-de-sac of consumption' (Edensor, 1998: 214). The Dionysian (Greek god of pleasure) desire of anti-structure, disorder, transgression and abandon are marketed as attractive imagined possibilities but then sanitised, structured, bounded and turned into tradable assets – ready for easy, safe consumption. Major event strategies further emphasise the 'closed' city as the demands of event owners require citizen exclusion, superficial (passive) participation and performative labour, not to actively involve 'citizens' in a democratic, participative and empowering manner, but as a means of profiling positive signs and symbols saleable to a passive watching audience.

Summary

In this chapter, it has been suggested that events have moved from being somewhat 'unplanned' – or at least not as clearly 'created' for a specific purpose – to the point where they are planned by 'experts' with intended outcomes in mind. These outcomes (the new functions, they can be termed) are so powerful that they can alter the very fabric of the event as originally conceived. This is important because, from the point of view of local and central government officials (in an age of entrepreneurial governance), events are increasingly deemed unsupportable unless they achieve economic goals, thus limiting the events that are given 'permission' to take place in public places, for example, and to secure public support. During the nineteenth century, many events were banished from the calendar in the name of civilisation and new ones were 'invented' to fulfil a more meaningful social function (Hobsbawm, 1983a). This practice is even more pronounced in the contemporary period as ritualistic practice is threatened by the logic of regeneration.

Critical review questions

- Events and festivals have long played a functional role in pacifying unruly populations. How have their uses changed over the last century?
- Can you identify any problems with events that were created by local communities subsequently being used to attract tourism and inward investment?

Recommended reading

Hobsbawm, E. (1983a) 'Introduction: inventing traditions', in Hobsbawm, E. and Ranger, T. (eds) *The invention of tradition*, New York: Cambridge University Press.

Malcolmson, R.W. (1973) *Popular recreations in English society 1700–1850*, Cambridge: Cambridge University Press.

Waitt, G. (2008) 'Urban festivals: geographies of hype, helplessness and hope', *Geography Compass*, 2 (2): 513–537.

3 Trends in events and festivities
The policy panacea

Introduction

This chapter examines and evaluates the volume, value and scope of events in terms of local, national and global economies. It also considers the types of measures that are being used to evaluate events and festivals, how these measures are decided upon and both the standards of research practice and the underlying economic concepts chosen. It goes on to reflect upon the reasons for measurement and ends with an analysis of the politics of the measurement agenda. In turn, this feeds directly into Chapter 4, which scrutinises the evaluation of events in more detail.

Making the case for events

Until recently, the literature surrounding the justification for staging events and in estimating their associated impacts has been almost wholly derived from economic analyses (Crompton, 2001). Despite this almost global tendency, Emery (2002: 328), quoting Bunce (1995), suggests that only seven per cent of public sector agencies in the UK use economic impact studies in making decisions about the merits of events and festivals. Whereas the use of economic impact estimates was unusual in 1995, it now appears to be an essential prerequisite for securing political support for staging events and demonstrating their relationship with revenue and employment generation.

Since the early 1990s economic impact assessment has become the norm, and the impacts being estimated now frequently extend beyond the economic to the social, the cultural and the environmental – as simply being able to demonstrate economic 'success' or impact is likely to be insufficient to satisfy a policy agenda increasingly described using the terminology of the 'triple bottom-line' or the 'balanced scorecard' (Gratton, Shibli and Coleman, 2006). For example, the Sports Industry Research Group at Sheffield Hallam University and the Birkbeck Sports Business Centre at the University of London have routinely conducted a range of economic impact studies of sport events. However, it is only since around 2004 that social and cultural impact assessments have been conducted rigorously, accepted more widely and (crucially) used as part of the policy process (Garcia, 2004). Moreover, where these estimates are absent in bidding or in wider policy considerations it is now more common for questions to be asked of the robustness of the case (Walters, 2008). That is not to say that events have not (in the past) had significant local, national and international impacts; rather, it is only recently that these analyses have been conducted coherently, widely and authoritatively and are being exploited more fully in developing the role of events as effective interventions in economic, social and public policy. This has both followed in the wake of, and been partially responsible for, local authorities, state governments and individual politicians across the world becoming much more aware of the political impact that peripatetic events can have on both their cities and, concomitantly, their personal careers. Not surprisingly, the danger attendant upon this self-conscious approach to bidding is that competing for such events can sometimes focus, as Emery (2002: 331) observes, 'on personal and political conviction' rather than the logic or merits of the specific event for that city.

Walters (2008: 11) discusses how aspects of increases in either sports development or social and cultural impact are difficult to measure 'due to the need for the long term evaluations'. This no doubt inconvenient and perhaps resource-aggressive opportunity to reinforce 'one-off' impact analyses with a follow through into demonstrating lasting, sustainable and embedded benefits (or otherwise) is missed easily from the political agenda. This is partly because of an assumption that political power and influence will be different in four or eight years' time, or because localised 'boosterism' will have either reaped personal rewards to its exponents within a short planning cycle or it will have run its course and may not offer fruitful (positive) media coverage.

So it is clear that impact assessment of events is on the increase – in the expectations of planners, policy makers and citizens and in the practices of consultants, academics and government. That the forecasting and assessment of economic return has retained primacy in the field says much about the (relative) ease of measurement in the economic realm compared to other possible analyses of impacts, the tendency of economic arguments to domi-nate political debate and the portability and replicability of the models in use (Blake, 2005).

Events and global tourism impacts

Events and festivals are, in economic terms, considered to be net generators of tourism, producing both additional visitation and revenue to a destination. Chapter 1 reviewed the 'broad' scale of events for global, national and local areas. This chapter now considers some specific geographic concentrations and attempts to show how global public agencies (e.g. the World Tourism Organization) monitor and measure touristic arrivals to countries in five grouped regions throughout the world. Later in this chapter the changes in these arrivals are charted to show a dramatic increase in some segments of the world since the early 1990s (e.g. East Asia and the Pacific, and the Middle East). These increases in tourist arrivals have been linked to the strategic changes in bidding for events and marketing in these regions. Summary data will be used to demonstrate pictorially where a large-scale or mega-event has taken place to chart increases in touristic visitation and to draw some correlations between the two – broadly linked to specific strategies of competing in the events bidding circuit (e.g. Doha, which hosted the Asian Games in 2006 and failed in its bid to host the Olympics in 2016).

In terms of measurement, International Tourist Arrivals (ITA) is a standard tool used throughout the world, so it provides a useful comparative base figure. Although it allows the interpretation of trend data, measurement of arrivals offers little in terms of reasons for visitation, so it is hard to connect these directly to the hosting of major sporting or cultural events. Where possible, regions' strategies for events and tourism will be linked to arrivals in the ensuing discussion.

A further significant measurement indicator is the contribution to Gross Domestic Product (GDP) that an event can claim – most countries around the world provide this and it will be commented on in relation to events. However, such claims are fraught with hazard – both as absolute measures of impact and contribution and as comparators with other nation-states. Analyses are seldom clear about the additional contributions being made by an event – i.e. the extra economic impact that would not have occurred had the event not taken place, known as additionality. For various reasons, that may be less than the impact given because some visitors would have visited the region anyway and spent their money there regardless of the event being staged. Equally, events may have unexpected, and hard to quantify, costs and benefits – known as externalities – such as environmental consequences, increases in crime or long-term increases in the image of a destination. What is presented below needs to be treated with caution for these reasons.

The Keynesian multiplier is the estimate most often and most widely used, but is also increasingly the measure that is most criticised (Horne and Manzenreiter, 2004; Chalip, 2006) by both academic analysts and industry professionals. Criticisms fall into two broad areas. First, the underlying assumptions of expenditure patterns that must prefigure any data gathering and analysis, when combined with the process of measurement, lead to methodological concerns about the reliability and validity of findings. This criticism is most frequently ventilated when the political ramifications of any 'findings' are inconsistent with, or inconvenient for, the preoccupations of any particular interest group. Second, there are concerns, particularly among professional event directors, that multiplier analysis, by its very nature, does not account for the social and cultural impacts of major events (Crompton, 2001). There is a danger, therefore, that what gets measured is what can most easily be measured, rather than a connection made, via an evaluation strategy, to the objectives of the host, the event owners or the other stakeholders – a situation that offers its own challenges to, and implications for, strategies and policies for events. Thus, the impact of a major event on a country or region is often heralded only in economic terms, particularly where the numerical representations of the analysis seem very large and where media and PR considerations are to the fore. It is not uncommon for the communications strategies of major events to address specifically the possible political damage caused by coverage of escalating costs, dubious local connections and benefits and (apparent) environmental costs – all three can provide journalists with fruitful material, once the euphoria of bid-winning dies down and the process of preparation and early investment begins. Political stakeholders often associate themselves strongly with event bids as part of their assertions of local or national identity, global cultural connectedness, recognition and emerging civic pride. Demonstrable, and apparently authoritative, estimates of income and employment generation are obviously helpful in ensuring that perceptions of success and the 'halo' of the event continue for some time after it has ended. The multiplier is, thus, generally used to show flow after the event but is often criticised for over-estimating returns over costs (Hall, 2006), a criticism that derives from the technical and political imperatives outlined above. For example, McCartney *et al.* (2009), in a report on the legacy of events conducted for the Scottish Government in anticipation of the Commonwealth Games in 2014, have shown that there is mixed evidence on the economic impact of hosting mega sporting events and suggest that governments need to consider carefully the likelihood of actual, realised economic growth, the likely impacts of such growth and the unintended consequences of such a strategy. More fundamentally, Gratton *et al.* (2006) suggest that calculating the economic impact per day is a more appropriate indicator of the success of an event than estimating total expenditure and that the latter is what causes many of the over-estimations and subsequent problems. Undoubtedly, spectator-driven events are more likely to generate income than competitor-driven events (although they will also generate greater costs, some of which will be far harder to measure accurately than, say, direct income at turnstiles), and Gratton *et al.* emphasise the need for agencies to first forecast and then analyse actual spectator numbers for a truer economic impact analysis.

Thus, an overall problem appears to be that agencies are estimating and predicting impact before the event has been allocated to justify bringing it to the host city, to satisfy political interests and to invest in media (and thus popular) support. This is unsurprising, especially as the cost of bidding for major events has escalated considerably, and the financial costs of failing in that bid are considerable, notwithstanding the risks to international reputation and local confidence. So even a failed bid will seek economic justification when the post mortem is conducted, drawing on the inevitable political terrain of the necessity to compete to maintain global profile and to demonstrate civic ambition.

After that, the problem appears to be that there is no uniform approach to gathering data on the impact of major sporting or cultural events, and while it is impossible to get governments around the world agreeing to such a uniform methodology, there is increasingly a need for some form of impact assessment that each sporting or cultural agency can agree to, if the credibility of impact assessments is to be secured.

The politics of measurement

When bidding on and winning the right to host events, countries are not only heralding their success or otherwise solely in economic terms but also in terms of demonstrable improvements to their nations' health, wealth, safety, general tourism profile, and social and cultural environment. This suggests that longitudinal analyses of variables that have been notoriously difficult to measure would have to be conducted, taking account of externalities, additionality and direct causal links between the event and the desirable social impact. This last issue has been especially intractable for policy analysts when seeking to correlate – not least because of the time needed to embed some of these in communities and in general social consciousness. Not surprisingly, then, there is little convincing evidence of such impacts being sustained beyond the short term, and there is little evidence of the reasons for perceived or asserted positive impacts (Daniels, Backman and Backman, 2003). What is less clear is whether these analyses have been conducted and have been found wanting in some respect, or whether they are simply too expensive, too difficult technically or politically unsustainable to consider in the first place.

The lack of 'quality' evidence is more likely to be the case with cultural festivals or events. Sporting events tend to be criticised for the cost of capital investments, and the over-run of capital costs budgets often tends to be blamed – thus comments like 'London 2012 runs millions over budget'. Preuss (2004) cautions against this approach and suggests it is dangerous to attribute such costs to a two- or three-week event when the lifespan of the capital investment could be fifty or so years. The 'common sense' assumption is that any impact is wholly attributable to the actual sporting or cultural festival, but, as Vrettos (2006) suggests, that is unsustainable because of inconsistencies in measure-ment and because few analyses (in terms of cultural festivals) consider whether the impact is because of the artistic nature or the social nature of the festival. This could equally be applied to sporting events, where assertions of general health benefits or community engagement cannot be solely attributed to any single factor, as with an Olympic Games. Such concerns lead to questions about whether the inevitable, media-driven raising of consciousness of 'sport' or 'culture' attendant upon the process of facility and infrastructure develop-ment is either important or measurable compared to the actual actions of sport and arts development professionals 'on the ground'. It seems likely that both are important, but that only spawns more questions about the security of measurement, rather than informing strategies for embedding the benefits of an event locally and nationally.

Once again, these difficulties question both the tools of measurement and the rationales and strategies for measurement. The overwhelming status quo seems to be concerned with the technical considerations of reliability around the tools of measurement and the accuracy of predictability of the impact rather than matters of validity in what is being measured and for what reasons. So it is likely that non-locals are visiting a city because of a sporting or cultural festival, but equally it is at least possible that they are visiting not to see the actual event, but for the social and cultural festivities that surround the event, thus making the city a more attractive place to visit, a place to be at the time of a global focus upon that region. Currently, this is being overlooked as a possibility in many studies. More work is needed to look at what is being measured and why, and what this says about impact, rather than technical, rational aspects of measurement practice. Policy makers now concentrate their considerations upon economic analyses, largely because these predominate, are widely quoted and acquire authority by continued use. Academics look to these forms of analysis too, and they have become a standard part of assessments of the contribution of events to the destination. Numerical assertions are more media friendly as well as being attractive to politicians who often want numbers as opposed to nebulous assertions.

The volume of events: tourism inflows

Notwithstanding the conditions placed upon the numerical data used to calculate economic impacts, to gain insights into the principal trends in events and festivities it is prudent to use the tools and techniques that exist and are in widespread use at present as a guide. Major events and festivities can regularly be associated with 'spikes' (literally, as demonstrated pictorially below) in tourism demand, measured in the form of arrivals and expenditure. Politically speaking, major increases in tourism flows and revenues in comparison to competitor economies are a 'good news' story. These apparently objective measures, which are broadly accepted as being globally comparable, have direct impacts upon national income and local economic development strategies. Many agencies with economic development objectives become involved in deciding which events to target in bidding and how and where the bid will be located. As recent events in other industries have shown, economic considerations and economic 'health' tend to have primacy over other policy preoccupations in what is broadly a neoliberal agenda for governments globally (see Chapter 5). It is simply not politically sustainable, or feasible in global economic terms, to run significant debt, or to fund solely via taxation, in order to host an event – even where 'estimated' economic growth associated with the event could lead to eventual payback. Where taxation implications apply, it is often necessary to demonstrate a spread of (positive and desirable) impacts (say, to a whole nation in the development of an Olympic Games) in order to justify a taxation impact that, because of its size, must be spread across a wide population of citizens, consumers and businesses to make it politically acceptable. While other areas of policy preoccupations may have recurring primacy over resources (health and education being the most obvious in liberal democracies), attempts to run a major event solely as a one-off economic entity are likely to be frustrated. Thus they have to associate themselves with influencing and supporting the wider public policy agenda (in what will often be characterised as 'joined-up policy'), usually through ideas of legacy, while demonstrating that they are not, in themselves, significant drains upon economic resources. Thus, cases for bidding and winning tend to revolve around ideas of 'leverage' whereby the event itself becomes a focus for activities, facilities and (asserted) benefits, some of which might have happened without it and all of which are political 'winners'.

This section now turns to an examination of the volume of tourist arrivals and links this, where possible, to mega sporting or cultural events to try to give a global snapshot of the scale of growth of peripatetic events. Simultaneously, it addresses the challenges of the legitimation of running events and why this leads to a probable over-reliance on purely numerical (and economic-orientated) measurement tools and techniques. The irony of the use of graphs and numbers is not lost on the authors here, but, where possible, these are framed within an interpretive framework, which until now, has been missing.

The general trend of worldwide international tourist arrivals since 1990 has been one of steady, if modest, growth, even in the period that is now termed an economic downturn of the global economy. Figure 3.1 shows a general

	1990	1995	2000	2001	2002	2003	2004	2005	2006	2007	2008*
- - - - World	441	538	681	680	700	690	763	802	847	903	924
—— Europe	264.8	309.3	384.1	383.8	394	396.6	416.4	438.3	462.2	484.9	488.5
·········· Asia and the Pacific	57.7	85	114.9	120.7	131.1	119.3	152.5	155.4	167	184.2	188.3
— — Americas	92.8	109	128.2	122.1	116.6	113.1	125.8	133.2	135.8	142.5	147.6
—— Africa	15.2	20.4	28.2	28.9	29.5	30.8	33.2	37.3	41.4	44.3	46.9
— · — Middle East	10	14.3	25.2	25	29.2	30	35.4	38.3	40.9	47.4	52.9

Figure 3.1 Global shifts in tourist arrivals.

*2008 data estimated.

Source: UN World Tourism Organization (2009).

stagnation in tourist arrivals between 2000 and 2003, followed by increased growth. A particular feature is that Asia and the Pacific has overtaken the Americas, from a difference of minus 35.1 million arrivals in 1990 to a difference of plus 40.7 million in 2008. This may be, in part, because Asian nation-states have been strongly marketing themselves as event destinations (e.g. Seoul Olympics; Japan and South Korea FIFA World Cup; several Formula 1 Grands Prix, the Asian Games; and numerous international conferences, such as the International Monetary Fund event in Singapore). This 'top-line' merchandising of a destination via such flagship events is part of the policy objective of showing that it possesses the ambition and the infrastructure to host any significant events and the attitude to set its sights in the comparative international arena of capable nations. For example, in 2007 the Qatar Olympic Committee produced a seven-year strategic plan for bidding for events, culminating in its (unsuccessful) bid for the Summer Olympic Games in 2016 and the (successful) soccer World Cup 2022 bid. All of this seems to suggest that, with rational planning and strategic investment, an event destination can be developed successfully.

Of particular interest here is the underlying methodology used by the World Tourism Organization (WTO) for the construction of these data, representing, as these do, one of the key, agreed, international tourism performance indicators to which almost all nation-states subscribe. These are based upon enumerated arrivals at international airports and thus amount to actual numbers, rather than estimates derived from additional methodological interventions with tourists or the sector.

Region- and country-specific graphs are shown in the relevant sections, highlighting growth in tourist arrivals and showing the presence of major events alongside these where appropriate. There is evidence to suggest that in some areas visitation would drop in the year of a major event (e.g. 2000 Sydney Olympics) but that the growth in visitors to a region in the years to follow shows a marked increase. This is now being posited as one of the benefits of a mediatised mega-event, showcasing a city's attractiveness as a destination for more than just a (transitory) sporting or cultural event. Of course, it also raises policy issues around the inevitable infrastructural improvements and investments in human and peripheral (at least, peripheral to the main, original mega-event) resources and thus reinforces the argument that analyses of the impact of events need to account for cultural and social impact in the medium to long term and not just the immediate economic impacts (Preuss, 2004). It is tempting to speculate that these wider and longer-term estimates are becoming a greater part of a policy-driven, expectation management needed to convince politicians, investigative journalists and sceptical citizens that benefits will surely accrue if a long enough timeframe is adopted. That is not to say that such benefits may not be directly attributable to the original event in many cases. However, policy development is bedevilled by the challenge of demonstrating a direct causal link between event and benefit. Already difficult to assert in the short term, this becomes increasingly tenuous as time progresses and other phenomena intervene both at the destination and in the wider strategic and operational environments.

Of most interest in the forecast shown in Figure 3.2 is the decline in projected market share for European destinations, and the significant, relative increases in market shares for destinations in Asia and the Pacific and the Middle East (100 per cent in the case of the Middle East). Noting that the WTO estimates that Asia and the Pacific will have over one quarter of the world's tourists in 2020 offers significant opportunities for these destinations in terms of their events and conferences industries – indeed, these industries play a significant role in the assembly of this forecast and in the underlying assumptions about restructuring of tourism demand globally. Moreover, the forecasts also represent significant challenges elsewhere, where events and their attendant tourism impacts may need to become part of the 'answer' to these possible reductions in demand.

Significantly, the forecast in Figure 3.2 is for the number of visits to each global region, i.e. international arrivals only. In bald economic policy terms, visits are merely opportunities for expenditure. Many destination managers now seek tourists with low environmental footprints and high per diem expenditure – low cost, high (economic) impact visitors. Where this can be achieved, significant reductions in actual visits can be offset locally by each remaining trip being of the highest possible net benefit. Particular visitor demographics are associated with this 'desirable' visitor type (of which more in Chapter 6), and it is reasonable to assert that certain types of major events attract these visitors, either directly at the event or, subsequently, as a result of effective merchandising during the event.

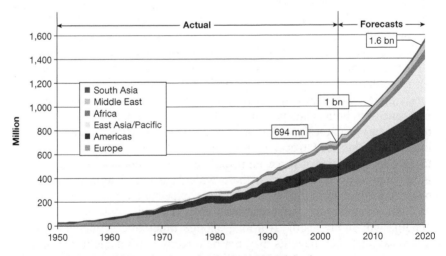

Figure 3.2 The World Tourist Organization's '2020 Vision'.

Source: 'The Tourism 2020 Vision', UN World Tourism Organization (2009); www.unwto.org/facts/menu.htm (accessed 5 July 2011).

During the general growth demonstrated in Figure 3.3, it is clear that many European destinations grew their short-break markets significantly (e.g. Prague, Dublin, Paris and Amsterdam) and that the removal of restrictions upon travel to and from Central and Eastern Europe had considerable impact on the overall size of the market. The evidence suggests that a lot more people were moving around Europe during this period, sometimes for relatively short periods of time. What is also clear is that major, urban-led and derived events became a particular feature of the European marketplace, highlighting various individual cities as embodying cultural, sporting and business excellence (e.g. Barcelona). Perhaps equally important was the idea of the city as a place where culture, sport and business could be conducted and witnessed and far more embedded in consumer consciousness, in industry marketing and in urban economic policies – and events located in any European city could provide possible benefits for almost all capital and 'second' cities, possessing, as many did, a wealth of resources ready to be consumed as either the focus of an event or festival or the backdrop to a holiday.

The crucial policy point here is the importance of the festival and the event in securing regional economic strategies within Europe. Most major cities developed a city-based function intended to develop their attitudes, infrastructure and capabilities to win and run large events, and even more worked to demonstrate that this was both desirable and successful as an urban development policy (e.g. Rotterdam).

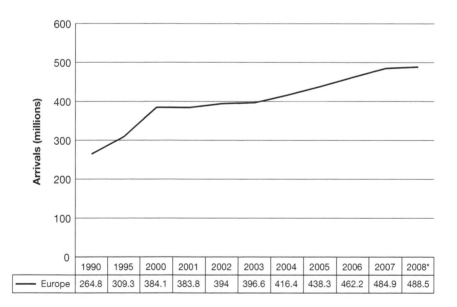

Figure 3.3 International tourism arrivals in Europe.

Source: 'Tourism Market Trends', UN World Tourism Organization (2009).

Figure 3.4 takes the specific example of tourist expenditure in Germany in the years up to, and following, the FIFA World Cup. What is obvious is the steady increase in expenditure, some of which is directly attributable to the event. More startling is the growth in expenditure up to the event, an important benefit of a long trailed event (qualification for the FIFA World Cup can take up to three years for some countries) where media attention reaches its crescendo during the competition proper but which highlighted the destination and host cities long before 2006. Of course, political changes in Germany since 1989 had a significant impact upon its desirability as a destination for its own and other European citizens, but its capability to exploit a growing media (and, thus, carrier, hotels industry and package tour sector) derived from emerging urban policies designed to capitalise upon all of the 'good news' stories about the country as a whole and to drive up expenditure (note, not necessarily visits – see above).

Of course, as an economic policy, this is inherently short-lived, if the 'halo' of political change and sporting infrastructure cannot be maintained. However, the management of the FIFA World Cup tournament, in various German cities and in using 'fan fests' outside stadia for the first time, emphasised the unity of the 'new' Germany (Frew and McGillivray, 2008) – offering clear marketing benefits that this was a destination for the 'new' Europe of many more members within easy travelling distance of its spectacular cultural and natural heritage.

Nation-states in the Middle East have been actively pursuing the sports tourism and event tourism market since early 2000 (see Figure 3.5). Abu Dhabi,

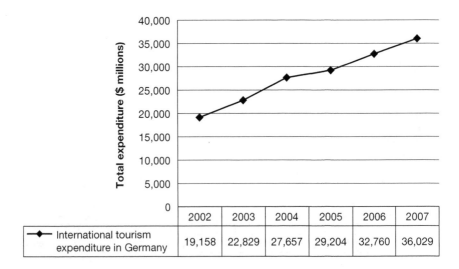

	2002	2003	2004	2005	2006	2007
International tourism expenditure in Germany	19,158	22,829	27,657	29,204	32,760	36,029

Figure 3.4 International tourism expenditure in Germany around 2006.

Source: 'Tourism Market Trends', UN World Tourism Organization (2009).

Dubai and Doha are close competitors in the market to secure the events capital destination of the Middle East (Foley *et al.*, 2009). Abu Dhabi won the right to host the F1 championships in 2007, and Dubai continued to host the Dubai Rugby Sevens part of the World Series, while Doha made it onto the events circuit by staging the largest ever (in terms of participants and global media coverage) Asian Games in 2006. The infrastructure, transport and facilities development necessary for the global events market has led all of these States to ensure they are now more attractive for touristic travellers generally, as well as for specific event tourists. Figure 3.5 reveals a 152 per cent increase in international tourist arrivals between 1990 and 2000, and a 109 per cent increase between 2000 and 2008.

Critical to policies in the Middle East has been the need for governments to diversify economies that have grown around commodities and money markets but which cannot sustain these in the long term as the only drivers of their economies. Many of these governments inhabit a policy environment that is radically different from the (generally) liberal democracies in Europe, most especially in the need to convince a political elite of strategic analyses and choices or avoid a media- or citizen-led opposition to policy directions. That is not to say that arguments have to be won, or that some elites have to be won over, but the processes of policy formation lie less exposed, and are more directive, than in some of the examples discussed previously. (See Chapter 10 for more details.)

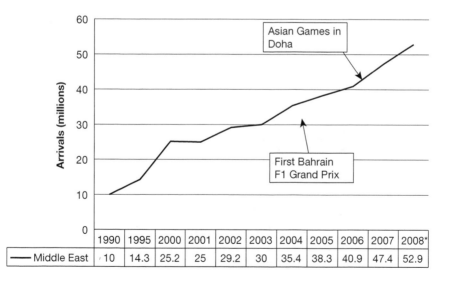

Figure 3.5 International tourist arrivals in the Middle East.

Source: 'Tourism Market Trends', UN World Tourism Organization (2009).

That many of the nation-states emerging into significance in terms of international festivals and events derive economic (and social and cultural) policies in these more directive forms is crucial to their eventual development in this part of the tourism sector. Planning of resorts, facilities and environments may be (superficially, at least) easier and perhaps more 'nimble' in reaction to economic and consumer trends. The need to show non-economic benefits to citizens individually and collectively can be more readily asserted – rather than argued and demonstrated in critical discourse. The long-term implications of this are yet to be demonstrated. In the short term, policies for tourism growth and events development in the Middle East continue apace.

Tourist arrivals in the Asia-Pacific region increased by 226 per cent between 1990 and 2008, and this is taking into account a nine per cent slump in 2003, put mainly down to the SARS epidemic. The strategy of this section of the world has been to actively pursue mega-events as part of their global economic policy (Horne and Manzenreiter, 2006).

Many nation-states in the Asia-Pacific region have set out their stall as global events 'players' during a period when their general growth (as so-called 'tiger economies') has been spectacular and their economic infrastructures and their associated politics of 'national identity as economic success' has been a crucial part of governmental credos – notwithstanding any underlying ideological frameworks. As these economies have become increasingly important

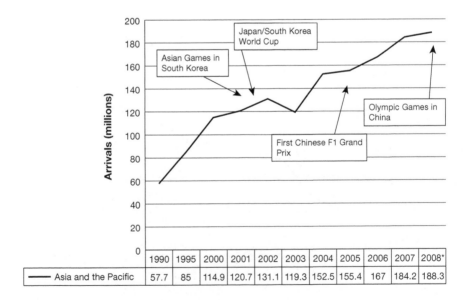

Figure 3.6 International tourist arrivals in the Asia-Pacific.

Source: 'Tourism Market Trends', UN World Tourism Organization (2009).

globally, public policies have sought to assert global connectedness by competing for, and winning the right to stage, international mega-events. For some, such as Singapore, where touristic bed-night supply is high but international, physical attractions are relatively few in number, events and festivities have become a significant part of the overall offering – encouraging incentive travel, business events and cultural experiences that are not always those that the host population either recognises or values. For others, such as China and India, their emergence into the G20 group of nations has coincided with their capabilities and capacities for international sporting events being showcased as part of a national policy of boosterism. In these cases, as with Japan and South Korea during the soccer World Cup of 2002, major economic investment to deliver state-of-the-art physical facilities and to 'grow' sporting cultures that can lead to successes at their own Games and in front of their own populations has been a significant policy expectation and deliverable.

Demonstrably, a range of (diverse) ideological and policy environments has led many governments to invest heavily in events and festivities as part of their growth, their arresting of decline or their diversification of economic approaches to governance. Critical to all of these policy directions has been the necessity for significant state intervention to ensure that the vagaries of market economics do not affect the overall 'message' – which is mostly not the event itself, but the externalities attendant upon the event. That these are often asserted and demonstrated as being greater than the original cause should be no surprise. Political, social and cultural influence may accrue from a major festival or event, but it is more likely to be positive over time and only after an initial demonstrable economic success (however measured) that is ongoing as a continued revenue stream.

Political rationale for event-led policy

The drive by local and national level politicians to secure exposure on a global scale has witnessed the rise of the mega-event (whether sporting or cultural) to super stardom in the race to reach the status of a global events city. It is a bit like an athlete's track record: countries and cities are now tracking their record in staging regional, national and worldwide events. Their ability to stage, host and manage a global media spectacle is on view for all to follow (Kellner, 2003). As was pointed out in Chapter 1, cities can achieve a level of status and capability for hosting mega-events. So, for example, Glasgow can host the Commonwealth Games in 2014 but would never be capable of hosting an Olympics. Cities need to be a certain size and scale and have sufficient infrastructure and capability for hosting the number of visits associated with the scale of the event they are staging. What the politicians recognise is that they want to be on that global events map – they want to compete with New York, London, Beijing or Sydney to host the Olympic Games, and if they are unable to meet that aspiration, then they want to be there with the next level of countries hosting Commonwealth Games or Asian Games or World Cup.

The status of the city and nation winning the event is now associated with the politicians and the celebrities that have backed the event.

Support for major events is now inseparable from the spectacle politics, which dominate political discourse. The announcement that Rio de Janeiro had won the 2016 Summer Olympic Games was not unexpected in some camps but it represented a surprise for Chicago, especially as the US President, Barack Obama, was flown in to Copenhagen for last minute talks to sway the voters. On this occasion it proved unsuccessful, a tactical error as the Brazilian President had impressed IOC members with his ongoing commitment to the Rio bid over a much longer time. The political strategy of the then-UK Prime Minister, Tony Blair, was more successful when London was victorious for the 2012 Summer Olympics. The UK Prime Minister spent three days in Singapore, wooing the voters. What is clear is that winning the right to host major events is about the political power that a country can put behind the bid alongside possession of the technical capacity to deliver on the strict conditions laid out by the IOC. The IOC also faces increasing political pressure to share the Olympic Games around the world (Rio will be the first time the Games have been staged in a Latin American country). As illustrated in Box 3.1, the 2010 soccer World Cup in South Africa set out to prosecute a developmental agenda built around the alleviation of poverty, reductions in crime and opening up of new possibilities for the host nation and the entire African continent. Increasingly, the owners of major events have to consider these supranational agendas in their decision-making.

The worry for policy makers is that the outcome of increasing demands for sophisticated technical bids is the ranking of cities capable of hosting particular events. There are already a number of examples of nations whose ability to host major games has been brought into doubt in the run up to the event. Concerns were expressed about Greece before the Athens Olympic Games of 2004, about South Africa (see above) before the 2010 World Cup and about India before the 2010 Commonwealth Games. While the criticisms have ultimately been unfounded, nevertheless, the presence of doubt does feed into the hands of established cities and nations desperate to communicate their credentials as the 'safe pair of hands' to host the highest profile events.

Summary

This chapter has discussed the use of measurement tools and techniques in bidding for, and securing, large-scale events, and has demonstrated the significance of the politics of the measurement agenda for event policy makers. The chapter provided a snapshot of the volume and value of tourism travel and changes in destination arrivals coinciding with large-scale events and festivals. It suggested that policy makers, to assert their position as competitive cities in the global marketplace, increasingly use these trends data. As barriers to travel diminish and a consumerist culture around festivity and events grows, the desire of large cities to host events becomes a key tool in the economic

Box 3.1 South Africa World Cup

The South Africa 2010 World Cup provides a clear demonstration that using economic arguments to attract large-scale events can also produce social and political by-products. The South African government have used this global event as a means show the world that they are addressing issues associated with inequality, race, security and infrastructural under-development. The soccer World Cup represented an ideal vehicle to address these issues because sport has been used for many years as an oppositional tool against apartheid (Ndlovu, 2010) in South Africa. According to Ndlovu, South Africa's foreign policy has been based on presenting Africa as a better place to the world. The use of cultural diplomacy as a strategy in securing a sporting event has been extremely beneficial to South Africa. Jacob Zuma, South Africa's President, has already declared that they will bid to host an Olympic Games on the back of their successful hosting of the FIFA World Cup 2010.

What this case tells us is that the policy of several African nations over recent years has been to accomplish economic and political objectives using the vehicle of major events (Cornelissen, 2004). Moreover, Africa has also employed an 'emotional' strategy to persuade event owners that this continent deserves its turn to host global games. This was clearly used as a bidding strategy by Abuja for their unsuccessful 2014 Commonwealth Games bid. The emotional arguments, when attached to economic outcomes, provide a powerful case for distributing major events more equally. The successful Rio 2016 Olympic bid put forward an emotional political argument that winning the event would bring economic improvement to the underdeveloped South American region. Brazil and South Africa share some similarities as both nations have struggled to alter negative representations associated with their treatment of citizens. But the success of using mega-events to win the hearts and minds of other nations and governing bodies and to catalyse social (as well as economic) development is certainly gathering pace. If the major event owners see political capital from awarding their events to nations with a developmental agenda, then perhaps the nature and form of future mega-events will be very different from those hosted in the developed liberal democracies of the West.

Further reading: Cornelissen, S. (2004) 'Sport mega-events in Africa: processes, impacts and prospects', *Tourism and Hospitality Policy and Development*, 1 (1): 39–55.

and image regeneration agenda of the country – although this agenda is not uncontested within cities and nations. This chapter has reflected on the use of economic impact studies and their political value during and after events, and has exposed the need for more coherent approaches to the analysis of social and cultural impacts of events on local, national and international communities (see Chapters 7 and 8 for further discussion). There is a danger that an over-reliance on political expediency in securing events could distract attention from the key task of securing successful sporting and/or cultural experiences. That said, it is clear that, for political leaders the world over, the use of state intervention to further economic, social and public policies is a key driver for event-led strategies. While in a neoliberal period this should be of surprise to no one, it is important that policy makers ensure that the benefits are embedded sufficiently to ensure that the positive impacts sought through events and festivals are achievable and sustainable, beyond the short term of political life.

Critical review questions

•   Why are economic impact assessments attractive to political decision makers when making the case for hosting major events?
•   What are the potential drawbacks of awarding major events only to a select few 'developed' nations on a rotational basis?

Recommended reading

Baade, R. and Matheson, V. (2004) 'The quest for the cup: assessing the economic impact of the World Cup', *Regional Studies*, 38 (4): 343–354.
Daniels, M.J., Backman, K.F. and Backman, S.J. (2003) 'Supplementing event economic impact results with perspectives from host community business and opinion leaders', *Event Management*, 6 (3): 175–189.
Preuss, H. (2004) *The economics of staging the Olympics: a comparison of the Games 1972–2008*, Cheltenham, Edward Elgar.

4   Evaluating event outcomes
A legitimation crisis

Introduction

This chapter extends the discussion in Chapter 3 and concludes Part 1 of the book by considering the growing importance of event evaluation processes in legitimating the policy interventions made by local, national and international 'actors' alike. Over recent years it has become clear that the monitoring and evaluation function is closely linked with policy development. The planned outcomes associated with sporting, cultural, corporate and other events are increasingly influenced by wider political aims, and the choice of what is evaluated and judgements on success or failure cannot be detached from the overarching political (and economic) environment of the time. As political actors from across the public, private and third sectors coalesce to produce event-led strategies (in the democratic Western world, at least), monitoring and evaluation become crucial mechanisms for legitimating policy objectives and contributing to the transparency and accountability of the process – a frequent criticism of the irrational decisions made by political elites in the past (Roche, 2000). This chapter draws on Jürgen Habermas's (1976) *Legitimation Crisis* thesis, to reflect critically on the politics of the evaluation process. It will consider how investment in events-led urban 'boosterist' strategies now requires justification on the basis of objective outcome and output measures. It will discuss the way in which the preponderance of economic impact assessments is slowly being complemented with an array of evaluation techniques that are the outcome of greater demands to include a wider set of stakeholders in the ownership of event-led strategies. However, the chapter also considers the challenges facing policy makers in developing appropriate models for measuring longer-term and more subjective social and cultural indicators associated with large-scale events, in particular. Moreover, it also discusses the rather Eurocentric nature of the debate on evaluation, drawing on examples from parts of the world where legitimation of the sort expected in much of Europe and North America is non-existent.

Why a legitimation crisis?

This discussion starts by outlining the choice of the term 'legitimation crisis' in the title of the chapter. To do so, it is worth returning to the latter part of the discussion in Chapter 2 regarding the implications of an over-reliance on the function of economic regeneration in the planned outcomes associated with events in the early twenty-first century. In this context, Hassan *et al.* (2007) have suggested that citizens of those cities (particularly in North America and Europe), which have followed a boosterist urban strategy, suffer from the narrowly defined nature of what they call the 'official future' (p. 48). This official future, they argue, is less about progressive ideas around 'citizen participation', 'ownership' or 'voice' and more concerned with who deploys power to condition and constrain the strategic direction of urban policy in these locales. Whitson and Horne (2006), among others, have expressed a desire for greater citizen participation in every aspect of the debate over the decisions to bid for and subsequently deliver events, and this is partly due to some concerns over the authorship, content and style of an official future that is common to many of those cities and regions across the world following an events-led strategy. Since the 1980s a host of cities have actively pursued entrepreneurial governance strategies, and their focus on market-led growth coalitions (involving business leaders and public officials) has meant that the interests of commerce have often been explicitly promoted over the traditional welfarist concerns of the state. In this period of what Habermas calls advanced capitalism, the local state then 'becomes the complementary arrangement to self-regulative market commerce . . . economic exchange becomes the dominant steering mechanism' (Habermas, 1988: 21). Following this line of argument, state power is reduced to a supporting role in the protection of commerce, the shielding of the market mechanism, and the regulation of the system to facilitate economic growth – essentially providing the foundations upon which consumerism can flourish.

The interests of private capital (e.g. commercial institutions) also frequently permeate the content of the vision for the official future. The terms 'step change' and 'transformation', 'world class (or global) city', 'opportunity' and 'choice' are ubiquitous in urban governance discourse, including in the realm of events strategy. The official future is one defined as doing better, promoting conspicuous consumption, affluent lifestyles and tourism, narrowly focused on free market private developments and economic growth. Stylistically, the content is communicated in impenetrable language that Hassan *et al.* (2007) argue becomes an impediment to public comprehension – while, at the same time, promoting the maxims of profit-orientation. This perspective paints a picture of a relatively autonomous and powerful economic sphere enabled by a supportive local state, but this view is not without its critics. Scholars in a variety of academic fields are increasingly concerned that the 'costs' of this version of the official future for the wider public(s) are disengagement and disempowerment (no point in participating as the future is planned out), disbelief and distrust (official future not aligned with citizens' values and ideas of hidden agendas and power building), and opposition and confusion (ulterior 'versions' of the city start to appear – crime, poverty, drugs and social collapse). These concerns are heightened due to a perceived tokenistic engagement with meaningful public involvement and consultation in the policy process. Existing in relation to a wide range of social and public policy terrains (e.g. education, housing and use of public space), these concerns are also evident in the field of event policy where there is growing unease with the lack of apparent commitment to citizen engagement in, and ownership of, major events. The emerging evidence base around the impact of major sporting events, for example, suggests that it is, at best, unclear that the needs of direct and indirect beneficiaries (Whitson and Horne, 2006) are being adequately served by the furtherance of an events-led urban strategy. Critics propose that a host of beneficiaries are proposed, often without substantiation, as a form of legitimating rhetoric (Chalip, 2006) for political elites. As Getz (2007: 319) suggests, 'It often seems like industry and the community's powerful elite realise huge profits at the taxpayer's expense, even while poor people are displaced or the middle class has its taxes increased to pay for the mega event or new event venue'. Whatever the veracity of claim and counterclaims, it is clear that there is a renewed interest in questions of how state intervention in major events and festivity is rendered legitimate to those in whose name the policies are implemented. The growth in the use of monitoring and evaluation of event outcomes is certainly one important legitimating vehicle.

In using the term 'legitimation crisis' in the chapter title attention is drawn to the thesis of the renowned critical theorist Jürgen Habermas, who has written extensively over the last three decades of the crisis tendencies inherent in the capitalist economic system. As a critical theorist, Habermas is committed to emancipation, in bringing attention to and, ultimately, changing the conditions of people so that they can realise their human freedom – a freedom that, critical theorists argue, has been left unrealised due to the conditions of domination and ideology, which are features of the capitalist system. Habermas goes beyond the internal dynamics of the capitalist economic system to consider wider political and cultural processes that act to legitimate the system itself. His work is useful for this discussion of evaluation as a means of legitimising event policy objectives because his theoretical tools can be used to unmask the 'interests' (economic and political, in particular) at work in employing specific techniques to validate narrowly defined market-led outcomes accruable from investment in events.

In charting the development of the capitalist economic system, Habermas contends that, in the move from primitive to traditional and, subsequently, liberal to capitalist social formations, market commerce has become the dominant player, relegating the political class to a secondary, facilitative role. Elements of what he calls the *system* (economic, political) interact with the *lifeworld* (the other 'level') in different forms and contexts. For Habermas, the accelerating importance of the economic system and the 'crisis' tendencies therein creates the need for management and planning to be displaced and transformed into the spheres of social and cultural life (the lifeworld) once largely free of direct involvement (e.g. in primitive social formations, kinship relations governed people's behaviour). Using the example of event policy, it is clear to see that economic and political systems are inseparable in those cities that are committed to boosterist strategies, and this increasingly spills over into the wider social and cultural spheres of life, too. The administration of events as an economic driver (see Chapter 2) acts to politicise them as governments (local and national) try to use their profile to facilitate growth (economic impact) and, at the same time, to alleviate the social costs (social impact) attributable to the self-same market-led policies. Furthermore, in the context of events, economic imperatives are 'translated into political problems' (Dandaneau, 2008: 208) to be solved by subsidising the hosting of major events or by absorbing the costs associated with providing the infrastructural framework for this to happen.

For Habermas, crisis tendencies exist (which might lead to a withdrawal of legitimation) when micromanagement moves from the administrative system or bureaucracies to the lifeworld or socio-cultural system. The lifeworld is constituted through communicative action, or mutual understanding achieved 'between agents and their common orientation towards shared norms and values' (Crossley, 2003: 291). This refers to personal identity and the sphere of cultural patterns and traditions that define people's sense of reality. In Chapter 2 it is suggested that there has been a shift from events as ritualistic practice to events as regenerative policy, and this can be associated with Habermas's concern about the 'colonization of the lifeworld' that, he argues, is a defining feature of advanced capitalism. Historically, traditions have played the role of useful legitimising activities, but their instrumental use potentially endangers the continuity through which individuals and groups can identify with one another and frame their sense of place. Overly invasive techniques into the cultural sphere are of concern to Habermas, and he warns that there are 'limits to being able to make up for legitimation deficits through conscious manipulation' (Habermas, 1988: 71). Yet recent evidence suggests that an instrumental desire to realise wider social and economic policy objectives through events is being implemented without much concern for the potential loss of cultural value that might accompany it.

The tentacles of economic and political interests are frequently extended into the cultural domain to assuage the crisis tendencies of advanced capitalism. However, the danger associated with this increasing colonisation is that further planned state intervention requires simultaneous legitimation, which might not be easily achieved. As Dandaneau (2008: 211) contends, 'For Habermas, it is not possible to replace traditional values and beliefs with an artificial culture constructed only to further some corporation's profit-maximisation strategy or some government's legitimacy'. Of specific concern for this chapter is the possibility that the effect of instrumental rationality invading the realm of events and festivity is that the colonisation of the traditional or cultural might actually work to destabilise and create disaffection and apathy on behalf of citizens, further drawing attention to the notion of who gains and who pays for events. If the evaluation process for events and festivity is, similarly, conceived in terms of instrumental rationality (i.e. demonstrating the economic value of events) bereft of meaningful participation or debate from 'public' stakeholders other than those from the realm of commerce and political elites, then the possibility of a loss of confidence in that system is real, as the form of legitimation is superficial and bound up in self-interest.

If the system of governance (and, of interest to us, evaluation) is 'democratic in name but . . . in myriad ways discourages genuine participation and denies average citizens a meaningful political voice' (Dandaneau, 2008: 211–212) then Habermas's prediction of a withdrawal of legitimation and of motivation is real (see instances of protest and mobilisation of campaign groups against numerous Olympic Games, as an example). Habermas argued that the space for two-way dialogue and debate in the public sphere, without the interference of political or market forces, is already severely curtailed. When the opportunity for such 'dialogue' does take place – say through consultation or engagement workshops – it is, at best, tokenistic and 'framed' in such a way as to generate the conclusions already envisaged (e.g. exaggerated benefits and minimised costs).

Moreover, in the context of events, the process (or procurement) of legitimation is increasingly consumerist in its logic and practice. For example, as a substitute to meaningful open public debate (i.e. in democratically accountable forums), there is a growing tendency to use marketing and public relations expertise to create innovative campaigns that exhort the host citizens to support a bid for major sporting (and, increasingly, cultural) events. The outcome of these campaigns is invariably an overwhelming show of support for the hosts' plans, and this is taken to reflect legitimation for the actions of political leaders and their growth coalition partners. However, it can be argued that there is a 'legitimation deficit' at work here as these campaigns are carefully choreographed through media management to ensure that commitment to 'support' a bid campaign needs no more effort than clicking a button or depositing a postcard in a collection box as you enjoy a café latte in the nearest Starbucks. 'Backing the Bid' (see Chapter 9 for a discussion of Glasgow 2014 Commonwealth Games campaign of the same name) is reduced to an act of consumption that carries with it little additional accountability or transparency – or, for that matter, participation of the individual. It is a show of generalised support as opposed to a commitment on behalf of the individual to pay additional taxes or accept housing displacement as a consequence of its delivery. In this respect, there remains a problematic deficit between making the case for hosting events in urban locations and the common practice of post-event evaluation, which has dominated the field for the last decade. Crossley (2003: 295), reflecting on Habermas's view of the degeneration of political debate, argues that 'public communication by politicians . . . has become a glorified public relations exercise, and genuine public opinion is drowned in the sea of manufactured opinion generated by the pollsters and image consultants'. When associated with the promotion of events and their imaginative bidding campaigns, then, the processes of legitimation can be described as increasingly superficial. To date, they exhibit few tendencies for the realisation of an effective public sphere where social actors are reflexive about their circumstances and which can offer the potential for greater 'public' ownership of events within host destinations.

The increased importance of the evaluation function for events provides an illustration of legitimation claims in action. Under the conditions of advanced capitalism where the market system dominates, events are no longer defensible on the basis of their intrinsic cultural value alone. Instead, they must be objectified, turned into quantifiable assets and measured according to the logic of advanced capitalist economic systems. However, at the same time, there are concerns that the 'publics' who are targeted as the beneficiaries of event-led strategies are left disaffected as the logic of evaluation continues to focus on criteria of value that assert the importance of private capital return over other, less easily measurable variables.

The politics of evaluation: the multiplier effect

In the preceding discussions a case for the inseparability of the economic and the political under advanced capitalism has been made. There is also a close relationship between wider political aims and the development of specific events-related objectives to the point where we can say that there are 'ideological underpinnings influencing the focus, goals and objectives of . . . event policy' (Whitford, 2004: 17). As discussed in Chapter 2, it is clear that, as event forms and functions have been subject to change (linked to the ideological commitment to advanced capitalism), so the associated evaluation processes have concomitantly been altered to align with these new agendas. In this sense, it is clear that the 'approach to evaluation, the choice of what is measured and the judgement as to what has been achieved cannot be divorced from the wider political or cultural context' (Moore and Sykes, 2000: 203). Moore and Sykes are referring to the politics of evaluation here. As political actors (in coalition with private capital) set the agenda as to the policy objectives of the central or local state, their decisions have then to be legitimated by a system of appraisal that is often narrowly channelled to ensure that the desired outcomes are forthcoming. If evaluation is conceived of as a method of judging whether there is a rationale for policy interventions, and to monitor progress in achieving these, then the selection and use of particular evaluation techniques is an important battleground for the question of legitimating event policy. Principally, this is because the appropriateness of evaluation techniques (e.g. economic impact studies) can become self-fulfilling if they demonstrate the achievement of (set) objectives. Of course, principally, legitimation crises relate to nations with democratic systems of governance, where governments are accountable to those that elect them. In many parts of the world, alternative governance arrangements exist (e.g. communism in China, theocracies in the Middle East, ruling families in the Emirates) and there is no such need to secure the legitimation of the populace. This is important because those nations outside of the democratic form of governance, in effect, hold a significant advantage when it comes to the bidding process for peripatetic sporting events as their investments are not subjected to the same level of accountability as is common in, say, the UK.

What is certainly clear is that, over the last two decades, a step change has occurred whereby events have been justified (or legitimated) on the basis of their contribution to the economic well-being of the city, region or nation. Investment in an event-led urban strategy as an alternative to social welfare expenditure needs to be justified, politically, on the basis of objective outcome and output measures (i.e. that it works). As there is 'significant public sector expenditure to develop, underwrite and promote' (Connell and Page, 2005: 64) events, the evaluation techniques employed in both public and private sector event contexts are now ever more connected to the managerialist language of Key Performance Indicators (KPIs). Here, policy objectives are broken down into a set of measurable indicators that are easily quantified and manipulated using statistical techniques. It is an inherently positivist approach to research in which numbers are turned into 'meaning'. In terms of events, these KPIs will invariably include the numbers, place of origin, length of stay and expenditure of visitors, the media profile generated by the event (turned into an economic value), return on investment (ROI) for public and private stakeholders, infrastructural legacy, and so forth. Each indicator (and there are now many) is part of a complex equation that justifies investment in events-led strategies. In the late nineteenth and early twentieth centuries large sporting and cultural events simply required political patronage from elite groups (Roche, 2000), but this is no longer deemed satisfactory. The need for 'hard', quantifiable data is reflective of similar managerialist developments that have transformed a number of policy environments, including cultural policy, where there was an increased emphasis towards a 'more rational and instrumental legitimacy in the 1980s' (Hitters, 2000: 184). This shift in emphasis is indicative of what Habermas (1988) called a move from 'value-oriented action' to 'interest guided action'. However, this move towards measuring the economic value of events (essentially how they contribute to private capital gains) is problematic when the economic rationale becomes autonomous and the pressures of legitimation (Habermas, 1988) are removed from the political sphere and occupy a space outside of the democratic process. Questions of accountability are sidelined as the menu of alternative models of governance is reduced. Others have suggested that economic impact studies have often been deliberately flawed (Crompton and Mackay, 1994) for political reasons.

However, while the flawed nature of previous methods is well documented, there is some evidence of significant improvements with respect to the development of comprehensive economic 'impact' evaluation tools usable in the events sphere, which at least focus their attention more clearly on the notions of 'additionality' and 'attribution' – what added value does winning the rights to host an event have on a city – that would not have otherwise accrued, and can this value be solely attributed to the event alone. Of the numerous economic impact models that have been borrowed from the economics discipline and utilised in the events field, the most commonly cited is the 'multiplier effect', but there are others, each of which has its relative merits. Carlsen (2004) summarises the main features of each approach and concludes that *cost–benefit analysis* measures both the tangible and intangible benefits of an event and analyses whether net benefits are positive (indicating an economically valuable event). However, it is a model that, relying on the estimation of future benefits and costs, is challenging, and the intangible also has to be given a value. The *input–output* model (but known as the multiplier effect) is a method of measuring the total economic impact of sectors that flows from an increase in demand for the output of those sectors (i.e. when an event takes place, what effect does it have on other economic sectors?). In calculating the overall economic impact, it takes into consideration effects that are *direct* (increased sales), *indirect* (effect on suppliers) and *induced* (increased spending by employees). It also uses historical economic data and models of transactions between sectors and the way they respond to increased demand, producing output, income and employment multipliers. In recent years this approach has been criticised for its tendency to overestimate returns over costs. Carlsen argues that it has suffered from a failure to consider exchange rates, labour market and price effects and from making unrealistic assumptions about surplus capacity in the economy (Carlsen, 2004).

The most sophisticated (and, therefore, most expensive) approach in use is *computable general equilibrium* modelling. It is used to evaluate the impact of 'shocks' on an economy's equilibrium (e.g. an Olympics arriving in town). It uses more economic variables and 'acknowledges that some of the growth effects of events may be offset by contractions in other parts of the economy' (Carlsen, 2004: 257). For example, this model might more effectively acknowledge that mega-events can have many negative outcomes with respect to land, labour and capital and might exert inflationary pressures on, for example, tourism products and services. Given that it also considers changes in prices, taxation, and labour market effects, this modelling approach tends (perhaps unsurprisingly) to produce much lower estimates of impact, although critics would argue that the estimates are much more realistic. What is clear is that the more thorough economic knowledge required to conduct impact studies, the more expensive and time consuming the process is and the less likely it is, it might be argued, that they will be commissioned by those agencies happy to secure a positive economic forecast at much lower costs. Linked to the need to develop a more robust evaluation too, with economic, social, cultural and environmental variables embedded within it, the triple bottom line analysis (Elkington, 1998) and Gratton *et al.*'s (2006) balanced scorecard approach are relatively recent additions to the field (see Box 4.1).

There is little doubt that, in order to maintain a semblance of legitimacy to those commissioning evaluations as well as to the wider stakeholder community, event-related evaluations need to consider the difference between what would have happened had the policy intervention not taken place and what additional benefits have accrued *because* of an intervention. To reach

Box 4.1 The balanced scorecard approach

Gratton *et al.* (2006), following the suggestions of others that there needs to be a greater focus on the 'beneficiaries' of event-related investment by city governments, have tried to develop a balanced scorecard approach to event evaluation. This, they argue would involve assigning value to media and sponsor variables, place marketing effects and sports development impact for sporting events, for example. This approach is more holistic and it is being adopted by several funding agencies as a mechanism for securing comparability of research findings.

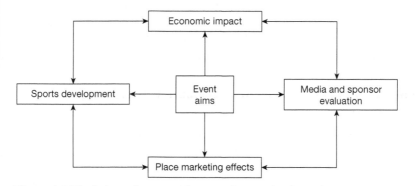

Figure 4.1 The balanced scorecard approach to evaluating events.

Further reading: Gratton, C., Shibli, S. and Coleman, S. (2006) 'The economic impact of major sports events: a review of ten events in the UK', *Sociological Review*, 54 (2): 41– 58.

net additional impact, value has to be assigned to variables including substitution (where policy-targeted investment takes the place of other investments), displacement (where additional activity from some sectors is counterbalanced by less output from others – e.g. tourism displacement as a result of Olympic Games hosting) and indirect impacts (additional spend in the local economy as a result of increased business for some firms).

In the democratic nations of the world, at least (legitimation is very different in the Middle East, for example) the important political (and economic) issue is whether public sector investment and support 'leverage' additional benefits and provide a healthy ROI for public and private stakeholders (e.g. London 2012 regeneration) or whether the beneficiaries are restricted to private capital and political elites – as some commentators have suggested (e.g. Whitson and Horne, 2006). Politically, the economic still garners more support as it has instrumental value and is more easily employed to legitimate interventions.

What has changed is that these economic models now take greater cognisance of more nebulous concepts such as image, perception and impressions than simply being concerned with immediate economic return. So while Hall (1992) was among the first to seriously consider the image effects of major events, there are now several examples of evaluation studies that consider the multi-dimensional aspects of image, including its economic value (e.g. Richards and Wilson, 2004).

It is important to offer a critique of the reliability of economic impact studies because, particularly when hosting large-scale events, there is a concern that public resources are effectively channelled through events to private corporations – and the 'benefits' thereafter are not always obvious to citizens (Mules and Faulkner, 1996), especially the poorer communities (Whitson and Horne, 2006). It is therefore prudent to ask not whether evaluation techniques confirm that net additional economic impacts are achieved through events, but instead whether this form of evaluation, and the discourse that sustains it, is what the wider 'public' wants from its event policies.

The conditions for (re-)action: evaluating alternative 'beneficiaries'

In considering the growing chorus of dissatisfaction with the standard economic impact models that are frequently disparaged for their overly optimistic forecasts, there appears to be a growing clamour for a more holistic approach to event evaluation that draws attention to a host of alternative possibilities and potentialities – not only for evaluation techniques *per se*, but for a dialogue on the desired outcome of events, too. The new possibilities are precipitated by the notion that 'the procurement of legitimation is self-defeating as soon as the mode of procurement is seen through' (Habermas, 1988: 70). Citizens now frequently mobilise (in more or less formal and informal groupings) to protest at the significant over-spends associated with major events. Invariably, these formalised social protest groups work to draw attention to the primacy of economic logic and the 'interest-guided actions' involved in producing economic impact studies, which corroborate the ruling political elites' official future projections. There are certainly intimations of change taking place whereby alternative 'value' systems (e.g. social, cultural and environmental) are gaining ground and subjecting the market logic, which has dominated thinking on event evaluation, to significant critique: 'with time, these shoddy and unethical practices will become impossible to continue in the face of public outrage and media scepticism' (Getz, 2007: 318). This does not mean that the economic rationale is now defunct. Instead, a wider understanding of social, cultural and environmental impacts is augmenting it. When utilising a Habermasian perspective, it can be viewed as the reclamation of the socio-cultural domain from the administrative system. Groups, varying in their formalisation, now regularly hold governments (whether local or national) to account, acting to expose conflicts over value in such a way as to draw attention to perceived inequities, often utilising what Habermas (1987: 392) calls the 'sub-institutional – or at least extra-parliamentary' realm to protest of the legitimation deficits experienced. Crossley (2003: 295) sees these groups as 'genuinely public, in that they stand outside of the stage show and bureaucracy of the political system'. The fact that they occupy oppositional or outsider status provides them with the distance from the institutionalised and bureaucratised political system to hold political leaders and their growth coalition partners to account. Most crucially, perhaps, is the idea that the system creates its own forms of resistance. As Crossley again writes:

> Having ploughed up traditions and stirred up a hornet's nest of political issues, the administrative system proves largely unreceptive to public opinion and pressure . . . the bureaucratic structures of the system are indifferent to communicative action and debate . . . thus, the system frustrates the very same projects that it sets in motion, amplifying the intensity of these projects and their tendency to follow 'alternative' and 'contentious', that is, extra-parliamentary, routes.
>
> (Crossley, 2003: 296)

As protest, in its myriad forms, is manifest, so the main governmental (e.g. local and national) and non-governmental (e.g. IOC, Commonwealth Games Federation (CGF), FIFA) agencies have slowly taken notice and the emerging outcome has been a renewed interest in the wider 'case' for the benefits of events for the social, cultural and environmental spheres. Some of these developments have fed into the evaluation process on a number of levels. First, there has been a renewed focus on the *leveraging* of planned benefits from events. Associated with the work of Chalip (2006), this approach emphasises pre-event legacy planning and evaluation instead of the preponderance of *post-hoc* economic analyses of event outcomes. The process of evaluation is also fundamentally transformed in a leveraging strategy as the focus is on pre-event desired benefits and seeks to ascertain 'why' certain outcomes were accrued. Leveraging then goes beyond legitimating public sector investment after the event has ended and seeks to develop what Crossley (2003) calls 'critical publics' who are involved more meaningfully in selecting and owning event-related strategies. As a result, this approach lends itself to more interactive participation and engagement techniques, although it must recognise that they are invariably difficult to implement, requiring a commitment to costly longitudinal study, which is discouraged in the (often) short-term nature of local government office. That notwithstanding, there remains merit in engaging with more innovative and creative methodological approaches as these have been conspicuous by their absence in event-related evaluations to date. As the authors have argued elsewhere, 'Policy makers need to look beyond the economic imperative to plan in social legacy using a strategic approach – engaging its beneficiaries early on in the process and matching the city's overarching policy drivers to the intended outcomes associated with the event' (Foley *et al.*, 2009).

Another way in which event evaluations have taken cognisance of a system largely unresponsive to public opinion and pressure is the detailed tracking of expectations that are associated with events. The approach adopted by the Italian city of Torino at the 2006 Winter Olympics is worth emphasising as part of a longitudinal commitment to monitoring and evaluating events. The city authorities monitored public opinion before, during and after the event, and their evidence showed that people were in favour of hosting the event four years in advance, and then post-event, people were found to be even more in favour, especially for tourism positioning, but not in terms of their hopes for jobs and infrastructure. After the games, concerns about corruption were reduced, but they increased in relation to excessive traffic and related expenditure. Overall, the public opinion surveys suggested that most pre-event fears were reduced with evident optimism for enduring benefits. There were, however, low levels of knowledge about the re-use of games facilities, which drew the organisers' attention to a problem of communication – this links back to the potential crisis of legitimation when public concerns are not addressed fully. Clearly, in the example of Torino, the monitoring function legitimated the public decision-making process and provides a new tool of governance as it helps create dialogue among populations about major events and their impacts, whether positive or negative.

In the UK context, there now exist a series of governmental and quasi-non-governmental agencies responsible for supporting events strategies, and they are looking to design evaluation tools that go beyond the crude economic impact studies of the past, recognising the overestimated benefits (and under-estimated costs) inherent within this system of measurement. These agencies increasingly work across national and, at times, international borders to produce more comprehensive event evaluation models that attempt to ascribe value to social, cultural, environmental as well as economic outcomes. Of course, politically, these agencies are looking for universal comparability to be enshrined across the range of event types, where in previous historical epochs, difference was to be celebrated. That said, an interest in values other than economic does provide some hope that the policy outcomes of events will be evaluated in a more holistic manner. For this to be successful, those in whose name events are delivered will need to be more meaningfully involved in setting objectives and in the monitoring and evaluation of proposed outcomes. So, for example, if social capital enhancement is a planned outcome of a community event, the evaluation method needs to be designed in such a way as to acknowledge the complexity of this concept and the time required to assess whether a specific intervention was successful or not.

Summary

If the work of Habermas on legitimation crisis is used, then democratically elected governments must be careful that, in their reliance on economic impact assessments as the principal method of event evaluation, the stakeholders other than those from commerce will feel disenfranchised from the process. The challenge facing policy makers is that the economic benefits of events are easier to document (through economic impact assessments) than the longer-term and more subjective social and cultural indicators. However, if the procurement of legitimation is self-defeating as soon as the mode of procurement is seen through, then there is a need for a review of evaluation approaches that can narrow the gap between the wider 'public(s)' and the events they are supposed to own. There can no longer be an artificial separation between the forms of engagement with citizens and the mechanisms of evaluation. Once forms of evaluation more clearly mirror the approach to engagement, then there is a chance that ownership and trust in both can be achieved. While a reliance on detached and complex economic impact assessments may lead to legitimation at the level of private capital, this is increasingly unsatisfactory as other criteria of value gain importance with events owners and governmental agencies alike.

Critical review questions

- Why is it important to consider the concept of legitimation when thinking about events?
- What are the main weaknesses associated with economic impact assessments and how have they been addressed in recent years?
- Why might extra-parliamentary groups be more effective in holding governments to account with respect to the costs of major events?

Recommended reading

Carlsen, J., Getz, D. and Soutar, G. (2000) 'Event evaluation research', *Event Management*, 6 (4): 247–257.
Connell, J. and Page, J.S. (2005) 'Evaluating the economic and spatial effects of an event: the case of the World Medical and Health Games', *Tourism Geographies*, 7 (1): 63–85.
Mossberg, L. (ed.) (2000) *Evaluation of events: Scandinavian experiences*. New York: Cognizant Communication Corp.

Part II
Event policy formations

5 The politics of events in an age of accumulation

Introduction

This chapter focuses on the way in which urban events policies are being created and shaped as one facet of the transformation, or restructuring, of social space. As they attract major events to the urban environment, local city policy makers and their central government counterparts are increasingly aware of the global 'neoliberalised' order that is emerging (Brenner and Theodore, 2005). The contention in this chapter is that hallmark, special or mega-events, along with associated culture-led regeneration processes, are part of the refashioning of urban governance in the context of the neoliberalised state and its roll-back of managerial welfare programmes. A key feature of this refashioning is that the principal risks associated with events are borne by a highly active entrepreneurial (local) state, with the involvement of the private sector being conditional upon the support of its public counterpart. The underbelly of this is that, having abandoned welfare programmes in the midst of neoliberal roll-backs, local and central governments face the threat of socially regressive outcomes, whereby marginalised groups experience an unequal distribution of the (apparent) rewards emanating from the new consumerism. Cities have taken over the mantle from nations as the most important focus of regimes of accumulation and the outcome is inter-urban competition involving intense city-branding and specialisation as a means of attracting private investment and inward visits. The last decade has witnessed the emergence of an entrepreneurial event policy in the affluent West (particularly, though not exclusively) marked by a reliance on largely unaccountable public–private growth coalitions that enable publicly funded entrepreneurship to flourish.

The emergence of neoliberalism in urban governance

Before paying attention to the specificities of how event policy could be said to have evolved along neoliberal urban governance lines, it is important to outline the wider context of neoliberalism and its relationship with urban development over the last three decades, especially in North America and Western Europe – although, as discussed later in the book, this mode of governance is now equally common across the developed economies of Asia and other parts of the world.

Commenting on the role of neoliberal discourses for the urban condition, Brenner and Theodore (2005) have summarised some of the main features of what they call the 'restructuring' of social, economic and political life in North America and Western Europe since the late 1970s and early 1980s. These authors, writing in the tradition of urban political economy, argue that an abundance of literature has been produced to describe the deconstruction and attempted reconstitution of urban social space. Variously, commentators in this tradition have employed the terms 'deindustrialization, post-Fordism, internationalization, global city formation, urban entrepreneurialism, informalization, gentrification and sociospatial polarization' (Brenner and Theodore, 2005: 101) to describe the transformations that have taken place within the global economy. In place of these terms, they offer the more general label 'neoliberalism' as a means of characterising 'the resurgence of market-based institutional shifts and policy realignments across the world economy during the post-1980s period (Brenner and Theodore, 2005: 101–102). In Chapter 2, it was suggested that the language of economic regeneration and the market determined the shape of institutions, limiting the policy levers available to the local state, and this is borne out in the most influential analyses of the dominant neoliberal order. Perhaps most importantly for this chapter is the acknowledgement that neoliberalism, as expressed in urban governance, hinges on the active mobilisation of state power in the promotion of market-based regulatory arrangements. Smith (2002: 248) agrees, arguing that the local state (he was talking of New York) works to a clear market logic without the 'pretense of regulation or steerage of the private sector towards results it could not otherwise accomplish on its own'. Smith believes that the new neoliberal urbanism avoids regulating the sway of the market – in fact, it actively courts free market exchange in every facet of urban life, including unprecedented state support or 'subsidized private-market subsidisation' (Smith, 2002: 440). As discussed in the next section, a good example of this mobilisation of state power (to support free market activity) is the development of public–private or quasi-autonomous organisations that can act relatively independently of local government to compete with other cities (inter-urban competition) for 'business' in the realm of tourism and major events (e.g. destination marketing organisations). That is not to suggest that neoliberal forms of urban governance are homogeneous, or that their outcomes are comparable across different global territories. To the contrary, neoliberalism is a process and has place-specific outcomes – at least to the extent that historical institutional legacies – perhaps more welfarist in orientation – collide with neoliberal projects. Uncertain outcomes aligned with intense contestation lead to 'variegated geographical implications' (Brenner and Theodore, 2005: 105). Moreover, a significant body of literature exists to suggest that neoliberal forms of governance exacerbate regulatory failure, generating increased levels of inequality, marginalisation and social polarity (e.g. Smith, 2002).

In order to tie this generalised discussion of neoliberal forms of governance to event policy, it is worth returning to the work of Brenner and Theodore (2005) in their discussion of neoliberalism as an important modality of governance. They argue that in the early twenty-first century, neoliberalism is a powerful 'framework' structuring the parameters for the governance of urban development, 'by defining the character of "appropriate" policy choices, by constraining democratic participation in political life, by diffusing dissent and oppositional mobilization, and/or by disseminating new ideological visions of social and moral order in the city' (Brenner and Theodore, 2005: 103). Considering the specific context of event policy, it is clear that neoliberalism, as a modality of governance, provides the parameters for appropriate choices around what the function of events is in the early twenty-first century. Clearly, within the structuring framework that naturalises market relations, events are deemed valuable only insofar as they contribute to economic restructuring. Moreover, the institutional arrangements that flow from this framework must also enable growth coalitions to form and public–private partnerships to flourish. In contextualising the discussion of neoliberalism to the notion of place marketing, Philo and Kearns (1993: 18) argue that places are increasingly 'rendered attractive, advertised and marketed', and that for this to occur a shift in discourse about how best to enable it at the central and local state level took place. Public–private partnerships, fostering entrepreneurship and self-help, were incentivised over centralised state planning. In policy terms, the 'strategies and alliances' of political elites under the conditions of neoliberalism are designed to promote policies of market-led growth – in favour of (inevitable) socially regressive outcomes. Events will be used, then, as boosterist strategies designed to assuage the problems associated with de-industrialisation, but in the process, there exists significant potential for what Hall (2006) calls a democratic deficit (or a 'legitimation' deficit).

In considering the way in which this discourse has been understood in relation to event policy, it is worth concluding this section with the observation that urban neoliberalism is a 'means of transforming the dominant political imaginaries on which basis people understand the limits and possibilities of the urban experience . . . this redefinition of political imagination . . . entails . . . the reworking of inherited conceptions of citizenship, community and everyday life' (Brenner and Theodore, 2005: 160). This is why a discussion of neoliberalism as the prevailing discourse of the late twentieth century is necessary in a policy text of this sort. Neoliberalism requires the reconceptualisation of the relationship between citizens and cities, between the central and local state and between events and the economy. It is to this relationship that the attention of this chapter now turns.

Neoliberal urban governance and event policy

Those writing specifically in the field of events and tourism studies over the last decade or so have been attracted to the neoliberal urban governance analysis presented in the preceding section. For example, Hall (2006) draws on political economy to stress the thin policies of competitiveness within the hard outcomes of neoliberalism, and Waitt (2001) has considered the 2000 Sydney Olympics as an example of civic boosterism in action. Furthermore, Whitson and Horne (2006) have also offered a critique of urban entrepreneurial neoliberal approaches to policy in their analysis of sporting mega-events. What each has in common is their identification of the importance of neoliberal governance on the field of events and, more crucially, their dissatisfaction with this policy preoccupation as a means of achieving stated social outcomes.

Hall (2006) has emerged as a significant critic of what he calls the 'hard' outcomes of neoliberalism, which can be traced through the field of mega sporting events in particular. He stresses that the creation of public–private growth coalitions is reflective of the dominant economic neoliberal discourse that has been embedded in local government since the 1980s, in the advanced liberal democratic nations, at least. He agrees with Brenner and Theodore (2005) and Smith (2002) in arguing that the local political system facilitates (even subsidises) entrepreneurial activity in place of welfare and secures the consent of the electorate (legitimation) on the promise of progress and growth – based on the notion that benefits will 'trickle down' to the majority of citizens. This analysis posits that market relations have been naturalised in local government as cities vie to attract the right sort of capital, people and images, yet in the process the private sector's needs are given precedence over other (often competing) claims upon public resources.

Also following in this tradition, Schimmel (2006) argues that the urban landscape of the US has been transformed along the lines of the neoliberalism documented by Brenner and Theodore (2005). Because, in the 1980s, 'local' urban policy makers were increasingly deemed responsible for providing city renaissance, inter-urban competition for investment was intensified to produce an hegemony of 'growth politics' (Schimmel, 2006: 162), operated on the basis of local state subsidy of private investment. The governance arrangements that flowed from this commitment to growth politics were focused comprehensively on attracting 'circulating capital' and 'footloose consumption' (Short and Kim, 1999: 39) to urban locales. In other words, the policy environment valued interventions that incentivised incoming visitation over investment in the social welfare of the host population. This perspective is also supported by Shoval (2002), who argues that the main transformation in cities (he refers to cities across the world bidding for Olympic Games) has been in urban governance from managerialism to entrepreneurialism defined by greater inter-urban competition and a commitment to the logic of 'consumption as economic salvation' (see Chapter 6 for more detail on the implications of a consumerist logic for events). In his analysis of the new phase of competition for the Olympics, Shoval suggests that cities with pretensions to be 'global' are 'fearful of competition' (Shoval, 2002: 596) and need to mobilise state institutions to 'promote market based regulatory arrangements' (Brenner and Theodore, 2005: 102) to stay ahead of their rivals by bidding, for example, for sports events. There is a generalised global policy emerging – one that necessitates 'playing the game' of events bidding because failure to do so could jeopardise cities' place in the globalised order of things.

Burbank, Andranovich and Heying (2002), in their discussion of sporting mega-events, urban development and public policy, also detail the transition from the use of tools such as tax incentives to attract new business growth and infrastructure investment towards the promotion of urban tourism for economic and social gain. They argue that the desire to bid for large-scale sporting events, for example, is tied in to the growth of the global economy and changes in federal urban policy in the US. First-wave federal policies, which included 'smoke stack' land-clearing initiatives, were replaced with second wave, riskier entrepreneurial development strategies that ended due to a reduction in federal funding. The third wave in the 1980s saw local government agencies taking increased risk within urban development, with the rise of cooperation between local government agencies at differing regional levels, public–private enterprises, and quasi-public agencies. In the US, from 1984, the federal government would not subsidise local economic development and encouraged cities to be self-reliant, financing developments through entrepreneurship. This is an example of a classic neoliberal strategy, with a small government acting in partnership with the guiding hand of the market to generate economic return that, it is argued, will distribute resources more effectively to those who need them.

In the US context, at least, the 'mega event as urban growth policy' was a response to the removal of federal funding. This led to cities diversifying development policies with the emphasis on consumption of leisure, entertainment and sport becoming more pronounced (Hannigan, 1998; Law, 2002). This policy shift into mega-event strategy has made tourism a pivotal part of the regeneration of American cities – and this is now frequently mirrored elsewhere. Events were designed to act as a 'stimulus' or 'catalyst' for local development projects, infrastructure, facilities and the attraction of sports franchises. As with other analyses of this urban entrepreneurial approach, city imaging is the backdrop upon which development proceeds. Cities, as the primary mode of activity in the global economy, want to be 'seen' to be dynamic. It is a consumption-centred process and the significance of image is accentuated within event-led strategies. Informal networks of local business leaders and elected officials assemble to provide the catalyst for a series of policy interventions. It is argued that this approach overcomes the inertia inherent within the disjointed power relations of (democratically elected) local government, producing a level playing field on which cities can compete. The case of Glasgow, illustrated in Box 5.1 is symptomatic of the shift towards market logic permeating public service in the realm of events.

Precedents are certainly available to illustrate the use of events and festivals as a means of refashioning urban environments – mirroring the 'city' branding depicted in Box 5.1. For example, Waitt (2001) suggests that the Sydney 2000 Summer Olympic Games offered the urban entrepreneurs and politicians

Box 5.1 Place marketing events: Glasgow City Marketing Bureau

The emergence of destination marketing organisations (DMOs), or place marketing agencies, across North America and Europe since the 1980s is indicative of a heightened urban neoliberalism that impacts the event policy process. Glasgow City Marketing Bureau (GCMB), established in 2005, is a place marketing agency that is relatively autonomous of the local authority structures (and strictures), permitting it to operate in a commercial manner, competing for business, including major events. The DMO has a wide-ranging tourism remit, but over recent years its events function has grown in significance. It undertakes conferences, meetings, incentive and exhibition sales, event creation, attraction, management and marketing. Within Glasgow's wider destination 'brand wheel' now sits a major events strategy, aligned closely with the 'Glasgow: Scotland with Style' brand. Crucially, this overarching brand identity governs decisions over whether to grow existing events or attract ambulant events to the city. For example, events that promote Glasgow's pretensions to be a 'stylish city' are more likely now to be in receipt of financial and related support as they produce place-imaging (economic) benefits. In contrast, local events that exhibit less clear brand 'fit' experience funding cuts or the withdrawal of agency support as they are perceived to be of less value economically to the city. 'Targeting events that reinforce the brand proposition is central to strategically positioning Glasgow on the national and international stage as a stylish, dynamic and cosmopolitan city' (GCMB, 2007).

The following success factors promoted by the GCMB further illustrate the dominance of the economic neoliberal modality of urban governance being followed in Glasgow, as elsewhere:

- an increase in annual hotel occupancy level since brand launch;
- an increase in additional tourist expenditure since brand launch;
- an increase in conventions booking;
- an increase in delegate days; and
- a positive shift in target audience's likelihood of visiting Glasgow in near future.

Essentially, progress in urban governance terms is restricted to economic development and the quasi-autonomous 'companies' created by Glasgow's local authority permits this to occur.

Further reading: Kavaratzis, M. (2004) 'From city marketing to city branding: towards a theoretical framework for developing city brands', *Place Branding*, 1 (1): 58–73.

behind the promotion of the city a tourism spectacle to reinforce their shifting economic and cultural offering, based largely on tourism, culture and the attraction of mobile capital. But, crucially, he also argues that the city leaders were able to use the mega spectacle (Kellner, 2003) of the Games to exert social control to address the loss of identity associated with class, age, ethnicity and of place brought about by the change in economic structure towards post-industrialism. As Waitt goes on to argue, elite economic and political interests, using a series of sites, signs and symbols, control the promotion of spectacle, distraction and excitement associated with major sports events. These help to 'legitimize political projects that function primarily in the interests of business and political elites whilst creating national consciousness that undermines internal social divides along class or ethnic lines' (Waitt, 2001: 254).

Of course, these 'propaganda exercises' are not new but they have increased in frequency and significance in the period of global capitalism because of the increased social polarisation that has been an outcome of this trend. In Sydney, for example, it was clear that the specially created public–private partnerships emphasised the entrepreneurial goals of the Olympics over the welfare agenda. The 'Share the Spirit' and 'Green Games' slogans were extremely effective – albeit on a superficial level – in stifling popular dissent around the Games. The 'Share the Spirit' slogan made an emotional connection with residents, emphasising the sacred, peaceful and harmonic element of the Olympic ideals. The latter promoted the environmental credentials of the Olympics bid that was a topical issue at the turn of the century. In sum, the promotion of urban spectacle continues to be a 'mechanism to stimulate consumption-led economic revival . . . and perhaps more importantly in a post-modern society noted for its fragmentary and volatile nature, as a propaganda exercise to generate feelings of civic unity' (Waitt, 2001: 256). That said, this does not mean that the benefits of the market model are shared equally, nor are they free of contestation. In the final two sections, attention turns to how an event policy governed by neoliberal logic creates division, dissent, and a number of winners and losers.

Neoliberal event outcomes: winners and losers

Brenner and Theodore (2005) and other critics document the regressive social outcomes resulting from a commitment to neoliberalism as a modality of governance. In the events area, Schimmel (2006: 166) is similarly sceptical of the sustainability of this model of capital accumulation, arguing that 'capital is mobile, cities are not', and that the outcomes of event-led policies are often temporary. Others express concern over the sharp contrast between the mobility-frozen (Ingham and MacDonald, 2003) residents and the affluent tourist tribes being targeted by entrepreneurial governments across the globe. Continuing the discussion introduced in Chapters 2 and 4, there is an important sense, then, that the processes of capital accumulation – driven by neoliberal forms of governance – are open to scrutiny in the prevention of 'unfettered capital accumulation' (Brenner and Theodore, 2005: 102).

Smith (2002: 443), critical of gentrification as a global urban strategy, argues that what he calls a 'class inflected urban remake' only targets certain groups, as 'the appeal to bring people back into the city is always a self-interested appeal that the white middle and upper classes retake control of the political and cultural economies as well as the geographies of the largest cities' (Smith, 2002: 445). Moreover, Smith (2002: 446) argues that the language of regeneration, from which events are inseparable (see Chapter 2), 'anaesthetizes our critical understanding' of the social polarisation wrought by these policies. These arguments have been rehearsed by urban sociologists for some time and are often framed in the terminology of what Marcuse and Kempen (2000) call the 'new divided city', whereby cities are deemed more inequitable – in terms of power, cultural and economic differences – than they have been previously. The argument goes that these divisions are exacerbated by the presence of privately owned leisure spaces that have transformed relations between residents in urban spaces. The increasing privatisation and regulation of leisure and recreational spaces, including parks, squares and events, has led to the 'cleansing' of cityscapes. Associated urban re-imaging projects have turned 'deteriorating urban spaces into areas for the middle class and their residential and recreational priorities' (Stevenson, 2003: 45). When globalising forces are considered, then the odds are weighted in favour of the instrumental use of public space and festivity for external audiences. In this context, celebrations (events and festivity) are deemed useful insofar as they generate positive signs and symbols of the city 'open for business' – in terms of investment, tourism and skilled workers.

Burbank, Andranovich and Heying (2002) also reflect on the potentially negative outcomes of an urban regime whereby cities use local coalitions or networks to fund and initiate sports event bid processes. They argue that the perceived risk with these networks is that the key interests of private stakeholders could drive the urban policy agenda and serve the goals of pro-growth business leaders rather than elected members or residents. For example, they suggest that citizen input in bid processes is minimal, and conclude that the process of bidding for an Olympic mega-event is conducted by an independent group of businesses, largely without the control of the local council. These views align closely with the work of Hall (2006) and Whitson and Horne (2006), who have provided significant empirical evidence from sporting mega-events in particular, to suggest that the 'impacts' of these events are not necessarily positive. Hall (2006: 59), in relation to the Olympics, argues that they 'have been associated with large-scale public expenditure, the construction of facilities and infrastructure, and urban redevelopment and revitalisation strategies which may have undesirable long term consequences for public stakeholders although significant short-term gains for some corporate interests'. Here, he is in tune with Smith (2002), Macleod (2002) and others when suggesting that bidding for a host of sporting and cultural events could be said to be at the vanguard of a dominant neoliberal logic in local government towards urban entrepreneurialism, subsidised by the public purse.

Hall goes further, providing evidence of the way in which corporate power is exercised with respect to event policy. Private capital now has significant influence over the development, planning and regulatory functions associated with major sporting events. While this might not be immediately problematic, questions of ownership arise when this influence is used to dictate exclusivity and regulate the use of public city space as an outcome of commercial rights agreements. As the local state is increasingly required (of economic necessity within the logic of neoliberal urbanism) to dance to the tune of major sponsors in bidding for and delivering events, there is a knock-on effect for 'local' stakeholder interests (whether citizens or businesses). Local objectives and interests can be sidelined as sponsor agreements exclude these in favour of the pursuit of their global corporate objectives. This apparent loss of control and influence is exacerbated by the introduction of legislation by numerous governments across the world designed to override the normal regulatory mechanisms in place within host nations (e.g. Glasgow has just undertaken this task for the 2014 Common-wealth Games as a means of 'protecting' sponsors' 'assets'). In the intense inter-urban competition to secure lucrative events, the power ratio between private capital, event owners (e.g. IOC, FIFA, the Union of European Football Associations (UEFA) and other governing bodies) and the local state has shifted in favour of the former over the latter. Whitson and Horne (2006) agree that, in the shift towards urban entrepreneurial neoliberal approaches to civic governance, public resources are often channelled through sporting mega-events to private corporations. They give the example of the 'construction firm Olympics' of Negano to illustrate how major construction companies benefited disproportionately from the public spending on infrastructure for large-scale events. They go on to suggest that political and business elites invariably benefit from the material rewards, while poorer communities bear most of the opportunity costs. Reflecting on Olympic Games, they suggest that the direct beneficiaries are construction companies, engineers and architects, local security firms, media outlets and advertising, marketing and public relations experts.

Perhaps most crucially, in line with the concerns over legitimation detailed in the previous chapter, is the concern that a market-led economic and social framework produces 'the development of structures and powers of governance that are opaque and unaccountable to public stakeholders and participation' (Hall, 2006: 64). As the language of urban entrepreneurialism, competitive-ness and growth permeates the realm of public life (or the lifeworld), so institutional arrangements and policy choices are also narrowly aligned with this justification. Of concern to Smith and Macleod is that this discourse becomes incontestable as stakeholders are coerced (there is no alternative) and co-opted (economic return will provide employment) under the weight of a positive media bandwagon.

Reclaiming public spaces: the role of events

However, before concluding this chapter by arguing that a market-led economic and social framework simply excludes the weakest and is structurally restricting and reproductive, it is necessary to draw attention to developments in urban sociology towards the cultural turn and post-structural analyses that offer a more positive outlook for citizens 'within' the strictures of neoliberal market models. Here, authors suggest that it is possible to consider fluidity, multiple meanings and the possibility that people 'use, experience, and relate to the same urban spaces in a range of ways often at the same time' (Stevenson, 2003: 41). For example, following this line of thought, urban public space can represent different things to different people at the same time, meaning that people are 'not necessarily the passive victims or recipients of dominant ideologies and oppressive power relations' (Stevenson, 2003: 42). Essentially, people may then create alternative 'narratives' of their engagement with, and use of, public spaces than can be easily read off from objective, structural analyses. De Certeau (1988) has made a significant contribution to the debate as to how everyday practices can be utilised by the disempowered to subvert dominant ideologies and power relations in urban environments. His work suggests that dominant power relations are 'incomplete', and meaningful practices can be enacted in urban spaces to avoid the nets of surveillance, policing and discipline indicative of the late capitalist city. What he calls 'tactical resistance' is possible, where space can be reclaimed, reinterpreted and shaped and identities can be reworked against prescribed or imposed meanings. Considering the possibilities here within the events realm, it is worth thinking about how audiences and participants colonise and use space in opposition to the planned outcomes of entrepreneurial governance. For many scholars the urban environment is a dynamic, lived space (including event spaces) open to 'unofficial' representations as well as the official (increasingly place marketing) approach. Despite attempts to fix meanings undertaken by the cultural intermediaries of entrepreneurial governance, these are invariably imperfect as lived histories and memories represent long-lasting and powerful narratives of the city. These narratives can act as sources of resistance to the place marketing hegemony where the possibility of the poor, women, ethnic groups and the elderly having their say is real and live. Despite attempts to bound and structure, social space remains an arena for social action to take place where negotiation is part of everyday life (Mitchell, 1995).

A good example of the negotiation of social space between place promoters and social actors is the 2006 FIFA World Cup held in Germany (Frew and McGillivray, 2008). This event introduced 'fan parks' at each of the ten host cities as a means of housing travelling ticketless fans and to allow corporate sponsors to generate increased returns on their investment with respect to merchandising sales and brand exposure. The fan parks were, in many respects, privatised spaces exhibiting the profile of managed brand environments, whereby 'local' produce and associated business interests were excluded. However, within the fan park spaces themselves, the attempt at managing the official representation of the event was less successful as those in attendance expressed their 'tactical resistance' by reconceptualising the performance space for their own purposes – reinterpreting and reworking official discourses in a creative manner. The creative dimension of event attendees was also apparent within World Cup stadiums as spectators engaged in forms of ambush marketing by wearing the colours of unofficial brands as a protest at the excessive power of headline sponsors such as Anheuser-Busch. In each case, there is, albeit symbolically, an attempt to subvert the dominant neoliberal hegemony that governs major event policy and practice.

Summary

In this chapter, it has been argued that the neoliberal governance structures formed, across the globe, to permit entrepreneurial activity to flourish can, at the same time, reduce levels of public participation and ownership of the policy-making process and produce an inequitable distribution of benefits. However, the displacement outcomes of this sort of public policy are often stifled as positive, pro-growth messages emerge from political leaders. The intensification in the use of events as a key facet of the capital accumulation process is marked. Moreover, the extent to which local actors are peripheral to the power play and decision-making processes that legitimate the policy objectives is problematic, especially as the economic growth of the last few years has shuddered to a halt. Events are now so closely aligned with neoliberal market logic that there appears to be only limited space for alternative discourses to effect change. Yet, as the final section of this chapter indicated, alongside dominant discourses comes resistance and there is some evidence that the neoliberal hegemony may be open to contestation as the creative engagement of sophisticated audiences transforms passive victims or recipients of dominant ideologies into active agents.

Critical review questions

- Why are cities across the world adopting an events-led strategy as a key facet of their urban policy objectives?
- In following an entrepreneurial event policy, who are the potential winners and losers, and why?

Recommended reading

Brenner, N. and Theodore, N. (2005) 'Neoliberalism and the urban condition', *City*, 9 (1): 101–107.
Hall, C.M. (2006) 'Urban entrepreneurship, corporate interests, and sports mega-events: the thin policies of competitiveness within the hard outcomes of neo-liberalism', *The Sociological Review*, 54 (2): 59–70.
Waitt, G. (2001) 'The Olympic spirit and civic boosterism: the Sydney 2000 Olympics', *Tourism Geographies*, 3 (3): 249–278.

6 Consuming events

From bread and circuses to brand

Introduction

Leading on from the critique of regimes of accumulation in Chapter 5, this chapter focuses more clearly on the role of events and festivals policy in legitimating a mode of consumption as the defining rationale for investing in an events-led policy. In the last decade of the twentieth and the early part of the twenty-first century in the developed West, it can be argued that events and festivals have been accorded significant value predominantly because of their contribution to economic development and place promotion. The outcome of the post-industrial commitment to consumption (Miles and Miles, 2004) and experiences (Pine and Gilmore, 1999) is that urban environments are now open to marketing activity in the same way that product promotion is understood. Moreover, destinations are frequently associated with an over-arching brand narrative, which describes the city's attributes and aspirations (e.g. 'style', 'uniqueness', 'authenticity'). In this chapter it is suggested that, in a shift from the use of events as distractions in securing feeling and affect, to their use as part of wider destination branding strategies, 'manufactured' events are often in receipt of investment in favour of indigenous events that fail to portray the desired aesthetic or represent the ubiquitous cosmopolitan ethos being sought in city place promotion. However, it is also suggested that there is a problematic emanating from the local state's commitment to branded events designed primarily to attract affluent mobile capital. While these events may satisfy the lifestyle aspirations of the sought-after tourist audiences, they may also exacerbate the exclusionary processes that exist within the urban milieu of post-industrial cities – in essence, the consumption-led events city may divide as much as it provides (Miles and Miles, 2004).

The consumption of place

Hallmark events (Hall, 1992) are often perceived to help cities define their sense of place. In event typologies, hallmark events are defined those that are inseparable from the place where they are held. In other words, Rio Carnival cannot be held in another location and generate the same imaginative connotations in the minds of visitors. Similarly, Calgary Stampede is synonymous with the western Canadian city and helps put it on a global map that its other economic assets find more difficult. What is certain is that cities are now increasingly the places of contemporary spectacle:

> In the city, the result has been a change in the relationship between its material and symbolic aspects with attention becoming focused on consumption and the nature and potential of urban cultures, diversity and creativity in their space, rather than on production and its spaces.
>
> (Stevenson, 2003: 93)

In recent decades, many would argue that as a result of the shift towards a neoliberalised order, lifestyle and tourism have become the major 'pivots' of the predominantly service-dominated economy. The symbolic elements of a city and its 'soft' attributes have become as important to economic development as what it produces – place identity is no longer simply read off from a city's industrial heritage (e.g. Sheffield and steel, Glasgow and shipbuilding, Detroit and motor vehicles). Rather, place identity is now frequently associated (in the minds of potential visitors, investors and residents, at least) with what it sells, what it creates and what it represents in terms of aesthetic attributes.

As long ago as 1938, Lewis Mumford distinguished between producing and consuming cities and, in the ensuing period, the balance has certainly swung markedly in favour of consumption as a fundamental ordering device for urban life in particular. There are, of course, those who are critical of the extent of this shift to consumption, arguing that cities are perhaps 'over-determined by the provisions they make for consumers' (Miles and Miles, 2004: 2), meaning that other forms of social organisation are left out of the equation and an unequal distribution of resources results. But, as consuming cities are a product of urban entrepreneurial governance (see previous chapter), the framing of alternatives is narrow.

As industrial economies have collapsed, so the realms of lifestyle and consumption have become the new battlegrounds of urban life. Many post-industrial cities now compete on the basis of image and amenity and have undertaken nothing short of a makeover – in how the city is perceived (and represents itself) internally and the impressions external actors have of it. The cityscape and its 'place' attributes is now *the* symbolic commodity being sold to lucrative markets of tourists, investors and workers. This requires the 'sale of what the city means, how it feels and what it looks like – both the tangible and intangible attributes of particular urban spaces' (Stevenson, 2003: 98). However, the dilemma facing destinations (as they are frequently titled) is to secure buy-in from the local (internal) and global (external) stakeholders with this re-imaging project, especially if there is little tangible benefit to the local arising from explicit place promotion activity. If local actors represent mere props on the theatre stage, which is designed for incoming visitors, then there is a danger that the consuming city becomes merely an abstract concept that generates impressive returns to the few (e.g. hotels, retail, PR, financial services) as opposed to the many. In Chapter 5, attention was drawn to the way in which sophisticated media marketing communicators compete to create an attractive transmission of urban symbolism, which strikes a chord with savvy consumers. In the case of Glasgow, this city has courted the most influential opinion formers in place promotion (e.g. Lonely Planet and Conde Naste) to alter perceptions of the 'no mean city' towards 'Glasgow: Scotland with Style'.

A good example of a city that has experienced a transformation from producing to consuming is Manchester, UK. In the 1970s this city was a dilapidated industrial powerhouse, but through the 1980s and 1990s it became synonymous with 'play' and 'spectacle' as a blueprint for the renaissance of its city centre, in particular. Mellor (1997) has argued that the process of transformation began in the period 1984–1989, when a loose coalition of public and private stakeholders began to revitalise the city centre through an investment in heritage, tourism and leisure. This policy was pushed by the business-led coalitions of the time. Culture was effectively commodified and used to generate economic activity in the city centre. Focusing on lifestyle and consumption, the city centre attracted a younger audience for the multitude of popular culture attractions and, as a result, tourism was kick-started. Moreover, planning regulations were loosened to facilitate round-the-clock-revelry (and revenue). This was also accompanied by what Mellor calls a 'conspicuous reversal to privatism' (Mellor, 1997: 59), which relied upon a change whereby 'sociability in the cities was increasingly public, in the street, weather permitting'. The 'prestige' bid for the Olympics in 1993 was a further illustration of the model of urban regeneration being pursued. In Chapter 1 it was suggested that mega-events can redefine a city's (and nation's) sense of itself, but it also true that even the process of bidding for a major event can lead to the sort of step change that Manchester was looking to achieve. Flagship developments and signature facilities were also initiated to define the city and lead to its play and spectacle growth. City image promotion was traded for the 'relegation' of the backstage neighbourhoods. This is a policy that has drawn criticism in other urban locations across the globe, especially in connection with sporting mega-events, where the argument goes that entrepreneurialism has been supported in favour of social welfare (Waitt, 2001). Despite their being winners and losers in this revitalisation agenda (see Chapter 5 for discussion of these), Manchester continued to emphasise the city centre as a consumption zone, creating sociable spaces and an intense public life – Albert Square, pedestrianised streets and sponsored public festivities (fun days, carnivals, fiestas, fireworks, festivals of the arts). The local authority became the 'manager of spectacle' (Mellor, 1997: 65). However, the story of Manchester, as with other cities from as far afield as Singapore to Seattle, is one that targeted a selective audience, the new service class, who colonise the civilised space of the city centre, with its arts, its heritage and its cool entertainments. While the café society, urban promenade, public squares and urban village concepts are attractive to workers and visitors, this is a vision of a planned spectacle, lacking spontaneity and diversity. It is about 'brand' as opposed to bonding. In this sense, Miles and Miles' (2004) view that consumption is an ideological project is pertinent. The way Manchester went about its re-imaging was to reinforce a particular group's way of thinking – it was a form of socialisation that established the idea that there was no alternative to reverse post-industrial decay.

Selling places

Philo and Kearns (1993) have written extensively on the phenomenon of selling places and the policy permutations that flow from such a practice in the late twentieth and early twenty-first centuries. They argue that a range of economic (largely neoliberal in design) and social implications arise from a commitment to manage places. Specifically, they outline the practice of selling places as being about

> The various ways in which public and private agencies – local authorities and local entrepreneurs, often working collaboratively – strive to 'sell' the image of a particularly geographically defined 'place', usually a town or city, so as to make it attractive to economic enterprises, to tourists, and even to inhabitants of that place.
>
> (Philo and Kearns, 1993: 3)

They believe that this approach has both an economic and social logic – external promotion to inward visitors is accompanied by processes of socialisation for 'local' citizens. So some of the representational dilemmas created by the manipulation or exploitation of more or less 'authentic' cultural expressions cause conflict and tension once in the hands of place marketers, especially when these cultural intermediaries are in the job of creating desire for the city as opposed to being responsible for making it a socially rewarding environment to live in.

The role of the cultural intermediary in creating the consuming city, and selling it, is a crucial one. Everything is up for grabs as being 'faithful' to a prescribed history is less important than celebrating and making use of particular qualities of cities for economic gain. For example, historical occasions such as sports events, expositions, carnivals and other cultural festivals play a specific role in selling cities. At one extreme, Olympic Games or World Cups are more clearly about accumulation strategies disconnected from the specificities of the 'local'. In contrast, the carnivals and other cultural festivals do tend to have a historical reference point, although they are also subject to the vagaries of capital in an increasingly instrumental manner. This approach is comparable with the Romans' bread and circuses, containing social pacification and entertainment at one and the same time as a means of 'persuading' local citizens of the beneficence of the events on offer. However,

Philo and Kearns (1993: 18) suggest that the views other people may have of the city – views that are not in keeping with bourgeois culture promoted by consumption – cause problems for the sales agents of cities:

> The marketers have assumed that the places being sold are the spaces of bourgeois culture . . . the problems arise because in the process the marketers also try to sell places that mean other things to the 'other peoples' of the city, who thereby resist the form that the selling takes and who also resist the 'bread and circuses' element of this selling.

Despite these potentially deleterious ramifications, it remains clear that the 'symbolic' values that are attributable to consumption are promoted in terms of place selling rather than their use or utility value. City managers certainly want to emphasise the positive symbolic elements of their 'product' as a means of differentiating it from competitors – these assets are more than the built environment of signature or 'iconic' architecture (although Bilbao's Guggenheim, Dubai's Burj Al Arab hotel and Beijing's Bird Nest Stadium are also valuable symbolic resources) but also soft, emotional, intangible features of place (e.g. vibrant, dynamic, confident, cool, edgy) that are deemed attractive to the tourist tribes with cultivated lifestyle aspirations. In symbolic terms, visitation or consumption of a city can take on magical (Campbell, 1987) qualities as desire replaces need.

As a host of authors have suggested (Philo and Kearns, 1993; Zukin, 1995; Miles and Miles, 2004), there always exists the potential that, in selling places on symbolic assets that bear little resemblance to stories of the city handed down from generation to generation, a universal ubiquity can be created whereby the uniqueness of places is eliminated in the march towards the fantasy city (Hannigan, 1998). City success, according to the logic of market forces, is, ironically, most threatened by homogeneity, as destinations work to

> [G]ive themselves basically the same sort of attractive image – the same pleasant ensemble of motifs (cultural, historical, environmental, aesthetic) drained of anything controversial – with basically the same ambitions of sucking in capital so as to make the place in question 'richer' than the rest.
> (Philo and Kearns, 1993: 20)

As cities and regions around the world coalesce around a discourse of growth and economic return, then the activities that will be in receipt of local state investment (financial and otherwise) are invariably restricted to those that correspond with consumption logic. As an outcome of this framing of alternatives, there is a narrowing of the acceptable 'meanings' and 'memories' that are valid and will be given space in the promotional plan. For example, meaningful, yet controversial, memories are more likely to remain hidden or reworked for public consumption in the official city narrative (as decided upon by the place marketers). This might, in itself, be seen as a progressive step if these memories are deemed unacceptable to the standards of tolerance and diversity expected of a liberal democracy in the early twenty-first century (e.g. religious marching), but there are also legitimate concerns that *meaning* is being traded for *money* as the importance of place identity for external consumption overrides the needs of the internal constituency.

Events and destination branding

As cities seek to exploit their (unique and distinct) symbolic assets, this, ironically, becomes more difficult as other cities follow the same formulaic approach. There is a spectrum of approaches to the process of urban re-imaging. At one end you have the high-profile promotion of entertainment (and events) and pleasure placing consumption centre stage. Here, the attraction of 'signature' national or international events is a significant strand. At the other end of the spectrum is the promotion of local cultural identity and of the possibilities associated with the creative and cultural sectors. This approach also seeks to revitalise public space and the public sphere but there is an argument that the commodification of this cultural uniqueness can lead to the very opposite effect where exclusive cultural spaces are created (see Chapter 7 for a more in-depth discussion of the cultural events terrain).

It is clear that the event or festival – whether mega sporting (Roche, 2000) or cultural – has become one of the key strategic tools in repackaging a city for tourism consumption. It focuses attention, kickstarts or showcases image enhancement projects, galvanises local political actors and pressurises governments to ensure the watching and visiting world leaves with positive impressions of the locale. It is a strategy based on enhancing the desirability of the urban cityscape. Of course, this positive story overlooks the lack of accountability of the pro-growth coalitions that are behind these projects and the oft-cited lack of recognition of the need and interests of local people (see Lowes' discussion of the Molson Indy Car race in Vancouver as an example). What is certainly true is that in the promotion of events and festivals as cultural and economic resources for the city, 'leisure, enjoyment, spectacle and pleasure are produced, packaged, marketed and consumed' (Stevenson, 2003: 100).

In order to take the discussion of consuming cities to the next level, it is important to consider how they are increasingly subject to the preoccupations of the branding process and the role played by events within this configuration. Brands are more than a name, a logo, a series of images or a place – although each might form an important dimension of a brand identity. Strategic brand management has become synonymous with the most successful corporations (think Apple, Nike or Starbucks), celebrities (think David Beckham, Michael Jordan or Tiger Woods) and cities (think New York, London, Toyko or Paris). As Chalip and Costa (2005) suggest, a strong brand is a prerequisite for imparting perceptions of quality and value, whether this is for a product or a destination. For the purposes of this discussion destination branding refers to the

[O]verall impression that the destination creates in the minds of potential tourists, including its functional and symbolic elements. The brand encompasses the destination's physical attributes, services, attractions, name, logo, reputation, and the benefits that those provide the visitor. A recognisable brand facilitates a tourist's choice of destination because it encapsulates what the destination has to offer.

(Chalip and Costa, 2005: 219)

The brand narrative or story is clearly important in communicating appropriate messages about a destination to its target markets. In the period of urban entrepreneurial governance (see previous chapter), these target markets are invariably international visitors, investors and potential workers. In this environment, formulating the correct brand message is more important than the social and economic circumstances of the resident population. A powerful brand imparts perceptions of quality, adds value, reinvigorates and reanimates memories and generates emotional experiences. Since the 1990s, in many parts of the world, there has been an 'expansion of city marketing techniques and their progressive transformation into city branding strategies' (Garcia, cited in Smith and Fox, 2007: 1127). Essentially, cityscapes are now in global competition with each other where 'if a cultural project [event] is going to succeed . . . it is crucial that it does so as part of a holistic destination' (Tibbot, 2002: 73). This holistic view of destinations is evident in the view that city image is cultivated to communicate dynamic, vibrant, affluent, healthy, tolerant, cosmopolitan and sexy places (Waitt, 2008). Waitt calls the strategy of boosting city images through the *hype* of public–private partnerships geographies of 'hope' (Waitt, 2008). In other words, cultural intermediaries (e.g. advertising and PR agencies) create positive impressions of destinations on the way up by carefully exploiting hopeful motifs. Events represent a particularly useful mechanism for achieving the hype of hope as they represent the 'organization of spectacle and theatricality' (Harvey, cited in Smith and Fox, 2007: 1126). However, as part of the holistic destination, events have to 'fit' within the core 'umbrella brand' (e.g. Glasgow: Scotland with Style, or Enchanting Singapore). Yet it is no longer enough for cities to create events themselves, organically, to align with the city brand. Instead, a trend has emerged over the last decade where cities buy into, borrow or manufacture 'already-branded' events to complement their aspirational destination brand. In an accelerating world (Gleick, 1999), cities face intense pressure to buy rather than make their events portfolio in order to keep pace with established destinations. A good example of this process in action is the case of Auckland, New Zealand. In 2008 it published a major events strategy document, *Positioning Auckland as a major events destination*. In this document, major events are prioritised on the basis that they

•   are consistent with Auckland's brand, values and strategic objectives;
•   deliver net economic benefit to the Auckland economy without significant negative environmental, social or cultural impacts;

- provide leverage and showcase Auckland's distinctive landscape and culture;
- are likely to be welcomed and well supported by a wide cross-section of Auckland residents;
- efficiently maximise the use of existing regional infrastructure and enable new infrastructure development;
- increase visitor activity, particularly outside the traditional peak season periods;
- bring significant international broadcast and electronic/print media coverage enhancing Auckland's national and international profile and reputation;
- generate commercial opportunities for Auckland businesses;
- are aligned with the priorities of other regional and national strategies; and
- offer a pathway or entry to hosting larger events owned by the same body.

(Auckland Plus, 2008)

Only one of these objectives is driven by a concern for the residents of Auckland itself. The remainder are about destination branding and economic return. Leading from these criteria, Auckland has proposed an approach to create a portfolio of major events, most of which are derived from a buy rather than make decision. It proposes to identify, evaluate and nominate Auckland's interest as a candidate city for a mega and major event; create an annual or regularly hosted signature event that plays to Auckland's unique assets and strengths (this is, in essence, a hallmark event strategy); secure the right to host one of an international series of events (a special event strategy); bid for 'second tier' supporting events; and develop a cluster of events around an anchor event. These alternatives demonstrate the need for a relatively peripheral (at least geographically) destination to create major events as a means of securing brand recognition. Auckland is trying to bid for events that will bring consumption credibility to its destination in as short a timescale as possible. Of course, in dealing with top, or even second, tier events, the destination has to be aware that its own brand pretensions will have to engage with the brand requirements of the major sponsors who invariably accompany these events.

In this sense, cities are also taking on a new challenge – how to engage with brand communities, which Muniz and O'Guinn (2001: 412) describe as 'a specialized, non-geographically bound community, based on a structured set of social relations among admirers of a brand'. Brand communities can be attractive for destination agencies as they are perceived to be liberated from geography, well informed by the mass-media, less ephemeral, more committed and explicitly commercial. If the recognised brand (e.g. Red Bull) is aligned with the destination's events, then there is a greater chance that the brand community will generate more intense support and commitment. However, this also creates new challenges for event policy makers and for those concerned with ensuring that the benefits of events are shared more equally across the population. If events become synonymous with a corporate sponsor that has significant power and influence over the nature of the activities being delivered, there can be tension with the interests of the host destination. Moreover, if the industrial context of the brand is not deemed socially beneficial, policy makers face another challenge in deciding whether to accept economic value in exchange for political principle. Over recent years, tobacco and alcohol companies have been the subject of particular interest with respect to major events sponsorship. The former was a major sponsor of Formula One Grand Prix races until 2005 (e.g. Marlboro), and the latter continues to be a significant contributor to a series of major sporting events (e.g. Budweiser). In some nations, alcohol sponsorship is banned (e.g. France), but in others (e.g. the US) it is one of the most significant income streams for major (particularly sporting) events. The salient point is that as major corporations of all sorts (attractive or otherwise) target major events as brand vehicles, the local policy makers are forced to decide between the financial inducements and the long-term brand aspirations of the destination. This is not only in terms of the major sponsors; it is also relevant to the nature of the event itself. If a city is looking to develop its style credentials, it may not view the hosting of a motorsport event with a 'petrolhead' fan base as being suitable.

Event spaces in the consuming city (Miles and Miles, 2004) are now places within which cultural consumption is performed. Certain 'types' or genres of events are deemed necessary by the place marketers (or urban myth makers) as a symbol of cultural appreciation to attract the 'right' sort of tourism visitation. This necessitates the presence of a gastronomy festival, a visual arts festival, a gay pride event, an architectural festival and an art fair as each corresponds with the aspirational lifestyles of the new urban middle class for whom culturally coded consumption is the means of distinction. Events and festivals that drew from an earlier era of industrial capitalism (perhaps those that were justified on the bread and circuses motto) are replaced by deterritorialised, decontextualised, rootless events that celebrate placelessness in the name of a generalised cosmopolitanism that is easily amended and (re)packaged 'to attract the hordes of 'international, high income, bohemia' (Wilson, 2003: 219). A good example of the development of a portfolio of events to generate destination profile is the approach taken by Melbourne (see Box 6.1). This city has worked on a clear strategy to make it the 'world's event city'. It has achieved world renown and has ameliorated the economic challenges of the 'soft' or 'shoulder' off-peak season by developing an attractive calendar of events, both sporting (its main asset) and cultural. This was no accident. Instead, the regional government initiated a major events partnership to leverage the economic return desired. It is an exemplar for other cities with pretensions to enter the world stage.

Branded space and divided places

Before drawing this chapter to a close, it is necessary to return to the problematic that was identified in the introduction. It was suggested that, while

Box 6.1 Destination Melbourne: the world's event capital

Many cities around the world provide public sector investment for major events strategies on the basis that there exists an opportunity to grow visitor activity (and visitor expenditure) in the destination as well as a chance to raise its profile as a visitor destination and a place to live, work, play and invest. However, while major events have the potential to generate significant benefits that are widely distributed across industrial sectors and geographically, this does not lead necessarily to commercial viability for the private sector. As a result, the public sector frequently invests in major events to ensure that socially efficient outcomes are generated, that aggregate benefits outweigh aggregate costs and that benefits are widespread. If left entirely to the market, the argument goes that many potential beneficiaries would either (a) not realise they were going to be beneficiaries, (b) become free riders – realise the benefits but fail to invest, or (c) be unwilling to invest in advance to ensure benefit. In this (common) situation, public sector investment is investing on behalf of society to secure well-distributed benefits. In Melbourne, this was certainly the case. Major events have become a more significant component of the Australian city's economic transformation over the last decade. It has also helped to build the Melbourne brand to produce a range of tangible and intangible benefits. This was achieved through a series of planned interventions starting in 1991 with the formation of the Victorian Major Events Company (VMEC). This organisation was established as part of a Victorian government initiative to raise Melbourne and Victoria's profile on the world stage. VMEC markets Melbourne and Victoria to event owners. It does not stage events itself, but instead puts in place an organising structure to ensure the event can be delivered in keeping with the region's stringent requirements. As one of the world's best sporting event destinations (recognised as such by SportBusiness International in 2007), Melbourne hosts six of Australia's ten most popular events: Australian Open, Australian Formula One Grand Prix, Australian Rules Football Grand Final, Melbourne Cup, Australian 500cc Motor Cycle Grand Prix and the Volvo Ocean Race (Melbourne Stopover).

Moreover, with its Food and Wine Festival (March), Fashion Festival (March), International Flower and Garden Show (April), International Comedy Festival (April), International Jazz Festival (April), International Film Festival (July) and International Arts Festival (October), Melbourne is an exemplar for a consuming city, which has aligned an events strategy with its overall destination brand. It sustains its tourism industry with a staple diet of year-round events, supplemented by a series of one-off 'unique' events. Over the last few years, this has included the

International Rugby Board (IRB) World Cup in 2003, the Melbourne
Commonwealth Games in 2006 and the World Swimming Championships in 2007. Melbourne is utilising events (sporting and cultural) to
help achieve its aspiration of being recognised as a chic, sophisticated
destination with style, romance and attractions. Ultimately, this destination has established a public–private growth coalition (VMEC) to secure
major events that help grow the city's economic value.

Further research: Misener, L. and Mason, D. (2008) 'Urban regimes and
the sporting events agenda: a cross national comparison of civic development strategies', *Journal of Sport Management*, 22: 603–627.

these events may satisfy the lifestyle aspirations of the sought-after tourist
audiences, they might also exacerbate the exclusionary processes that exist
within the urban milieu of post-industrial cities. There is certainly evidence
to suggest that the consumption-led events city may divide as much as it
provides (Miles and Miles, 2004). Some commentators have suggested that
spectacle-based city projects (of which events are certainly a part) provide
only 'temporary illusions' of urban cohesion, 'papering over' real-life existing
social problems. Boyer's (2005) notion of the 'figured' and 'disfigured' city
is certainly relevant here. She argued that the figured (visible) city represent
grids of isolated, carefully designed consumption nodes for well-off sectors
of society. The disfigured city, in comparison, is a neglected sector, which is
unimaginable, operating as a specific place for the poor. In the urban rhetoric
of entrepreneurial governance (see Chapter 5), the figured city is designed (or
branded) to generate economic return, which will trickle down to assist the
latter. However, the urban studies literature suggests that the intensified
surveillance and 'gating' evident in many US and UK cities actually act to
sustain the 'divide' rather than ameliorating it.

Taking this debate of equitable distribution of resources further, Waitt
(2008) uses the term 'geographies of helplessness' to denote contemporary
urban spaces that, while liberating certain social groups, also constrain,
disadvantage and oppress. In the attraction of major events under the banner
of economic salvation and building a visitor economy there is unavoidable
tension between the interests of consumption and those of inclusion. As
Smith and Fox (2007: 1125) suggest, '[T]he main beneficiaries of event
strategies are seldom the most deserving and needy candidates'. Elsewhere,
it has already been suggested that the event-led benefits of 'hard' physical
regeneration of spectacular event strategies do not necessarily 'trickle down'
to local people and small businesses (Smith and Fox, 2007: 1128). Potentially,
this brings the power of destination branding into disrepute. As one response
to this challenge, Smith and Fox (2007) suggest that public policy makers are

now engaging with event-*themed* rather than event-*led* strategies – or at least a blending of the two. The rationale for this is that it is unsatisfactory to simply use events as promotional vehicles with no sustainable legacy for host cities other than a catalogue of wonderful images.

Event-themed strategies focus on the social and economic conditions that can be enhanced through the careful use of events to connect people and communities together around specific event-related projects (Chalip, 2006). The idea is to use events as vehicles to improve skills, employment and the competitiveness of associated small and medium enterprises (SMEs) or to develop cohesion through community participation. This, it is argued, brings a local 'buy-in' effect as well as the much sought-after external recognition – a branded 'win–win' scenario. Event-themes are designed to develop and leave a tangible legacy where the 'hard' benefits are complemented with the 'soft'. In the achievement of this success, the destination brand is strengthened and can ensure the loyal patronage of its associated brand communities.

Summary

In this chapter it has been argued that, as an extension of the neoliberal urban entrepreneurial approach, cities across the globe have become sites of intense consumption. Previously reliant on an industrial economic base that required the exploitation of land and labour, cities now sell their softer, less tangible assets to the visitor, investor or potential resident. In the clamour to have the city's assets promoted holistically, destination brands have emerged, an umbrella term representing the city's most saleable material and symbolic goods. While retail, hotels, restaurants and visitor attractions are significant features of the consuming city, events and festivals act to animate the cityscape and generate a plethora of alluring mediated images for touristic consumption. Major events strategies are now an essential component of the aggregate brand narrative of a destination – albeit at a cost. The indigenous history of place is increasingly threatened by the need to buy (into) rather than make events. In developing competitive events portfolios, the pressure to purchase a profile in the form of major events is an attractive one. However, the creation and manufacture of saleable events with little connectedness to the host community remains problematic for a number of reasons. First, securing 'buy-in' for an event-led (as opposed to an event-themed) strategy has been shown to be a challenge for policy makers. Second, the unequal distribution of beneficiaries in the consuming events city leaves the potential for a disfigured city of event haves and event have-nots. But perhaps most crucially, as inter-urban competition intensifies, cities are engaged in a game of diminishing returns as more events (cities) compete for a finite population of event tourists. There will be winners, like Melbourne, but it is also clear that there will be losers. In policy terms, public sector investment in destination branding is justifiable if socially beneficial outcomes result – but it remains uncertain that these will be forthcoming.

Critical review questions

- What value do cities receive from aligning their events and festivals programme to their wider destination brand promotion effort?
- What challenges face local governments that pursue a place marketing strategy using major events and festivals as a vehicle?

Recommended reading

Philo, C. and Kearns, G. (1993) 'Culture, history, capital: a critical introduction to the selling of places', in Kearns, G. (ed.) *Selling places: the city as cultural capital, past and present*, London: Pergamon Press.

Smith, A. and Fox, T. (2007) 'From "event-led" to "event-themed" regeneration: the 2002 Commonwealth Games Legacy Programme', *Urban Studies*, 44 (5/6): 1125–1143.

Waitt, G. (2008) 'Urban festivals: geographies of hype, helplessness and hope', *Geography Compass*, 2 (2): 513–537.

7 Events and social capital

Linking and empowering communities

Introduction

This chapter goes beyond the narrow economic model of analysis that has dominated the events field for the last few decades to consider the wider social impact of events on a variety of stakeholders. It gives consideration to the direct and indirect beneficiaries of event policy formations in order to assess the real winners and losers in the event-led strategies employed by city governments. Here, the focus will be on the opportunity costs associated with the allocation of public resources to subsidise or support the involvement of private sector actors in attracting and hosting events. It also considers the proposed social benefits accruable from the hosting of events (large and small) and subjects these to critical scrutiny, examining the potential role of events in the development of social economy and social enterprise skills. Finally, the chapter concludes by arguing that certain types of events and their specific governance arrangements are more likely to secure the proposed social 'benefits' than others.

The social impact agenda

The social impacts of events and their measurement have not, until recently, been a priority (Waterman, 1998; Derrett, 2003) as the economic agenda has been the dominant imperative for cities and nations (see Chapter 3). Starting in the 1980s, several factors have contributed to the pre-eminence of economic discourses. These include the onward march of neoliberal economic systems globally, the introduction of entrepreneurial local state governance arrangements (Chapter 5) and the subsequent creation of consuming cities (Chapter 6). There is an extensive literature base on the economic impact of events and festivals focusing on the additional expenditure leveraged by hosting these celebrations (see Chapter 3), but over recent years there has been greater scrutiny given the veracity of the economic claims and of the relative contribution of events and festivals to the softer outcomes associated with social and cultural fields. As a result, a growing body of literature is now given over to verifying the social impact of events on host communities, or at least offering a critique of the actual beneficiaries of investment in events – certainly in the cases of mega-events, although not exclusively (Whitson and Horne, 2006; Misener and Mason, 2006). Hall (2006) and Whitson and Horne (2006) provide influential critiques of the proposed economic benefits, arguing that benefits are invariably overstated and suggesting that perhaps investment in smaller and more embedded events would produce a greater 'return' (in economic and social terms) than the vanity projects of major sporting events in particular. As discussed in Chapter 4, greater critical scrutiny is now being paid to the legitimating rhetoric of economic analysis, and several authors are directing their attention to consider how best to ensure that (if present) an economic return is distributed more equitably than has been the case to date (Chalip, 2006; Hall 2006; Whitson and Horne, 2006). This requires a focus on who are the actual beneficiaries from the hosting of events and festivals. Over the last decade, there has been a more concerted campaign to re-evaluate the ubiquity of economic functionalist arguments about the benefits of events, led by a series of interested parties including community groups, academics, anti-globalisation protestors, environmentalists and the media. These groups have begun to hold city governments and event organisers to account with respect to the resources invested in the delivery of their spectacles. Whereas pro-growth urban renewal strategies paid little attention to the potential social and community benefits accruable from investment in the consuming city, host cities now have to consider mechanisms for ensuring wider social benefits within their bidding strategies for major events. A good example of this change in emphasis in action is the introduction of Community Benefits Clauses in the tendering processes for the 2014 Commonwealth Games in Glasgow (see Chapter 9 for more details). Glasgow avoided compromising European Union freedom of trade legislation while sending a clear signal to internal and external stakeholders that it wanted the benefits of this major sports event to reside in the city and its environs, where possible. This is one small example of the growing recognition that the social outcomes of major events need to be demonstrable and meaningful. It is no longer acceptable to utilise public resources to attract and deliver a sports event, for example, without other positive externalities (or eventualities) being secured.

There is a growing body of evidence pertaining to the exploitation of event-themed regeneration (Smith and Fox, 2007) to achieve social objectives, including in the fields of health, education, crime and community development. For example, those responsible for attracting sports events to destinations have successfully aligned themselves with the health agenda, ensuring that the halo effect accruing from these events can contribute positively to the challenge of escalating public health costs. Public spending for large-scale events in culture and sport is also frequently justified by its contribution to education and employment, by helping people back to work, providing social economy skills, linking with curriculum development (e.g. the Olympics are often used in this way to engage students) and engaging communities.

In sum, there is certainly a growing recognition that, in bringing large-scale events to cities, public expenditure has to benefit more than just the gentrified middle class of the city centre boundaries. This is where city planners are using events as a policy vehicle, in what Richards and Palmer (2010) refer to as an 'eventful city' approach, one where sustainability is at the core. With greater scrutiny on public expenditure (in the liberal democracies of the West at least), events have to defend their impacts against increasingly robust criticism. At one historical juncture it was sufficient to provide 'bread and circuses' to assuage the concerns of citizens (Veyne, 1990), but some recent examples point to a more effective critique of this approach. Since experiencing the financial debacle of the Montreal Olympics in 1976, Canadian citizens have been perhaps the most fervent critics of the economic benefits of major sporting events. This criticism culminated in the formation of the non-profit organisation Bread Not Circuses, which was established in Toronto against that city's bid for the Summer Olympic Games. The organisation lobbied hard internally and through the International Olympic Committee for the social welfare of Toronto's citizens to be considered when bidding for the world's largest circus. Similarly, when Canada successfully won the right to host the Vancouver Winter Olympics in 2010, there was evidence of significant protest over the rights of First Nation peoples and the spiralling costs associated with the event before and during the Games themselves.

What these examples show is that for events to gain, or maintain, legitimation they need to demonstrate the achievement of beneficial social externalities. However, despite there being more emphasis placed on the social outcomes by policy makers and event organisers, history shows that the easily quantifiable is much more attractive to decision makers than the qualitative 'intangibles' often associated with the social outcomes of events. It is for that reason that there is a renewed focus on producing demonstrable evidence for the social case, building on the popularised notion of social capital and its role in linking communities.

Linking communities: social capital as an instrument of event policy

In order to empower those communities working with policy makers to maximise the positive impact of events in their environment, individuals and groups need the appropriate skill sets and competencies. Moreover, those responsible for the events themselves must also understand how to lever this involvement to secure more meaningful participation from each stakeholder. The concept of social capital has been seen as a means of explaining the potential contribution of events to social good. This concept has attracted a significant amount of attention in recent years as fears over the fragmentation of communities and a generalised decline in civic engagement has intensified. It is argued, by some, that the loss of coherent networks within communities is responsible for this fragmentation. Stokowski (1994) suggests that in response to the loss of geographical and spatial coherence, leisure networks could play a pivotal role because of their inherently social status. As some of the binding forces of the past are now replaced in a post-industrial era with leisure networks, connections made through shared experiences and spectacles could provide an antidote to the apparent loss of trust that defines this period.

There is certainly an argument that events, for example, are communal celebrations that create the conditions for *communitas* to be produced (Chalip, 2006), transcending existing social conventions. However, if the one-off opportunity for dialogue, sharing and the expression of identity is not sustained, then the positive benefits gained are likely to evaporate as quickly as they were formed. In order for events to be used effectively to generate sustainable social outcomes, a greater understanding of the dynamics of social capital is required.

The concept of social capital is now commonly used both in everyday language and policy debates. It refers to an individual's inclusion in a range of networks, structures or groups that allow them to develop and gain this capital (Portes, 1998). The political use of such terms and policies aimed at developing this form of capital has intensified in recent years. Bourdieu (1985: 248) defined social capital as 'the aggregate of the actual or potential resources which are linked to possession of a durable network of more or less institutionalised relationships of mutual acquaintance and recognition'. There is now broad agreement among academics about the benefits that individuals and groups secure by participation in social networks, clubs and groups (Coleman, 1988; Portes, 1998). Social capital has been popularised and is, for some, a panacea for solving a number of social problems. However, Putman (1993, 2000) has been criticised for de-contextualising the concept and for its misuse. That said, for this book there is merit in considering how durable networks, mutual acquaintances and reciprocal relationships can be formed through the vehicle of events as a policy instrument.

Drawing together some of the key theorists of social capital, there is agreement that it refers to networks (bonding or bridging); connectedness; feelings of trust and safety; sense of belonging; reciprocity; participation; citizen power and proactivity; values, norms and outlook on life and diversity (Coleman, 1988; Hall, 1999; Putnam, 1993, 2000). While acknowledging that the term should not be used as a catchall for any success in community development, the potential contribution of events and festivals in strengthening social capital is increasingly prevalent in building the 'case' for hosting a variety of large- and small-scale events.

There has certainly been a policy move in Britain and elsewhere towards the empowerment of communities and individuals to take control of their own community development and partnerships. At UK governmental level, community cohesion units have been put in place to assist with neighbourhood renewal and have a remit to develop a common vision and sense of belonging, the valuing of diversity, similar life opportunities for all and strong and positive relationships between people from different backgrounds and circumstances. Flinn and McPherson (2007) have demonstrated the potential utility of culture and events as a stimulus for community engagement, arguing that forms of art and culture can be used to engage citizens in local issues and democratic processes. There are plenty of recent examples of the use of events and related activities to address social issues. For example, projects funded through the London 2012 Cultural Olympiad focus on building social capital, especially the variables of networks, civic participation, citizen power and proactivity around the UK. In Glasgow the 'Govan Wave of Change' project, funded through the Cultural Olympiad 2012, has used a series of events and 'conversations' to engage local people to help change their communities and inform policy makers of their expectations for change. This type of civic engagement in regeneration initiatives is being mirrored throughout the UK and elsewhere and often they are constructed around the 'hook' of a major event, whether sporting or cultural. Of course, while well intentioned, there is a danger that such initiatives are merely about listening rather than acting upon the interests of one or two stakeholders. As Mitchell, Agle and Wood (1997) argue, not all 'stakeholders' have the same degree of power, legitimacy and urgency. Given the predominance of economic functionalist arguments about the benefits of events, it is reasonable to assume that local residents may certainly have the urgency, and perhaps the legitimacy, to bring their concerns to bear (e.g. if an event venue is to be built in their area and they are the representative group for residents), but that does not necessarily mean that they will have the power to enforce change or even to have their concerns heard. In this sense, the relative value of social 'capital' over competing claims for legitimacy in event policy remains uncertain at best.

That said, theoretically there is a cogent argument to be made for events and festivals working as the 'social glue' of communities by aiding capacity building and through cementing a sense of place identity (whether a nation, a city or a neighbourhood). In the UK context, the community benefits arising from London 2012 Olympics is a political issue as the Games are being hosted in the capital city but are, simultaneously, being promoted as the UK's Games. In order to assuage those critics who argue that the economic, physical and social benefits will reside only in London, elements of the event have been shared with other counties and regions of the UK. The ability of the London 2012 Olympics to act as the social glue for community bonding is becoming apparent and was in evidence in advance of the event itself. The county of Kent, for example, has secured a number of Olympics-related projects, which has given it a new vibrancy and focus for community development. This has enabled them to rebrand themselves as the gateway to the Games. The benefits have primarily been in terms of connectedness, a facet of social capital, as residents of the county feel part of the 2012 Games. Kent has more approved pre-Games training camps for London 2012 than any other region in Britain and has already signed deals with the Ukrainian and Belarussian judo teams to train there (www.insidethegames.com, 26 June 2010). Kent has used the Games well in helping the county feel like it is very much part of the event and demonstrating lasting links well before the Games, in the anticipation that by 2012 they will feel fully empowered and involved.

However, while these examples suggest that it is possible to empower communities, generate new networks (or re-energise existing ones) and secure citizen involvement through events, there remain significant question marks over the longevity of the positive outcomes secured and the nature of the beneficiaries thereafter. That is why attention needs to be paid to the most effective mechanisms for turning the theoretical benefits into practice-led initiatives. It is to this problem that the chapter now turns.

Leveraging social benefits for events

The development of social capital is inextricably bound to the process of community development and engagement, and supporters argue that events and festivals can assuage feelings of alienation and social isolation experienced in some of the most challenging community circumstances (Foley *et al.*, 2009). Festivals can, it is argued, 'reconnect leisure with the quality of community life, social engagement, and the achievement of the common good' (Arai and Pedlar, 2003: 199). Other 'social benefits' are linked to the feeling of pride in the host city engendered by the hosting of a large-scale event – but again, the evidence suggests that higher property prices, displacement of residents (Whitson and Macintosh, 1993), crowding and congestion (Fredline and Faulkner, 2002), inconvenience and the financial legacy of revenue funding can be punitive for lower-income groups in particular. Aligning with the renewed focus on social capital, McDonnell, Allen, O'Toole and Harris (1999) define a series of positive social impacts emanating from the hosting of events, including the shared experiences, which can replace other forms of collective solidarity (e.g. trade unions or political parties).

The development of community pride and subjective feelings of hope and renewed achievement orientation are used as evidence by many cities hosting peripatetic events. Misener and Mason (2006) argue that the positive impacts of large- and small-scale events do provide opportunities for community development and involvement, especially when decision-making is decentralised and when communities are empowered to decide on the most appropriate mechanisms for delivering their service needs. In other words, when residents and community groups have power as well as legitimacy and urgency. Tangible outcomes also need to be forthcoming if social capital gains are to be made. For example, the development of the social economy can be directly linked to successful events planning 'as individuals gain new skills and capacities in management, decision making, teamwork, fundraising, negotiation, etc, so the community is gaining new skills and competences' (Gould, 2001: 71). It is now commonplace for the wider skills agenda to be a key feature of major events bidding documents, illustrating the need to leave a social legacy for the most needy segments of the host city population.

However, despite all the well-intentioned rhetoric surrounding the social case for events, there remains a sense that these outcomes are hoped for and desirable as opposed to being expected and planned for. This has led to a call from some researchers for a greater focus on *leveraging* benefits rather than waiting for *impact* to occur. For example, O'Brien and Chalip (2007) refer to event leveraging as a new strategic approach, focused on processes and interventions prior to, and during, events. A leveraging approach 'implies a much more pro-active approach to capitalising on opportunities . . . rather than impacts research which simply measures outcomes' (Weed *et al.*, 2009: 13). Leveraging emphasises pre-event planning (and investment) and requires governments (central and local), events organisers and other stakeholders to agree on their social objectives at the earliest possible stage. Whereas in the past, decisions to bid for major sports events were often made on the basis of political reasons (Roche, 2000), the focus on leveraging is an indication of a maturing events field concerned with how the circus can help make more bread. The recognition that the event spectacle can help focus the minds of policy makers is now being taken to another level with a series of policy objectives being tied into the activities of planning and delivering major sporting and cultural events. The development of leveraging strategies also necessitates a more fundamental engagement with techniques like stakeholder theory, whereby the individuals or groups affected by a particular activity or event are evaluated and questions are asked as to which interest is most important and why. Only then can appropriate decisions on investment, engagement structures and decision-making approaches be made. Take the example of Mark Lowes' insightful thesis *Indy Dreams and Urban Nightmares* (see Box 6), which demonstrates how a community can be mobilised successfully to a proposed major event arriving on their doorstep.

Box 7.1 provides an example of where socially oriented stakeholder interests can prevail, gaining power as well as legitimacy when they mobilise in a coherent manner. While the eventual outcome was a 'forced' compromise for the city of Vancouver and the event owner, Molson Indy, if city authorities were to create the structures within which alternative visions of the role of events could contribute to planning decisions, then greater ownership and stakeholder management could be the outcome – as opposed to the confrontational politics that often accompany these decisions.

The development of strategic approaches to leveraging benefits is certainly required as there are plentiful examples of flawed attempts to use events for social gain, many of which failed on the basis of the absence of effective involvement with a wider range of stakeholders. For example, in her studies of Barcelona, Glasgow and Sydney, Garcia (2004) remains unconvinced of linkages between spectacles and the participation and representation of local populations. She argues that it is necessary to exploit major events to extend cultural horizons and experiences rather than simply creating new showcases of cultural experiences that are flown in and out of the host destination without leaving an imprint on its population. Flinn and McPherson (2007) echo this concern, arguing that more needs to be done to work with local communities to secure meaningful participation in the Glasgow 2014 Commonwealth Games well in advance of the event to ensure that the new partnerships,

Box 7.1 Molson Indy Vancouver

A good example of stakeholder theory and the development of social capital in a community around an event-related issue is the case of the Molson Indy Vancouver (MIV). In this case, an urban neighbourhood turned its back on the professed economic benefits of hosting a high-profile motorsport event in its environs. The Hastings-Sunrise community mobilised itself to resist the relocation of the MIV from its existing site to the Hastings Park location.

This example is a story of the competing visions of the Indy-boosters versus the Hastings-Sunrise neighbourhood activists – two competing stakeholders with different degrees of power, legitimacy and urgency in their involvement with the MIV. As part of their campaign to "sell" the Indy to their opponents, proponents of the MIV employed a combination of strategies ranging from *brinkmanship* (if the Hastings Park relocation bid fails, the race will move elsewhere, taking with it millions in economic spin-offs to the community); the promise of *financial inducements* (3,000 discounted tickets and a free one-day pass; 1,300 part-time jobs; and money for a park restoration fund, to be generated through a special ticket surcharge); and an appeal to civic duty by highlighting the *symbolic benefits* of the MIV for Vancouverites (it puts the city on the world map). This was a contest between those promoting the urban entrepreneurial discourse of events (and indicating that there was no alternative) and those interested in ensuring greater involvement, empowerment and voice for those affected by the imposition of major events on their locale. The resident groups stood firm in the face of inducements, hype and the threat of withdrawal from Vancouver on the Molson Indy altogether. However, because the Hastings Park communities had already fought long and hard for park restoration and the principle of local community control, the boosters found it difficult to break down their resolve. Effectively, the Hastings Park community used its bank of social capital (networks, trust, participation and citizen involvement) to force the MIV management to back down and keep the event at a reconfigured and expanded False Creek track. Lowes, in his Ph.D. thesis on the case, suggests that the local activists constructed and successfully promoted an alternative common sense for their space, which is a lesson for other attempts at community mobilisation around an events-related issue.

Further reading: Lowes, M.D. (2002) *Indy dreams and urban nightmares: speed merchants, spectacle, and the struggle over public space in the world-class city*, Toronto: University of Toronto.

community groups or social networks formed continue to exist long after any physical structures or formal funding is gone. Misener and Mason (2006) provide some advice on the most effective means of leveraging social benefits, based on the experience of Manchester's 2002 Commonwealth Games. Manchester focused much of its social regeneration on its most disenfranchised communities and drew on the advice of Chalip (2006) in viewing the Games as an opportunity not merely for the evaluation of impact, but rather to engage in organisational learning – with communities in receipt of this learning. Most fundamentally, Manchester's policy makers secured involvement from community interest groups and related stakeholders by enabling them to participate in strategic activities related to the Games (i.e. the bid process, management and legacy planning). While most major events will engage in some type of formal 'consultation' with stakeholders as they plan their events, it is the degree of openness with respect to communication and collaborative action that differentiates the Manchester case from others. If events are to effectively bridge the democratic deficit and contribute to a community's bank of social capital, then their organisers need to embrace the core values of residents, community groups and neighbourhood associations. This process also needs to involve respecting the community's definition of place and space and not only those of private capital. The local state needs to intervene sensitively if it is to lever the desired benefits from its communities. Acting as a 'catalyst, convener and facilitator' (Misener and Mason, 2006: 45) is preferable to the imposition of roles and norms upon communities. Building trust between the local state and its residents is perhaps as important as those between residents themselves. Specifically, in terms of social capital, vertical ties are more valuable than horizontal ties. Vertical ties are those linking ties between, say, a community group and its local government or political representatives and (say) the event owner. These ties are more valuable because they create dialogue, which can aid understanding on both sides and also develop reciprocity and sustainable lines of communication that may not have previously existed. However, if the structures created for a one-off event are temporary and evaporate once the event is over, then the charge of tokenism may be laid at the door of the local state. Furthermore, it is vital that the composition of groups representing community interests is diverse, so that they act to alleviate as opposed to increasing marginalisation. This in itself is a challenge, as communities are complex, multifaceted and contested, and not all interventions will lead to positive outcomes for all of their members.

To the contrary, there exists a fairly significant body of literature that illustrates the less positive social outcomes of events. Some of these are connected with overly instrumental or interventionist strategies employed by the local state, and others are attributable to the intentions of those promoting events as forms of social control. Waitt (2004), for example, asserts that the creation of spectacular events (he is primarily referring to sporting events) could be seen as a means of exerting social control to address the loss of identity associated with class, age, ethnicity and place that was brought about by the change in economic structures towards post-industrialism. Others have suggested that many negative impacts arise from the hosting of major sporting events. For example, most of the recent Olympic (e.g. Atlanta, Sydney, Athens and Beijing) and Commonwealth Games (e.g. Delhi) have attracted negative press coverage for the displacement of residents and the compulsory purchase of people's houses to create the desired showcase venue. McDonnell *et al.* (1999) add to the list of negative impacts by suggesting that major events also bring community alienation, feelings of being ignored with respect to decisions about bidding and delivery and the practice of legislative fast-tracking to circumvent normal democratic processes pertaining to planning and environmental impact assessments, for example.

Other commentators have referred to the opportunity costs that arise from expenditure on large-scale infrastructure for events and the subsequent diversion of funding from mainstream leisure activities. Additionally, the loss of amenities in the run up to, and during, the event also has a detrimental effect on the lives of local communities. Some residents feel excluded from their own city when events are in town, and if this becomes part of a cyclical trail, it can affect the perception of the quality of life in the city – very different from the professed commitments in most bid documents and government event strategies. While there is certainly an argument that having more sporting and cultural opportunities enhances the desirability of a locale, it is the distribution of benefits arising from this strategy that generates criticism. As discussed in Chapters 5 and 6, destination branding approaches involve 'selling places' in order to attract tourist visitation and investment. However, neither of these outcomes is necessarily to the benefit of the majority of the destination's citizens – at least in terms of immediate return. If events are at the core of a city's sporting and cultural plans, then 'the integration of events with civic goals becomes even closer' (Richards and Palmer, 2010: 37), but this continues to require the meaningful involvement of citizens at every stage if it is to be sustainable in the longer term.

Beyond the debate over the most effective structural mechanisms to secure meaningful community involvement in, and outcomes from, events, it may also be time to question whether certain types of events and the specific arrangements governing them are more suited to developing social capital (and, by definition, positive social outcomes) than others. For example, are shorter events better than longer events at securing social benefit, or are cultural events more effective than sporting events? In the cultural terrain, securing the title of European Capital of Culture (ECoC) is a hotly contested competition. The ECoC is a coveted title that allows a city (and country) to badge itself all year round as a place in which to experience cultural events and performances. Recent title-holders include Glasgow (1990), Rotterdam (2001) and Liverpool (2008). This event can permit event leverage because hosts invariably plan to both showcase their existing cultural assets and develop new ones through investment in internationally renowned cultural products as well as local cultural practices. In the latter – what could be called the expression of local culture – community values and norms of behaviour are given space to be promoted to a wider audience and a panoply of other social policy outcomes are tied to the ECoC title. For example, Liverpool used its time as ECoC as much to promote its own unique cultural tapestry as to commission internationally renowned performances and showcase events. This was because Liverpool won the title on the basis that it wanted to lever culture to contribute to the city's renaissance as opposed to merely displaying its high cultural assets. Liverpool was also innovative in the way it evaluated the wider economic, social and cultural outcomes of its year of activity. Impacts 08, or the 'Liverpool model' as it is now being referred to, has demonstrated how evaluation can complement the event itself as long as it is planned at the start and conducted independently of the event organisers – a key attribute of leveraging strategies. Impacts 08 engaged proactively with residents, citizens and other stakeholders throughout the year on their experiences of the ECoC and the transformations the event brought about for the city. This process generated an extensive research archive that provides an evidence base not only for the outcomes of the EcoC event, but also for the means of achieving these outcomes – in other words, it is as much about the process as the product.

However, it is important to remember that there is a need for the case to be argued for the social outcomes of events so that those involved in the conception, planning and delivery of events and festivals take full cognisance of their social meaning to local residents. Alongside the work of Impacts 08 and related projects, there is a growing body of work now focused on the 'intangible' or 'soft' outcomes of events (community pride and community regeneration), culminating with the publication of a free database, EventImpacts, for use worldwide, to help people plan and evaluate national-level event impacts (see www.eventimpacts.com, 2010).

While the Liverpool case provides an example of the way a year-long event can engage proactively with the social cause, others claim that a focus on major events (whether sporting or cultural) is, in itself, the major barrier to sustainable (and positive) social impact. Hall (2006), for example, suggests that policy makers would secure more significant long-term benefits from investment in smaller, but more embedded events rather than pursuing the pot of gold which mega-events are said to represent. However, a policy shift of this sort looks unlikely in the short to medium term, especially as competition for these mega-spectacles is intensifying as more destinations enter the circuit. In this context, working from within to extract the greatest level of social benefit for stakeholders is the most that can be expected.

Summary

This chapter has highlighted the need to recognise that events are now used as a key part of city strategies for social regeneration. The policy process now involves the use of events in transforming social spaces, sustaining communities and the development of the social economy as well as developing economic growth, inward investment and reputation. The role of events in developing social capital is not now just an add-on or political rhetoric; it is a key addition to bidding for events, and more than that, the key component of engaging and sustaining communities. Until the last few years, events planners and policy makers often failed to address the social impact of events because of the difficulties associated with quantification, the cost of longitudinal work and the less immediate political outcomes attached to it. However, alongside the economic and physical impacts being scrutinised in depth, there is also a greater emphasis being placed on measuring the social value of events, especially when policy makers stress these benefits as part of the bidding and delivery objectives for sporting and cultural celebrations.

The drawbacks of hosting large-scale events are nearly always presented as being about the negative social issues that face the host community, but until long-term longitudinal studies of the social impact of events (both positive and negative) on host communities are conducted, it will always be easier to highlight the negative impacts on the host. Now more than ever, event hosts are exposed to the watching gaze of the global media and event owners, who do not want to be seen to adding to a country's global and social problems especially around issues of displacement and poverty.

Future government policy needs to take greater cognisance of the distribution of benefits arising from an investment in an events-led strategy. It is increasingly unsustainable in public accountability terms for large-scale 'public' events to transfer 'profit' to private corporations and to consult with other social stakeholders only tokenistically. If there is to be a meaningful triple bottom line appraisal of the value of events and festivals, then lasting social infrastructures need to be created. In the development of these infrastructures, consideration needs to be given to how strong community networks, relationships of trust and reciprocity and participation can be formed. In keeping with the major tenets of stakeholder theory, the involvement of all stakeholders in strategic and operational activities helps to assuage concerns about the usual suspects benefiting. But more than this, meaningful involvement in pre-bidding, bidding, planning and delivery will produce a more socially sustainable model to help cities realise the benefits beyond the narrow economic logic found to date.

Critical review questions

- Discuss the positive social impacts that an event or festival can produce for a destination.
- What are the main differences between a leveraging strategy and one based on the measurement of impacts?
- Identifying the main stakeholders involved in an event of your choice, discuss the relative power, legitimacy and urgency each has and why.

Recommended reading

Chalip, L. (2006) 'Towards social leverage of sport events', *Journal of Sport & Tourism*, 11: 109–127.

Flinn, J. and McPherson, G. (2007) 'Culture matters? The role of art and culture in the development of social capital', in Collins, M., Holmes, K. and Slater, A. (eds) *Sport, leisure, culture and social capital: discourse and practice*, Eastborne: Leisure Studies Association.

Misener, L. and Mason, D. (2008) 'Towards a community centred approach to corporate community involvement in the sporting events agenda', *Journal of Management and Organisation*, 16 (4): 495–514.

Richards, G. and Palmer, R. (2010) *Eventful cities: cultural management and urban revitalisation*, Oxford: Butterworth-Heinmann.

8 Events as cultural capital
Animating the urban

Introduction

This chapter will explore and evaluate the ways in which policy makers have embraced the concepts of cultural capital and escalated the events industry to a new level of symbolic engagement. Policy makers now battle to have their cities or nations seen as able to compete at the top tier of bidding for large-scale events and express their 'personalities' in global place wars. The chapter presents a discussion of the concept of cultural capital and its use in the promotion of the cultural economy, and debates whether cities are now contested cultural spaces for event-led regeneration rather than civic public spaces.

Events and the cultural economy

In the first part of this chapter, it is necessary to address two important distinctions in the way cultural capital is evaluated. First, there is the growing recognition that cultural forms (e.g. the arts, sport, music or dance) contribute to the economies of cities and nations and, as a result, should be the subject of investment as a means to achieve a range of associated externalities – including positive economic impact. The second use of the term cultural capital derives from the sociological field and is concerned with the unequal distribution of cultural taste, which derives from access to the educational system. Both conceptualisations of cultural capital inform the content of this chapter. However, it is first necessary to provide a context for the transformation of cultural forms (often defined by their expressive qualities) into commodities, which are invariably important drivers of the economies of cities and nations in the early twenty-first century.

Building on the discussion of the neoliberal economic model in Chapter 5 and of consumption-oriented cities in Chapter 6, it should be clear that entrepreneurial approaches to managing urban areas rest on the exploitation of the unique assets of a 'place' – whether in the form of the physical environment, a distinctive cultural heritage or a set of manufactured narratives. The cultural terrain, often valued for its intrinsic qualities as opposed to its extrinsic (instrumental) ones, has, over recent decades, been subject to the effects of market conditions. In academia, a number of scholars have commented on what is termed the culture economy thesis (Du Gay and Pryke, 2000) over the last two decades. This thesis, it is argued, suggests that culture is itself the business of cities, fuelled by an increasingly important symbolic economy of images, signs and spaces (Zukin, 1995). Event-led policies are increasingly important contributors to this cultural economy as they are viewed as effective vehicles in mediating the relationship between cultural symbols and entre-preneurial capital. Major events and festivals are now seen as part of the cultural (including sporting) strategies of those cities that embrace the concept that the cultural industries are there to showcase symbols, adverts, experiences and images that policy makers seek to project. Utilising the currency of the so-called creative and cultural industries, the mass commoditisation of major events allows cities and nations to project themselves in the great place ident-ity battle for cultural authority (Pratt, 2005). Events are selected and delivered under umbrella brands (e.g. 'Glasgow: Scotland with Style' or 'Uniquely Singapore') and are strategically designed to construct a 'brand family' or network of sponsors who wish to be associated with the event and the cities' wider message (e.g. cosmopolitan, culturally advanced and innovative). Selected images are transmitted through the mass media spectacle, which represents and, some would argue, misrepresents destinations' cultural assets. The spectacular ceremonies associated with sporting mega-events, in particular, are essential tools to place market cities as they project alluring images for visitors to ensure secondary spend opportunities can take place in them. The value of such symbolic images to cities is enormous in terms of promoting the city well beyond the period of any major event. That events can play such a significant role is in part due to the economic transition that has taken place across much of the developed world over the last two decades, whereby economies have moved from 'extracting' to 'making' to 'delivering' to 'staging' experiences that engage and emotionally connect audiences in intense memorable moments (Pine and Gilmore, 1999). As Frew and McGillivray (2008) have commented, events, as spectacular off-world creations, allow people to assume new performative identities where they can immerse them-selves in hyper-experiences. Events are attention grabbing, making them desirable both as a branding platform and as a policy vehicle for local and central governments.

Events and cultural policy

Events are now being seen as part of a circuit of cultural competition to the point that demonstrating the ability to stage them is crucial for a destination's competitive positioning. Culture is a contested concept and has been understood to have two main definitions. First, culture can be conceived as a concept that gives regularity, unity and systematicity to practices (Bourdieu, 1992). In this view, culture serves to reaffirm, further develop and elaborate those aspects of reality that hold a particular group of people together in a common culture (Geertz, 1957). In the other main definition, culture is conceived as an activity, a context or an aesthetic judgement. Culture is segmented into various activities that are created, or performed, by creative people and are judged using aesthetic criteria. Events and festivals are often seen as contributing to both definitions of culture – they are seen to represent a way of life, or to hold people together in a common culture (e.g. carnival or national days), and they are often the most visible representation of diverse cultural forms (e.g. art, dance or film festivals). However, in policy terms, dealing with the cultural terrain has proved challenging, mainly because of the different values assigned to the activities of cultural practitioners vis-à-vis their policy counterparts. As cultural policy is a relatively bureaucratic process (Miller and Yudice, 2002), it works to govern what counts as creative and cultural practice through funding, promotion and evaluation. Of course, in the furtherance of this process, there is a tension between those espousing the intrinsic value of a particular cultural form and those responsible for justifying its instrumental worth in terms of social and economic externalities. As Garcia (2007) has argued recently, there is a problem in that creative practices are not easily 'framed' to fit with the bureaucratic, systematic and regulated processes of policy formation and implementation and, therefore, can be easily dismissed – unless these organisations engage with the 'framing' device of entrepreneurialism that has become influential within many policy terrains in recent years.

Over the last twenty years in the US, the UK and most of mainland Europe, there has been a cultural turn towards exploiting the instrumental value accruable from the expressive industries. Garcia (2007) argues that culture-led regeneration is about using cultural activity as the catalyst and engine for the transformation of a place that has displayed the symptoms of environmental, social and/or economic decline. She suggests that the main approaches to culture-led regeneration include investment in major cultural events (e.g. European Capital of Culture), in iconic cultural infrastructures (e.g. Bilbao's Guggenheim Museum) and in creative and cultural quarters (e.g. Dublin's Temple Bar). In Singapore, this formula was followed as a means to establish an alternative brand identity. First, city officials developed the cultural esplanade, before attracting cultural events and now large-scale sporting events.

There is little doubt that events (regional, national and international) are increasingly programmed into the culture-led regeneration strategies of many cities (McGuigan, 2005; Crespi-Vallbona and Richards, 2007) with the intention of revitalising their economies. This regeneration often focuses on repositioning urban centres as part of a branding exercise to attract tourists and inward investment and retain talent, but it can also work as a means to upgrade the service provision for locals and visitors, through better quality transport links, shopping and cultural attractions. The common denominator of culture-led regeneration approaches is that they are driven by instrumental motives – events, like sport and other cultural forms before them, are now being used to achieve specific social and economic goals (Burnham and Durland, 2007). Urban spaces that were often seen as places to avoid even a decade ago, now through the guise of culture are being transformed into events venues, attractive living spaces and locations for inward investment. It is the economic discourse that is now synonymous with events-led cultural policy in the developed (and increasingly the developing) world (McGuigan, 2005). Policy makers are prioritising the entrepreneurial outcomes over the perceived intangibles of social regeneration.

Crespi-Vallbona and Richards (2007) argue that cultural festivals have taken on greater economic, social and political importance in recent years – some view this as part of the 'cultural turn'. In policy terms, the public sector (often in partnership with private equity) has invested heavily in cultural regeneration strategies on the premise that culture 'is central to promoting the continued renaissance of the city . . . culture creates jobs, attracts invest-ment and enriches the lives of people who live and work in and visit the city' (Ali-Knight and Robertson, 2004: 6). McCarthy (2006) also writes extensively about the creation of cultural quarters, especially in Dublin and then in Leeds, Dundee and Glasgow as part of a British response to regen-eration. These are often developed using cultural events, initially, as an artificial bond to create local vibrancy and belonging. This is then developed into an identity that can be attached to the area and creates a space and place identity for the city. Alternatively, events can also follow on from physical regeneration projects – for instance, Sydney Opera House was developed to showcase the city as able to bid for cultural touring companies and used as part of their cultural regeneration arguments to win events and create identity.

Large-scale events, in particular, are perceived as being useful in achieving the three 'Rs' of regeneration, re-imaging and rebranding. Events are now used in Britain, (e.g. Glasgow, Manchester and London), Australia (e.g. Sydney and Melbourne) and elsewhere in Europe (e.g. Bilbao, Barcelona and Paris) as part of processes of *cultural planning* by city policy makers. Crucially, cultural planning does not refer only to the planning of cultural activities like art, dance, film or music. Instead, it refers to a more fundamental commitment to planning the shape of the urban landscape with culture in mind (Ghilardi, 2001). Singapore, for example, has addressed the perceived absence of creative and cultural assets in its offering by investing heavily in producing cultural products and showcasing them on a global stage. It initially branded itself as the 'eventful city' in an attempt to convince the West that it was capable of staging, if not producing, large-scale events. The development strategy for this started in the 1990s, and probably culminated in the staging of the Singapore F1 Grand Prix (see Chapter 12), which indicated the city was worthy of hosting big events.

One of the main reasons for using culture instrumentally is that, as Zukin (1995: 9) suggests, '[V]isual display counts in American and European cities today, because the identities of places are established by sites of delectation'.

Culture attracts attention and can be used as a valued commodity. The proliferation of cultural festivity can be associated with similar trends towards a 'cosmopolitan ethic' that defines a neighbourhood or city as vibrant. In 'created' or 'manufactured' events, the cultural message is carefully choreographed. Festivals and events are the vehicle with which to animate static cultural forms and promote them to new markets through the pervasive media-tourism complex (Nauright, 2004) – events can spectacularise fixed structures (Richards and Wilson, 2004), lighting them up and displaying them in an easily consumable format. Festivals and events provide civic governments with a relatively inexpensive means of securing a plethora of suitably colourful and multicultural images to circulate around the globe (e.g. Sydney Mardi Gras, Rio Carnival and London Notting Hill Carnival). The process often involves recreating a historical narrative, one that the governing agencies can swallow and is exploitable as a tourism resource and is easier to create than hosting large-scale sporting events. Using Singapore as an example again, Foley, McPherson and Matheson (2006) have highlighted how the Thaipusam Festival (see Box 2.1) is used by policy makers and marketers to showcase a local Hindu religious festival as a symbolic spectacle that can attract and detain visitors in Singapore. Events such as these are increasingly being used as part of that city-state's cultural tourism strategy to increase the dwell time in the city and highlight that local culture can be showcased globally.

However, despite these positive examples, this is not to say that the realm of events and cultural policy is uncontested. On the contrary, proponents of the intrinsic value of culture question the sustainability of the cultural economy if localised culture is being expropriated and if meaningful rituals are packaged and performed for simple pecuniary motives. It is to the contested nature of cultural capitals that the chapter now moves.

Contested cultural capitals

While it is clear that governments across the world have recognised the value of culture as an exploitable economic asset, this does not mean that cultural producers or the citizens of the host destination accept this approach uncritically. In fact, there exists a strong lobbying force arguing that the forms of cultural expression chosen to lead culture-led regeneration do not reflect the cultural experiences of the host audience and are overly instrumentalist and economic in intention. This is where the alternative conception of the term 'cultural capital', mentioned in the opening part of this chapter, is a useful explanatory device. In the sociological field, Pierre Bourdieu (1984) theorised cultural capital and made the term famous. Bourdieu argued that within cultural fields (e.g. the arts, sport or education), various class groupings possess different levels of capital that 'have value and can be traded or exchanged for desired outcomes within their own field or others' (Webb, Schirato and Danaher, 2002: 109). Possessing the desired cultural capital (Bourdieu, 1984) conferred by the educational field normally enhances individuals' opportunities for distinction (the division between the holders of cultural and financial capital and the different dispositions they display towards culture itself). Other sociologists had previously linked culture and leisure to social class, but it was Bourdieu who demonstrated how this form of capital (alongside economic, social and physical) could be acquired and deployed as a means of creating distinction from others.

Bourdieu believed that because cultural capital was distributed unequally, knowledge of and participation in certain cultural forms and practices serve to exclude some groups and reinforce the privilege of others. In terms of access to, for example, cultural events and festivals, city or national policy makers must be aware that access is potentially unequal and these events may work to reproduce and reinforce the social inequalities that presently exist in cities and society. Large-scale cultural (and sporting) events do appear to embrace mass audiences through their cultural, entertainment and sporting programmes – although that has been achieved primarily through mass spectatorship and media spectacle. Certainly, most people with access to mass media (and, more recently, social media) are able to engage in a conversation about the Olympics, a World Cup, or even an opening ceremony of one of these events. Opening ceremonies appear to have crossover appeal, engaging the uninitiated with the historical and contemporary cultures of host nations. Of course, the appeal of these cultural ceremonies is often as much about their spectacular staging and production quality as it is a reflection of a cultural curiosity, and participation is mediated.

Outside of the major sporting event ceremonies, governments must also tread a careful path to ensure that the cultural (and sporting) festivities presented as part of the urban touristic offering are able to secure economic, cultural and social outcomes – if they are to be sustainable. So, while events do offer urban policy makers an intriguing opportunity to increase inward investment and quality of life and to encourage residents to return to inner city living, there remains a concern among critics that the creation of overly commercial event portfolios threatens to marginalise competing 'value' claims, which can lead to the creation and promotion of more formulaic cultural events (Quinn, 2005).

Over recent times a fairly significant body of literature has been developed that questions the effectiveness of cultural festivals and events in achieving the social externalities expected of them. Garcia and Miah (2007), for example, contend that in relation to the Olympic Games' cultural programming there is a tendency to showcase either 'elite or folkloric expressions' of art over more inclusive art forms. Moreover, there is also a view that when culture is used instrumentally, for economic gain, the hallmark cultural projects that are promoted and resourced can leave the host city with a realm of showcase performances or events but local cultural forms lose out (Garcia, 2004). For example, the Cultural Olympiad for the London 2012 Olympic Games was heralded as a major cultural innovation to run alongside the development of the sporting event, four years out from the Games. Yet it took until March

2010 before a leader was appointed to run the project, and by then it was acknowledged that the original Cultural Olympiad proposals were too ambitious and they moved to run an extended cultural festival starting in June 2012. This shift in policy from their bid document reinforces Flyvbjerg's (2005) suggestion that event bidders say what they need to win a bid rather than what they can actually deliver – and in the process the cultural dimension frequently loses out because of its lack of political power.

As discussed in earlier chapters, governments (of all persuasions) have moved to establish strategic events agencies (public–private collaborations) to exploit culture economically as part of strategic event portfolios. These agencies require cultural events to develop a tourism product that attracts an educated and relatively affluent audience to the destination. However, some critics see inherent contradictions in the securitisation and privatisation of public space, which can accompany the commoditisation of culture (Zukin, 1995). Instead of opening up the city and its civic spaces to a wider section of the population, corporate culture can colonise, mark space and define who belongs and who does not. As private capital is accepted, and welcomed, by civic authorities, the cultures of cities become contested as sites of conflict about who has the right to use them and which types of events are staged. Take the example of New Year celebrations and winter festivals across the world. These cultural events (they are shared celebrations of a common culture) are increasingly choreographed and involve major sponsors looking to secure international profile from media exposure. However, these events now essentially colonise civic space and then proceed to make this space like a gated community where barriers are erected, security guards are employed and CCTV cameras are ubiquitous. An event like Edinburgh's Hogmanay has moved from being a relatively organic celebration of specific place identities to an increasingly managed (and mediatised) cultural experience for the consumption of a watching audience across the globe from Sydney to New York. The 'public culture' expressed is controlled and contained rather than being spontaneous and negotiated. By way of contrast, Barcelona's La Merce Festival, although scheduled, is much more free flowing with few security barriers and little obvious management in operation. The policing approach is to facilitate a party atmosphere as opposed to crowd control. As a result, the civic spaces encountered are inclusive rather than exclusive. In other words, they do not simply cater to a gentrified middle class with the necessary cultural capital to participate.

Policy makers engaged in culture-led regeneration have to stay ahead of transnational cultural competition, and one possibility is a shift, as discussed in Chapter 6, from event-led to event-themed (Smith and Fox, 2007) policy – from an investment in 'hard' infrastructure regeneration to 'soft' social and economic projects linked with events. In this policy shift, cultural events return to their more organic roots, as important means of connecting people and place and in providing sustainable skill sets for community members. This approach aligns closely with the cultural planning developments alluded to earlier in the chapter, whereby culture is embedded more meaningfully in the practices of government, across all of its activities. Additional benefits to this approach include the sustainability of cultural legacies arising from major events. In bid documents for major sport events and large cultural festivals, there is a trend towards incorporating more local involvement in the development of policies and programmes. As public investment in events faces constraint in the global economic downturn, the organic traditions of cultural events will be crucial to their ongoing existence. It is only relatively recently that cultural events have been brought into the framework of state subsidy – if funding restrictions continue, then the cultural product of a destination will be more dependent on events that have an integrated system of meanings that provide a web of significance for groups and individuals independent of the operations of bureaucratic cultural policy makers. Ironically, it is the uniqueness of these self-sustaining cultural events that might prove to be the key asset of a cultural tourism product, as place marketers need content to promote. Herein lies one of the main dilemmas for cultural producers and for policy makers alike – how to ensure that cultural events are a performance for participants and other community members, while also extracting value for the host destination. In achieving this, there is a need to take the advice of Jackson (1999: 96) who argues that 'the complexities and contradictions of commodification are easily missed by those who adopt a rhetoric of moral outrage and blanket disapproval'. In other words, while there are clearly dangers inherent in forms of cultural expression being hijacked by the market and becoming detached from their original meanings for participants and spectators alike, the benefits of commoditisation must also be taken into consideration.

If the perceived negative outcomes of cultural commoditisation are to be avoided, then those claiming ownership of these events need to be engaged with the content, management and ultimate outcomes, rather than stay as passive bystanders in their own communities. Over recent years, Harvey (1989) has warned that global events can become repetitious and homogeneous, and Rojek (1995) has also suggested that increasingly standardised events would lead to the production of a universal cultural space. At the start of the twenty-first-century governments began to recognise the danger of this over-globalising tendency and appeared to be adopting a strategy more attuned to Robertson's (1992) glocalisation thesis – involving the promotion of local distinctiveness on an international stage. In other words, the strategy changed to focus on investment in local event themes and traditions for exportation abroad; local culture was being transmitted globally rather than becoming a global culture (Foley, McGillivray and McPherson, 2008).

Another critical perspective on the way in which cultural festivals are utilised in the early twenty-first century is to view them as assets to enhance recognition abroad. The way cities are marketed and promoted 'operates as a form of socialisation which is intended to convince local people that the commodification of the city is entirely positive' (Miles and Miles, 2004). Cultural events can, therefore, be viewed as a device to pacify populations (or, more positively, extending them with the cultural capital needed to engage with the symbolic economy as presented to them). As discussed in Chapter 5, there is a clear attempt by policy makers to reduce the reliance on high season visits by 'manufacturing' new festivals and events and conferring them with some historical or 'local' significance – creating authenticity and uniqueness. But the danger associated with manufactured events is a perceived lack of authenticity – producing alienating effects and outcomes (Crespi-Vallbona and Richards, 2007). Yet, as Pratt (2005: 41) suggests, '[I]f cultural policy is not to become obsolete or irrelevant, it has to be drawn into a new conception of governance that acknowledges the existence of the market, but is actively involved in the shaping of that market'. This is a more positive opportunity for proponents of culture to engage with the language of the market and of policy makers so that their legitimate claims to be an important field of social activity is upheld.

There are certainly differences to be found across the world in addressing cultural regeneration, which are worth rehearsing here. Stevenson (2003), in her appraisal of the response of post-industrial cities to the development of consumption, has argued that there is a clear difference between Americanisation and Europeanisation approaches. The former is dependent on the creation of festival marketplaces and waterfront developments that, despite promising differentiated spectacle, theatre and the replacement of the dilapidated industrial landscape, actually end up producing sameness, betraying the hope invested in their apparent local uniqueness. By contrast, Europeanisation (as Bianchini and Schwengal [1991] termed it) has been more focused on nurturing local cultural and expressive activities and the creative industries. This approach has been used effectively in the UK to revive local economies and differentiate places. It proceeds on the so-called European model that local culture is marketable through its diversity and unique character. It is about promoting a sense of place and belonging through the incentivisation of local cultural production and the creation, on occasion, of cultural spaces (or quarters). This approach is perceived to be more democratic and participatory, but this claim can be subject to some criticism, especially as cultural quarters can be exclusive enclaves for the bohemian middle classes and exclude segments of the population by their absence of cultural capital (in the Bourdieusian sense). However, what is clear from the discussion of this chapter is that there is a renewed focus on the use of cultural events, not just infrastructural developments, as a means of enhancing civic pride and citizenship and reinvigorating the public realm. The theory goes that by working from the bottom up, active citizenship can be encouraged and the so-called 'divided city' can be integrated as ethnic groups, ages, classes and sexualities come together, animated through public space (e.g. local festivals and events).

However, in contradistinction to this argument, as city marketers fund spectacles, so local cultural events are squeezed as their aims and intentions fail to align with the global pretensions of city leaders. Public spaces remain commercial spaces, branded and bounded, controlled and surveyed. Cultural strategies have effectively created spaces that have been commodified rather than protected. Rather than help link politics and city life, public spaces are privatised and there exists, in this set of affairs, a 'fear' (of difference in the city), which encourages the separation of people from public spaces.

What remains clear is that, if it is to be successful, urban revitalisation arising in part from staging events needs to be an integral element of the 'eventful city' strategy that Richards and Palmer (2010) have proposed. Policy sustainability must be premised on measures to ensure greater involvement, participation and outcomes for a wider group of stakeholders – the challenge is that, unfortunately, 'trickle down' benefits are historically limited and the impact is often visual, economic and political rather than social and community based.

Box 8.1 Notting Hill Carnival

Cultural events such as Mardi Gras, New Orleans and Rio Carnival offer the historical legitimation of the authentic carnival alongside being able to exist in the marketplace and contribute to the cultural economy of their host destinations. As hallmark events, both are staged and managed to become synonymous with the place. Notting Hill Carnival, in London, has aspirations to be considered a hallmark cultural event, although there are differences in the way this event was created and sustained. Like the others, it has historical, cultural and urban authenticity, but it is funded by local government and was formed in response to racial tensions in inner London. The event was created to celebrate Afro-Caribbean culture in London and has grown, very successfully, to encompass a range of ethnicities and cultures in its parade. If organisers offered the event to the marketplace, its social and cultural purpose would be compromised, excluding the very people who participate all year round to make the event the showcase of multicultural London that attracts a significant spectatorship. Not all events are easily transferred to the marketplace and out of state intervention or investment. The Notting Hill Carnival case provides a demonstration of events being organised for ideological and political reasons rather than commercial ones. However, with public support (in terms of funding and policing), this cultural event contributes positively to London's position as a global city.

Further reading: Burr, A. (2006) 'The "freedom of the slaves to walk the streets": celebration, spontaneity and revelry versus logistics at the Notting Hill Carnival', in Picard, M. and Robinson, M. (eds) *Festivals, tourism and social change: remaking worlds*, Channel View Publications.

Summary

This chapter has addressed the complex and contested field of cultural capital as applied to the field of cultural events. As culture-led regeneration has become a familiar urban policy response to de-industrialisation and post-industrialisation, the value of culture has become the site of hotly contested debate. Whereas in previous epochs, forms of cultural expressions were valued for their intrinsic value and aesthetic qualities, the last two decades have witnessed a significant shift in policy towards culture being valued for the contribution it can make to a host of economic, social and political agendas. Cultural narratives have been instrumentalised and brought into the bureaucratic, regulated and systematic frameworks governing policy formation and implementation. That participation in the arts or other cultural activities represents a public good and should be supported for its intrinsic value has given way to a discourse that requires an evidence-based justification for culture. This need not necessarily be bad news for those involved in cultural events and festivals. Instead, by borrowing from the language of commerce and policy to assert their societal contribution, cultural events can be strengthened. However, a wider (cultural) democratic process is required to achieve a greater political voice whereby a greater cross-section of citizens are empowered to participate in, and secure positive outcomes from, engagement with an often alien set of cultural narratives. If culture is to represent a policy panacea, then it needs to overcome criticisms of exclusion on the basis that only those with educational cultural capital are able to participate. A mixed economy model of funding for the arts and cultural terrains will define the cultural economy of the early twenty-first century. If policy makers, participants and the corporate and third sectors can work together effectively, then the two conceptualisations of cultural capital outlined in this chapter can be managed in tandem, whereby the economic contribution of events and festivals is married with a more democratic, inclusive and participatory culture.

Critical review questions

- Cultural events are often used to animate urban civic spaces. Give an example of a cultural event that you think contributes to the animation of the urban environment.
- What are the main reasons why cities invest in culture-led regeneration as a solution to urban decline?
- In policy terms, what problems are generated when cultural capital is distributed unequally among a city's population?

Recommended reading

Crespi-Vallbona, M. and Richards, G. (2007) 'The meaning of cultural festivals', *International Journal of Cultural Policy*, 13 (1): 103–122.

Foley, M., McPherson, G. and Matheson, C. (2006) 'Glocalisation and Singaporean festivals', *International Journal of Event Management Research*, 1 (2): 21–16.

Richards, G. and Palmer, R. (2010) *Eventful cities: cultural management and urban revitalisation*, Oxford: Butterworth Heinemann (Chapter 4).

Part III

Event policy implementations

9 Glasgow 2014
Demonstrating capacity and competence

Introduction

This chapter takes Glasgow's bid for the twentieth Commonwealth Games (CWG) as its focus to explore the complex policy debates that coalesce around event bidding. To contextualise the bid for the 2014 CWG, insights will also be drawn from the preceding two Games – Manchester 2002 and Melbourne 2006. The chapter outlines the emotional strategy employed by Glasgow to bid for the event at a time when the global economic climate made significant investments of this sort uncommon. It will also explore how Glasgow used its successful model of economic, physical, social and cultural regeneration over the last two decades to persuade the event owners of its capacity and confidence to host this second tier major sporting event. The chapter draws on primary research gathered by the authors during the bid campaign of 2007/8 when they were seconded to participate in preparing the cultural element of the bid document. These experiences will provide rich insights into the strategic approach taken by the bid team alongside the more local tactics used to convince internal and external stakeholders of Glasgow's merit as a host city. Specifically, attention will be focused on the promotional campaign designed to secure the support of Glasgow's citizens and the wider Scottish population – the 'Back the Bid' campaign. Throughout the chapter, the preceding discussions of policy rationales, formations and implementation will be evaluated against the Glasgow 2014 bid process.

The Commonwealth Games: a brief history

First held in Hamilton, Canada, in 1930, the Commonwealth Games is a multi-national, multi-sport event, often referred to as the 'Friendly Games'. Following the example of the Summer and Winter Olympics, the Games take place every four years and are controlled and directed by the Commonwealth Games Federation (CGF). Seventy-one countries currently compete in the Games and two billion people, or thirty per cent of the world's population, make up the current Commonwealth family. At first called the British Empire Games, in 1950 the name was changed to the British Empire and Commonwealth Games, in 1970 to the British Commonwealth Games and finally, in 1978, to the Commonwealth Games. Close to 5,000 athletes now compete at each Games in up to seventeen sports in front of an increasingly global television audience. The Games embrace many faiths, races, languages, cultures and traditions, and underlying the decisions of the CGF are three core values: humanity, equality and destiny. It is these values that underpin every bid to host the Games. The CWG has been revitalised over the last two decades as the desire to host sporting events as a facet of place making has increased. While the historical legacy of colonialism is a permanent undercurrent of critical commentary on these Games, their international appeal and recent high-profile promotion (e.g. in Manchester, Melbourne and, more controversially, in Delhi) has generated extremely competitive bidding processes. It is to the agenda for event bidding that the chapter now moves.

The need to bid

Historically, Roche (2000) has argued, the successful hosting of mega-events (including Olympics, soccer World Cup and Expos) was a way for the power elites in a nation to promote hegemonic ideologies to their populations. Attracting positive media coverage and instilling (or strengthening) national pride and identity were seen as worthwhile reasons for hosting. However, in the late nineteenth and early twentieth centuries there was little competition for hosting these events – the economic and political powerhouses of their time offered to host to promote their particular contribution to the world whether in the form of science and technology or sport and culture. In the last fifty years, in particular, there has been a marked shift in the competition for hosting major sporting and cultural events – those described variously as peripatetic, footloose or ambulant according to their moveable status. Whereas only two decades ago events like the Summer Olympics and the Common-wealth Games were literally on their knees and were deemed unattractive to potential hosts, since then competition for sporting events, in particular, has intensified, to the point that they are now viewed as something of a panacea in relation to urban and regional growth and place competition (Hall, 2006). In part, this is because globalised media technologies now allow sport and wider cultural forms to communicate powerful messages to a global audience about what a city or nation has to offer. Sport events are seen as particularly suitable because 'sport' is seen as a good thing and these events permit the dominant discourse of pro-growth neoliberal urbanism to be continued (and intensified). As a result, from Copenhagen to Auckland, state-driven units have been formed over the last decade to provide strategic and operational support for event bidding. In the case of Toronto, the city tourism department set up its own events strategy department, 'Toronto International', to 'proactively facilitate bidding on major events' (Clark, 2008: 165). In Auckland, New Zealand, a Major Events Strategy and associated structures have been produced to enable the region to compete with its (very successful) Australian counterparts for major sporting and cultural events.

Event bids are, then, perceived to be a powerful catalyst for change in cities – whether these bids are ultimately successful or not. The Mayor of Barcelona, Jordi Hereu, has stated that his city used the 1992 Olympics 'as the organising idea for a new kind of strategic planning, one that looked deep into the future, and long back at our past, and enabled us to believe that we could be a leading city once again' (Clark, 2008: 11). There is little doubt that Barcelona's elevated status in the circuit of global cities owes a lot to the 1992 Olympics. The repositioning they achieved also gave their citizens and investors a strong local dividend from the Games (Clark, 2008). In the case of Barcelona, the Mayor attests that the benefits of the Olympic Games have allowed them to continue to attract inward investment and development of new quarters of the city well into the early twenty-first century.

The benefits of major events to a city extend beyond economic return, even if you are not attracting the top tier events. The Commonwealth Games provide just such an example. As Gold and Gold (2005: 1) state, '[A]lthough less prestigious than premier sporting festivals like the Olympics or football's World Cup, the Commonwealth Games are still events of some pedigree', and it is clear that hosting the Games has a number of tangible benefits for a city. The case of Manchester's 2002 Games is worth highlighting. A total of £200 million was spent on sporting venues, with a further £470 million expenditure on other non-sport infrastructure investments in East Manchester, and around 20,000 new jobs were created as a result of the Games, although when converted to full-time equivalents (FTEs) to take account of temporary or part-time jobs, the actual number of full-time jobs generated in Manchester is estimated at 4,900 (Gold and Gold, 2005). Spending by overseas visitors was shown to have increased from £190 million in 2000 to £245 million in 2002, an increase of 28.9 per cent (Gold and Gold, 2005), and cultural initiatives such as The Spirit of Friendship Festival saw over 2,000 events take place within the city. There was a "Let's Celebrate" programme to develop processional and celebratory arts, and Festival Live aimed at street entertainment and live sport. The passport scheme went beyond this to provide 13,500 young people with access to arts and cultural activities with the aim of leaving a cultural legacy behind for the city. This array of programmes attracted nearly a million people to the city. The Games legacy has left a Commonwealth Film Festival and a Let's Celebrate programme that has increased cultural capacity in Manchester.

Manchester also used the Commonwealth Games to contribute a wider social legacy for the city and its citizens through its much-cited volunteer training programme. The Manchester 2002 Commonwealth Games 'helped 7,500 in their personal development by participating in a range of activities related to the Games by the end of 2001. Furthermore, 70 per cent of the Volunteer programme participants said that the Games made them feel more part of the wider community and 46 per cent said that it had enhanced their personal development' (2014 CWG Feasibility Study: 76). Manchester has been seen as a standard bearer for how to bid for, and deliver, a major sporting event. It is worth noting that this city has twice failed in its bid for the Summer Olympic Games before successfully securing the Commonwealth Games. Crucially, Manchester showed that even losing an event bid is of enormous benefit in terms of rebranding a city. The city's political leaders and business community learned significant lessons from their failed bids and used these to host the 'most significant multi-sport event to be held in the United Kingdom since the 1948 Summer Olympics' (Clark, 2008: 109). These Commonwealth Games heralded a change in the way that cities bid for events and in their assertions of the legacy that would be borne out of them. For example, 2,423 people gained an accredited qualification in event volunteering as part of the Single Regeneration Budget (SRB) programme to engage local communities: 'The scheme was commended as an exemplary scheme for engaging disadvantaged persons and promoting volunteering as a means for social engagement' (Cambridge Policy Consultants [2003], B1.6: 2).

Before focusing attention on the specific strategic and tactical approaches utilised by Glasgow for its 2014 bid, it is briefly also worth highlighting the strategy of the Melbourne 2006 Commonwealth Games organisers. In an attempt to involve the local population and develop the social economy, Melbourne developed a 'Getting Involved' scheme, which gave each Council in Victoria State A$20,000 and further grant funding to co-ordinate activities aimed at strengthening their communities through the CWG (2014 CWG Feasibility Study: 76). Funding was conditional upon councils setting up a Get Involved Team. This could involve anything from small- and large-scale celebrations, single-day state-wide activity, to involving local communities, adopting a second team, celebrating local sporting history and heroes, developing civic and community infrastructure and looking after their heritage infrastructure. Alongside this, Melbourne also launched a programme called 'Getting Trackside' to get locals involved in watching sport first hand, especially those who had not accessed this type of activity previously. On the cultural front, they developed a cultural programme aimed at celebrating the diversity found across the Commonwealth whereby citizens were encouraged to take an active role in the cultural programme with leading artists working with community groups to put together musical performances and public art programmes. Added to this, they championed volunteering, school education and workforce development programmes. The development of the social economy was an obvious positive outcome for the Games and a legacy that others are seeking to follow.

As bidding for, and delivering, major sports events become more professional, the importance of knowledge transfer from one host to the next also becomes more pronounced. A significant body of critical literature exists around the impact of hosting one-off major events and this is increasingly informing bid teams as they seek to persuade internal (i.e. citizens, businesses and funders) and external (event owners, sponsors and the media) audiences of the lessons learned from preceding events. Taking a Commonwealth Games example, the 1998 Kuala Lumpur event 'provided a legacy of empty sports stadia, suppressed public demonstrations and the policing of media coverage' (Higham, 1999: 86), showing the failure to engage (or the desire to engage) with the host population at the bidding and preparation stage. Furthermore, Jones' (2000) study into the impact of hosting the 1999 Rugby World Cup in Wales highlights that for a year or more before the start of the event, tenants and homeowners adjacent to the Millennium Stadium had to deal with dust, road closures and construction noise, that little or no profit accrued from gate receipts and that the longer-term benefits for Wales are at least open to question.

As discussed below, before making the decision to bid for the 2014 Commonwealth Games, Glasgow was well aware of these potentially negative impacts and, as a result, tried to counter them at the envisioning stage. Glasgow has a (relatively) recent history of bidding for major sporting and cultural events and it is against this backdrop that the approach the city took to the 2014 bid must be understood.

Glasgow's promise: the strategic narrative

As a city Glasgow has its origins as far back as the eleventh or twelfth century. Certainly, the twelfth century is cited more as founding of the burgh of Glasgow. The Scottish crown granted certain towns trading and self-governing status, but they in return paid the crown revenues. It is not possible to give a detailed account of Glasgow's history as a city here, but for a more in-depth description please see www.theglasgowstory.com/storya.php (accessed 23 June 2010). This chapter will draw on some of the information contained in The Glasgow Story to highlight the transformational nature of the city and its forefathers to bring it from one of poverty and squalor pre-industrialisation, through its 'second city of the empire' stage from 1830 to 1914, when it was 'progressing' at a pace only compared with the likes of Rome and Venice, then its 'no mean city' image developed through a tough industrial period, to the present where it has once again reinvented itself through a cultural transformation of its spaces and image (Garcia, 2004). Glasgow's bid to shed itself of the 'no mean city' image started in 1983 with the 'Glasgow's Miles Better' campaign. The city's urban renaissance plans aimed to transform Glasgow into a place that was attractive to residents, tourists and inward investors while renewing the city's damaged sense of civic pride following its period of deindustrialisation. Following the launch of the 'Glasgow's Miles Better' campaign, the city then hosted the Garden Festival in 1988, won the European City of Culture (ECoC) title in 1990, opened the Glasgow Royal Concert Hall in 1990 and the Gallery of Modern Art in 1996 and held the title of UK City of Architecture and Design in 1999. Since the turn of the millennium, the city has gone on to host the UEFA Champions League Cup Final in 2002, collect the European Capital of Sport title in 2003 and host the UEFA Cup Final in 2007. Each of these events helped lay the foundations for the ensuing Commonwealth Games bid for 2014.

Glasgow's growing reputation as a city of consumption, focused on 'events', the creative and cultural industries and tourism, was strengthened in the 1990s with place marketing strategies being used more widely (MacLeod, 2002; Gibson and Stevenson, 2004) to sell the city's assets to international markets. At the start of the twenty-first century, the city rebranded again, launching its 'Glasgow: Scotland with Style' campaign with major events and festivals a central means of attracting new business and animating the city's fixed physical assets (Richards and Wilson, 2004). Glasgow's present reputation as a 'safe pair of hands' to host major sporting and cultural events owes much to the long-term strategy of its city leaders focused around cultural regeneration, infrastructural investment, civic engagement and an unwavering belief that it could transform itself into a global competitor on the events circuit.

Despite the many problems that continue to face post-industrial (or de-industrial) Glasgow, the city is now frequently cited as a model example of economic, physical, social and cultural regeneration, with Mooney (2004: 328) stating that 'Glasgow is widely acclaimed as the benchmark for other de-industrialized and/or "second cities" to follow'. It was the first ex-industrial city to develop a cultural-led regeneration programme and to be designated as European City of Culture (ECoC), indeed the first non-capital city to win the award. It was also the first city to run a year-long festival showing that Glasgow did things differently. 'Doing a Glasgow' has now become a recurring theme in discussions of urban cultural policy and place marketing in many of Europe's older industrial cities (Mooney, 2004). Glasgow's approach can be summarised as building first and then securing sufficient 'business' to ensure ongoing utilisation of its impressive venues. Bidding for the 2014 Commonwealth Games was the next logical step in moving the city from the semi-periphery to the centre of urban place competition (Whitson and Horne, 2006). As Tucker suggests, '[H]osting the Games could put Glasgow among the global elite of urban economic powerhouses' (Tucker, 2008: 20). Glasgow realised it could never, realistically, host an Olympic Games, but it was certainly going to be part of a Commonwealth Games bidding process and in doing so, continue to shine on the international sporting, cultural and political stage with the likes of Paris, Milan, Barcelona and others.

Glasgow's political leaders were not, however, naive to the challenges facing those wishing to host a significant sporting event. Early on in the process there was a recognition from Glasgow's Bid Director, Derek Casey, in a presentation on major events and their impact, that the 'benefits are usually exaggerated and the costs usually underestimated' (Casey, 2008). This is a view corroborated by much of the academic literature on the subject, with Flyvberg (2005) indicating that over 90 per cent of major event costs are underestimated. The costs of hosting the second largest multi-sports event after the Olympics is colossal. The 2006 Commonwealth Games in Melbourne is estimated to have cost the State of Victoria A$697 million (Reed and Hao, 2005). Glasgow did not have the capacity to bid for the 2014 Commonwealth Games on its own, yet the major benefits were likely to reside with the city. Bid campaigns are becoming events in their own right with significant public and private sector budgets being expended on the 'hope' of securing the rights to major sporting spectacles. Glasgow required the support of the Scottish Government at the bid stage, though it was the city that took most of the financial risk at that time (80:20 ratio of funding). Were the bid to be successful, the funding ratio would change to 20:80, with Scottish taxpayers picking up the majority of the bill for delivering the Games themselves. With the bid estimated to cost £288 million (Summary candidate file: 13), there needed to be a carefully prepared and logical rationale for submitting a bid.

Glasgow's bid strategy

One of the key issues for any major event bid is how to develop a strategy that combines internal stakeholder needs, sanctioning body priorities and the need to out-manoeuvre other potential host candidates. In terms of internal stakeholder needs, Shaw (2008) has argued that there are three main propositions in 'Olympic Framing' that also apply to 'selling' the Common-wealth Games to a potential host community. These propositions are the economic proposition, which promises fantastic outcomes to the greedy and needy; the patriotic proposition that declares 'your country deserves to host this event!' and the idealistic proposition that highlights the dreams of people that have trained their entire lives to take part in such events (Shaw, 2008). While the ideal strategy would be to perfect the mix of the three frames to ensure maximum public support, different bidders will inevitably give greater weight to certain frames, depending on their relative political, economic and/or social circumstances.

With regard to out-manoeuvring other potential host communities, there are two main routes bidders may choose to take. First, they may choose to focus on a proven track record of hosting major events, and in this case, Glasgow's ability to show its own past record (e.g. ECOC, 1990; UK City of Architecture, 1999; UEFA Champions League Final, 2002; and UEFA Cup Final, 2007) provided the city with a significant advantage over its main competitor, Abuja (Nigeria) in the bid. The second approach can be described as an appeal to the heartstrings, and two examples of this strategy being successfully employed are Liverpool's bid for the European Capital of Culture in 2008, and South Africa's bid for the 2010 World Cup, as evidenced by the statement 'the World Cup is not only important for football, but it will help strengthen and consolidate our democracy' from the South African bid team. Glasgow tried to use the 'Friendly Games' slogan, as the Commonwealth Games are known, to match its posited status as 'the Friendly City'.

Alignment with sanctioning bodies' priorities, the third key issue, involves a process that combines the key strategic points across all three areas (i.e. internal, sanctioning bodies and out-manoeuvring), through the creation of a coherent narrative. Brighenti *et al.* (2005: 51) point out that

> as competition to host sports events is becoming much fiercer, it is no longer enough to simply meet the requirements of the event specification.

In order to win over the evaluators, the media and the decision makers, it is often necessary to add a strong emotional and/or cultural element to the bid.

Black (2007) argues that three narrative types are identifiable with sport event hosts in Delhi/India (2010 Commonwealth Games), South Africa (2010 FIFA World Cup) and Vancouver/Canada (2010 Winter Olympics). These are:

- Unity: The bidders' narrative stresses that hosting the event will help bring together people in the nation, and also even the region.
- Transcendence: The narrative encompasses themes of transcending both historical divisions and economic problems.
- Cosmopolitanism: Here the narrative seeks to highlight the diversity and harmonious multiculturalism of the bidder.

(Black, 2007: 266–268)

Black (2007: 266) highlights that the bids of these three countries demonstrated the ability to 'transcend historic divisions and build a new, pluralistic, democratic and multiracial identity' that has had the effect of opening up these events to new audiences. Transferring the ideas contained in Shaw's three propositions (economic, patriotic and idealistic) and Black's (2007) narrative perspective (unity, transcendence and cosmopolitanism) helps to analyse Glasgow's strategic approach to its 2014 Commonwealth Games bid.

In terms of Shaw's ideas, Glasgow clearly emphasised the economic and patriotic propositions in its bid, and it also drew upon each of Black's narratives to a greater or lesser extent. Glasgow was chosen as the Commonwealth Games Council for Scotland's (CWGfS) preferred city in 2004, and in November of that year the Bid Assessment Group was set up to explore the viability of a bid and the long-term economic benefits of hosting the Games (Shaw's economic proposition) to Scotland (not just Glasgow) and to start work on the development of the city's bid strategy. By May 2005 a report based on a study by PMP Consultants concluded that there would be six main objectives in presenting a bid for the 2014 Commonwealth Games. These were:

- To meet and exceed the quality standards set by the Commonwealth Games Federation for the Games, through provision of world class sports facilities, Games village and media operations.
- To ensure that there is a solid infrastructure of transport, technology, security and accommodation, to support the games for Glasgow and Scotland.
- To ensure sustainability in relation to future use of facilities, and ensure the sporting and economic legacies of the Games, for Glasgow and Scotland.
- To promote an inclusive approach, by ensuring the involvement of the whole community and partner organisations, in the Games and associated cultural events.

- To demonstrate that the bid is well grounded, taking account of the track record of the city in hosting previous major events, and of the aspirations of the local community.
- To be realistic about likely capital and revenue costs, based on current knowledge and expectations.

(PMP Legacy, 2005)

From these six objectives it is clear that Shaw's (2008) economic proposition was fundamental to the proposed bid, though not framed in isolation from the patriotic proposition or Black's notions of unity and transcendence, described earlier. In a Cultural Strategy published by Glasgow City Council in 2006 it was suggested that 'a Commonwealth Games in Glasgow would play a central part in the city's long-term process of social renewal and economic development with a lasting legacy that would contribute to a wide range of economic, health, tourism, community and volunteering objectives' (Glasgow City Council, 2006: 18). The Glasgow 2014 Candidate City file itself put forward the idea that

this investment will . . . contribute to the key objectives of improving the health of our population particularly around physical activity, smoking control and the prevention of obesity. These in turn will contribute also to overall levels of confidence, well-being and mental health . . . for the local community increased pride in their city, renewed confidence . . . an ability to be part of a major initiative and a demonstration of . . . more sustainable ways of living will all be vital.

(Glasgow City Council 2006: 11)

In attempting to engage the nation (the patriotic proposition and the unity narrative) Glasgow ensured that they tied their bid to the health and well-being agenda of the Scottish Government's 15 National Priorities, thus linking with the wider national agenda rather than just a local city agenda. An independent review in 2005 concluded that Glasgow 2014 had 'considerable merit and should be subject to serious consideration', estimating that 1,200 jobs would be immediately created by the Games, as well as a positive economic impact of £81 million (Candidate City File, Operational Review: 3). Glasgow certainly made a significant commitment to unity in its bid, stressing that hosting the event would help bring people in its diverse communities together around a common purpose. The social regeneration agenda was utilised as a means of framing the commitment to volunteering in the city around the Games and to building the social capital of the city's most deprived communities.

In the spirit of unity and in building upon Glasgow's impressive record of developing its major event hardware (infrastructure and venues) and software (people), a formal bid team was set up in 2006 to incorporate an array of talent from across the public, commercial and voluntary sectors and from throughout Scotland. This inclusive approach extended to the recruitment of expert secondments from around Scotland – including architects, senior police officers, cultural advisors, medical professionals and environmental planners. All were required to support the specialist staff recruitment and to help write specific elements of the bid.

Glasgow also drew on Black's (2007) transcendence and cosmopolitan narratives (and Brighenti *et al.*'s [2005] emotional features) in its approach to promoting the 2014 bid to the seventy-one voting Commonwealth nations. However, instead of focusing on the *internal* dynamic of Glasgow and Scotland, the bid team focused on what a Glasgow 2014 Commonwealth Games would do for the Commonwealth as a whole, for sport development, for the revival of Commonwealth ideals and for the prestige of the Commonwealth Games itself. The bid team visited sixty-seven of the seventy-one voting nations over the course of a year from 2006–2007, far more than rival bidders Abuja (Nigeria) and Halifax (Canada). While this approach was acknowledged by the bid team as being ambitious, it represented an important opportunity to promote Glasgow's bid on a *personal* level, face to face, and the team noted that 'the Commonwealth Games Associations [CGAs] were very welcoming, with many making it clear that they placed a high value on the efforts made in visiting their home countries' (Candidate City Operational Review, pp. 18–19). The strength of the bid team certainly came from the fact that Louise Martin, Secretary to the Commonwealth Games Federation and Chairman of the Scottish Commonwealth Games Association, was well acquainted with a lot of the CGA Chairs personally and sought to engage with as many as possible to secure their vote. The Chair of the Scottish CGA and the Bid Director, Derek Casey, was also well respected internationally in sports administration circles. He made many of the presentations himself, and this personal effort proved to be a key element in securing the Games.

By May 2007, the 250-page City Candidate file had been completed and submitted, highlighting sixteen key themes that the bid team argued made Glasgow an ideal host for the Games (all bidders had to highlight these themes, which are now identical to the structure of Olympic Games bidding). At this point there was only one other city, Abuja in Nigeria, left in the running, after Halifax in Canada had pulled out in March. Interestingly, Halifax had lost the support of its citizens and the media were keen to exploit this, leading to their eventual withdrawal from the bidding process. This citizen-led campaign provided Glasgow with a stark reminder of the need to ensure popular consent and support for the bid. Glasgow's strategy to secure this popular support, as part of the patriotic proposition, was to create a 'Back the Bid' campaign throughout Scotland alongside the external-facing promotional activity.

Securing citizen consent: the 'Back the Bid' campaign

For cities and nations, bidding for events is justified on the basis of transformation to the economic, physical, social, cultural and (more recently) environmental landscape. In order to justify the support of the host urban population, sporting events such as the Commonwealth Games need to be legitimated (Hiller, 2000). Examples of legitimation could be the enhancement of young people's life chances, infrastructural improvements, the promotion of greater diversity, enhancement of the quality of life and so on. In order to secure legitimation at the bid stage, prospective hosts invariably look to secure the support of public opinion – in fact this is now enshrined as one of the IOC's bid criteria for the Olympic Games. Hall (2006) has argued that Sydney 2000 succeeded in securing support because organisers co-opted a community of interest (the media, business and political elites) and this enabled the bid committee to persuade the wider population of the benefits of securing the Olympic Games. This strategy of coercion and co-option has been used successfully elsewhere, including, it will be argued here, by Glasgow through the vehicle of its 'Back the Bid' campaign.

The 'Back the Bid' campaign started in early 2006, and by March of that year, prior to the Melbourne Games, the campaign had officially attracted 1 million supporters for the bid, rising to 1.5 million by December 2006. The campaign was promoted by a number of initiatives associated with the bid's main sponsors, such as branded trains, buses and stations from First Group, a Sporting Heroes Exhibition co-ordinated by O2, the branding of over a million bottles of Highland Spring Mineral Water and promotional gifts and hospitality opportunities from Diageo. The bid team also noted that

> throughout the campaign we maintained strong media relations at the highest level, ensuring delivery of consistently strong messages and high profile events, keeping the media enthused and positive about the Bid. This ensured regular, positive coverage, and a belief that we were doing everything possible to win the Games for Glasgow.
>
> (Candidate City Operational Review)

This strategy aligns closely with the argument made in Chapter 4, that the process (or procurement) of legitimation is increasingly consumerist in its logic and practice. Marketing and public relations techniques are now frequently used as a mechanism to procure citizen support for a bid for major sporting events. However, as Hall (2006) cautions, these campaigns are carefully choreographed through media management and 'Backing the Bid' requires little accountability or transparency – or, for that matter, participation of the individual.

After the completion of the Candidate City File in May 2007, the final push for the 'Back the Bid' campaign was enacted, with an intensification of the marketing and PR strategies employed by the bid team. As the team puts it: 'The focus shifted from how a Glasgow Games would look, to how Scots were showing their support for the Bid. This was segmented further across various sectors including business, young people, sports clubs and the community' (Candidate City Operational Review). This 'final push' helped the total official number of bid supporters surpass 1.75 million, and a research survey carried out by Ashbrook Research showed that in June, prior to the final campaign, public support for the bid was 78 per cent, rising to 84 per cent by September. The approach was almost like an American road trip. A 'Back the Bid' car was sponsored and a marketing assistant toured the length and breadth of the country, taking the campaign to the people to show that they wanted and needed their support. In the main, the press were co-opted, welcoming the attempts at public engagement (however superficial it may have appeared), and any negative publicity was kept to a minimum. This level of public support was in stark contrast to the situation that emerged in Halifax, where public support for the bid had waned and indeed an anti-bid campaign had been set up including the 'Halifax No Way' website. This certainly gave Glasgow an advantage over its rivals and they were able to present comprehensive evidence of support from a range of stakeholders throughout the nation.

Summary

Glasgow's successful bid for the 2014 Commonwealth Games was built upon twenty years of regenerative efforts, which provided the ideal political, economic, social and cultural context for bidding. Since the beginning of the 1990s, Glasgow had invested (politically, economically and socially) in a strategy of place promotion and consumption as a means of addressing the deep-rooted social and economic problems associated with its de-industrialisation. Politically, Glasgow has been a pioneering proponent of urban entrepreneurialism, creating public–private partnerships to drive the transformation of the city. Economically, the city's reliance on heavy industry has been replaced with a significant dependence on the service sector for employment and imaging. The city has been perceived as a model for the utilisation of culture as an economic and socially regenerative vehicle, which has produced an impressive cultural hardware and software. Finally, socially, Glasgow has tried to use its major events and festivals to address the social inequalities that continue to be the city's Achilles' heel.

In bidding for the 2014 Commonwealth Games, Glasgow drew upon all of the above to address internal stakeholder needs (Scottish Government, Glasgow City Council, business, citizens) and the interests of the sanctioning body (the Commonwealth Games Federation) and to out-manoeuvre the other host candidates (Abuja, Nigeria and Halifax, Canada). In addressing internal stakeholder needs, the city certainly emphasised the likely economic contribution of the Commonwealth Games to both Glasgow and Scotland. This approach was effective as the Scottish Government provided most of the funding for the bid, ably supported by the local authority and sponsors. However, Glasgow also played a more emotional card to indicate that the city was 'friendly' and would provide the 'welcome' that the Commonwealth Games deserved. One of is competitors, Abuja in Nigeria, had a strong case for emphasising unity and transcendence in its bid (the African continent has never hosted a Commonwealth Games), so Glasgow had to focus its bid on capacity. Ultimately, the city's track record of successfully hosting large cultural and sporting events over the period of two decades won over the emotional appeal of an African Games. The previous investment in facilities and associated infrastructure alongside clear evidence of citizen engagement and support overcame the bid of Halifax, Canada.

In essence, Glasgow's success is a reflection of its commitment to the creation of urban events policies to help transform or restructure the city. Its recent history of attracting major sporting events, along with associated culture-led regeneration processes, has led to a refashioning of its urban governance with a highly active entrepreneurial (local) state supported by private sector stakeholders. While the extent of citizen engagement and support can be subject to critical scrutiny, in the global events bidding game, Glasgow is competing at the top table.

Critical review questions

- Do you think that democratic governments have a duty to demonstrate the consent of the nation in bidding for a large-scale event? If so, why?
- In times of economic recession, do you think that it is right to use events as the master plan for physical infrastructure and social development?

Recommended reading

Black, D. (2007) 'The symbolic politics of sport mega-events: 2010', *Comparative Perspective, Politikon*, 34 (3): 261–276.

Clark, G. (2008) *Local development benefits from staging global events*, OECD.

Tucker, M. (2008) 'The cultural production of cities: rhetoric or reality? Lessons from Glasgow', *Journal of Retail and Leisure Property*, 7 (1): 21–33.

10 Destination Dubai
Event policy in an Arab state

Introduction

This chapter takes the context of Dubai as its focus to explore an alternative discourse of event policy – a discourse built upon the use of events (particularly, but not only, sporting events) as an economic generator and image enhancer in an Arab state with pretensions to become one of the world's most popular tourist destinations. The chapter outlines the development of Dubai from an Emirate reliant on oil to its current position as the Gulf region's dominant commercial centre with an economy that is increasingly oriented toward services, business and tourism. Dubai is positioned as a destination that utilises major sporting events and sports infrastructure as a way of developing tourism and commerce in the Gulf region, with the goal of 'gaining importance at international level via the development of high quality infrastructures, liberal trading laws and image enhancement via events' (Sampler and Saeb, 2003: 59). Significant investment has been attracted into the Emirate in the staging and sponsorship of the world's leading sports events and the building of sporting infrastructures. This chapter engages critically with the policy environment that makes these aspirations achievable and contrasts these with the experience of the other case study destinations discussed in this part of the book.

Background: from desert to Dubai Sports City

Dubai is one of seven Emirates that make up the United Arab Emirates (UAE) federation, located in Western Asia on the Persian Gulf. The other six emirates are Abu Dhabi, Sharjah, Ajman, Umm Al Quwain, Ras Al Khaimah and Fujairah. Each of the Emirates has their own ruling family (based on tribal monarchy) but they all share Federal Government with a President and Prime Minister (Amara, 2005; Henderson, 2006). The official language of the UAE is Arabic, although the area's long history and background as a trading port has resulted in a plethora of languages being spoken (including Persian, Hindi and Urdu). English is, however, used as the *lingua franca* of business.

Until the discovery of oil in the 1920s, the Gulf States consisted primarily of impoverished tribal desert principalities. The ruling British Government regulated the production of oil with concessional payments being made to local rulers, allowing them to cement their rule over their own tribal area. When the British withdrew from formal relations with the area in 1971, the Federation of the United Arab Emirates was created, and although local families continued to rule in each Emirate (in the case of Dubai this is the Maktoum family), the area shares Federal governance. There is a perception of Gulf countries as a grouping of oil-rich monarchies, sultanates and tribal states, and Dubai certainly continues to be led by a rich and powerful royal family that exerts a significant level of influence over policy matters. Although the chief of state is the Sheikh, the real state rulers are royal families and the population is made up of Bedouins, many of whom are rich (Amara, 2008).

Situated in a highly strategic area between the trading routes of the East and West, historically Dubai has fared well as a port and centre for pearling and trade. It was, however, the discovery of oil that led to the vast transformation of the Emirate, which is now renowned for its commercial success and quality as a business, trading and tourist destination (Sampler and Saeb, 2003). Dubai is successful partly because state–citizen relations are stable, based on 'a social contract – a reciprocal agreement, socio-economic stability in exchange for political rights . . . signed between the ruling families and the populations' (Amara, 2005: 497). This social contract continues to be effective in Dubai because of its economic prosperity (Henderson, 2006), but the spectre of global economic recession since 2009 produced greater pressure on the nature of the state–citizen relationship. Nevertheless, Dubai remains relatively unique among surrounding states in that it has proactively sought to develop itself as a commercial brand and tourist destination for Western consumption. While its neighbours in Abu Dhabi, Qatar and Bahrain are now also following a strategy commensurate with tourism promotion, sports events procurement and momentous infrastructural projects, Dubai is further advanced and has a more established position in the global mindset. The development of an integrated destination brand has been central to this success.

From tribes to tourism: destination Dubai

Dubai has developed significantly since the discovery of oil to become one of the world's most developed and commercialised cities. The Emirate's prosperity has been built on foundations 'of an entrepôt entity servicing the immediate hinterland, the export of gold to the Indian subcontinent, re-exports to Iran and other Arab neighbours, and its position as the region's dominant commercial centre' (Peterson, 2003: 138). In recent years, the ruling Maktoum family has sought to develop alternative income streams, diversifying from a trade-based, oil-reliant economy to one that is service-, business- and tourism-orientated.

Henderson (2006) argues that, to be successful, destinations need to be accessible and have high attraction and amenity standards, awareness and positive images associated with promotion and marketing, a supportive government and a peaceful and stable environment. Over the last three decades, Dubai has followed this blueprint and has been rewarded with growth in international tourist arrivals from 500,000 in 1995 to 6.7 million a decade later (Khalaf and Wallis, 2006). The historical perception of the Gulf States was previously of aridity, heat, dust and desert (Heard-Bey, 1982) when travel to these areas was limited and there was little or no tourism infrastructure in place. It was the oil crises of the 1990s that focused the attention of the Dubai authorities. Until then, vast wealth generated from oil reserves lessened the fiscal imperative to diversify the economic base. Alternative economic models were devised and tourism was at the forefront in the UAE, which includes Dubai. Dubai has been particularly successful in growing its tourism industry because, above all, it is stable, in economic, social and political terms. With a stable UAE federation and Emirate government, Dubai has no real democracy, but it is enjoying an 'uninterrupted period of political order and continuity' (Henderson, 2006: 91). Dubai has some autonomy from the UAE in economic policy and that has permitted it to exploit the opportunities presented by the free market economy, designing free-trade zones and industrial parks – including the recent Dubai Sports City development (Smith, 2010). Moreover, Dubai's safe reputation makes it an attractive mix for tourists, investors and residents alike. Although it is an Islamic state, 80 per cent of the population are expatriates, and Goodwin (2003: 125) describes it as 'Islamic pragmatism' in operation. Dubai's rulers have not permitted religious and cultural values to become an obstacle to progress in commercial terms.

Another of Dubai's great strengths is that it has a proactive government tourism and event policy. In the late 1980s and early 1990s the UAE government started to invest in tourism infrastructure – especially in Dubai and Abu Dhabi. As Henderson (2006: 91) suggests, '[T]ourism was positioned at the centre of the diversification programme'. It was overseen by the former Crown Prince, also in charge of the Department of Tourism and Commerce Marketing (DTCM) that was established in 1989. This demonstrates a clear vision in Dubai to grow tourism, endorsed and driven by the Emirate government. In order to understand the role of the ruling family in terms of policy and governance it must be understood that in Dubai the monarchy (i.e. the Maktoum family) is the government. The Maktoum family, by traditional tribal endowments, are the main landowners in the Emirate and it is therefore under their aegis that Dubai has developed, by gifts of land to foreign investors to build golf courses, resorts, hotels, stadiums, water parks, indoor ski resorts and, most recently, Dubai Sports City.

Beyond unparalleled government involvement, Dubai also benefits from its accessibility to international markets and its high quality amenities, including world-renowned hotel accommodation. Add to this the development of iconic attractions and you have a package designed to welcome the world's tourist tribes. Henderson (2006) argues that, as a tourism destination, Dubai has relied upon 'hype and hard sell', promoting its Islamic heritage but with a pragmatic twist on the new, modern and cosmopolitan. In this task it has been led by the vision of its monarchical rulers without the need to secure the consent required in the environments where democracies prevail. It has built, created, promoted and invested in a way that would simply not have been possible elsewhere, especially in the liberal democratic West. The model of development favoured in Dubai is of a high level of government involvement (some would say control) over both commerce and tourism. The model is very similar to that of post-colonial Singapore (Foley *et al.*, 2009). However, the notion of an Arab state such as Dubai opening its borders to the West, allowing tourism and encouraging a tourist infrastructure does not always chime well with the religious values of the region. It does, of course, suit the far-sighted ruling family's vision to create a viable alternative asset to oil and gas. Some view this suspiciously, noting that these 'manoeuvres are posited to be merely another strategy by the royal families to maintain their control over state affairs, in order to divert popular political energies into projects that actually sustain the very basis of the regime' (Amara, 2005: 498). However, while this strategy continues to reap rich rewards for residents, businesses and the ruling family alike, the so-called social contract is accepted and promoted as an indication of Dubai's 'integration to the norms of global culture and economy' (Amara, 2005: 498).

Having evaluated the features that have led to Dubai's positioning as the Gulf Region's most successful tourism destination, it is now necessary to reflect on the centrality of sport event tourism to the overall product on offer and the reasons for the Emirates commitment to this strategy.

Sports event tourism in Dubai

'Special events, particularly sports events, are being used by destination marketers with increasing frequency to enhance a host destination's brand' (Chalip and Costa, 2005: 219). The interest in promoting Dubai as a sports event tourism destination stems from the ruling Maktoum family, who have sought to use sport as a means of 'placing the country in the shop window and showing its credentials as a world resort and spectacular city' (Barclay, 2001: 50). As mentioned previously, Dubai is a destination that has sought to utilise major sporting events and the development of high-quality sports infrastructure as a way of developing tourism and commerce in the region (Smith, 2010). Sport is particularly popular in Dubai, but with few high-profile sporting teams of its own the trend has been to develop and fund iconic sporting events with lucrative prize money, such as the IRB-sanctioned Dubai Rugby Sevens. World-class athletes have also been attracted to compete in Dubai by the payment of vast appearance fees. For example, Tiger Woods was reputedly paid a $1.5 million appearance fee to play in the Dubai Golf Classic. Indeed, large investments are being poured into the Emirate in the staging and sponsorship of the world's leading sports events and the building of sporting infrastructures (Amara, 2005).

In destination branding terms, Dubai is following a (sport) event platform, though it is also increasingly exploiting its rulers' commitment to sport to build a 'place platform' strategy (Rein and Shields, 2007) whereby sport and Dubai become inseparable in the minds of potential visitors and investors. The (sport) event platform is less integrated to the notion of place, but is also less expensive to develop than a systematic process of integrating sports into the design of the destination brand. Interest in using sport as a facet for developing tourism stems not only from the Maktoum family's own interest in sports events but from the increased interest in sporting events that has arisen in the wake of a massive expansion in satellite and digital coverage over the past decade. However, there are also other reasons why sport has been viewed as something of a panacea within the Gulf Region. Principally, as Amara (2008: 67) indicates, modern sport is a 'symbol of modernization in Muslim societies and as a privileged tool for nation-state building'. Sport permitted monarchical regimes to mobilise their populations and to engage in nation-state building. International sport events also attract the attention of the world's media and have been deemed attractive to other Gulf states – Qatar, Bahrain and Abu Dhabi – in promoting integration with the international system and gaining recognition on the global map. Global sporting events attract private investment in terms of sponsorship, regeneration and destination brand value, and there has been coalescence in the Gulf region around the courting of commercial sport. However, it is important to note that the Gulf region, and Dubai in particular, has not simply developed strong relationships with global (read Western) sport at the expense of authentic Arab culture. In fact, the Maktoums' commitment to a traditional Arab sport, horse racing, is wholehearted. The Dubai World Cup of Horse Racing (US$6m is awarded to the winner) is one of the world's most prestigious events and it operates alongside Dubai's other modern sport events like the IRB Rugby Sevens, the Dubai Desert Classic Golf tournament, the Dubai Tennis Championships and its proposed bid for the 2020 Olympics Games, announced at the SportAccord conference in 2010. In the extremely competitive tourist market, many cities seek to increase their visibility via global mediatised sports events. As Henry (1997) argues, the positive symbolism surrounding such events has the potential to create city distinctiveness, transmitting an image of urban vibrancy and success (Smith, 2001).

Another key feature of Dubai's success is that it has sought to differentiate and continually refresh its offerings to attract international tourist arrivals. Bull and Weed (1999: 142) contend that 'many places which embraced rapid tourist development often concentrated on limited markets and may have provided few alternative attractions beyond the basic sun, sand, sea and hotel facilities'. This cannot be said of Dubai, which, as well as creating a sporting oasis in a desert environment, provides a plethora of entertainment facilities and a shopping paradise in addition to providing top-class hotels and facilities where tradition is embraced and encouraged not only as a tourist attraction but to retain the Emirate's Bedouin and nomadic past. Its attractions are awe-inspiring and ambitious and include projects in which iconic architecture abounds – Ski Dubai, Dubailand and Dubai Sports City.

The Dubai Sports City development is particularly interesting because it will, if successful, launch Dubai into the top tier of sport event destinations, which it is hoped will culminate in a successful bid for a sporting mega-event (Roche, 2000) such as the soccer World Cup or, more likely, the Summer Olympic Games. Smith (2010) argues that the clustering of sport facilities in specific zones has been designed to enhance their coherence and visibility, enabling effective place branding to take place (Rein and Shields, 2007). Whereas in the UK and Australia there has been a tendency to define a whole city as a 'sport city' (e.g. Melbourne, Glasgow or Sheffield), it is the sport city 'zoning' approach that appears more successful from a tourism promotion perspective. The intention here is differentiation from competitors and the branding of unique spaces or packaged landscapes where consumers and producers can come together. The Middle East has been particularly proactive in developing integrated sport cities to attract tourism and new residents rather than merely addressing the *post-hoc* use of event facilities, which has been the norm in those cities that have hosted major sporting events (e.g. Manchester 2002 Commonwealth Games).

Although Dubai has avoided the *post-hoc* use of event facilities, it has tried to secure strategic alignment between its sport city development and its major event strategy. Major event success legitimates the significant costs of development and permits the exploitation of sport event tourism potential. Moreover, as event owners, including the IOC, increase their demands of host cities, the Dubai Sports City initiative corresponds with the desire for a compact Olympic city. In that sense, Dubai's remarkable investment (mirrored by another Olympic hopeful, Qatar) can be considered as part of a long-term strategy to court the IOC with the promise of a breathtaking spectacle unparalleled outside of the 2008 Beijing Olympics. Dubai, therefore, has developed its Sports City to, first, cater to its growing tourist market and, second, continue to be able to compete for major sporting events because of the compact 'one-stop-shop' nature of provision. The challenge most destinations face is exploiting their Olympic or related sport facilities as they were either developed outside the main urban centre (to develop certain types of land) or the facilities were not designed to accommodate the tourism increases expected. Smith (2010) suggests that the Middle East examples (Doha and Dubai) are driven by a desire for tourism promotion and the attraction of affluent residents to these environments. They are also, crucially, driven by a desire to bid for Olympics and other multi-sport events in the future:

> Dubai's Sports City plans exist to build an Olympic-style collection of venues and facilities. A series of new sports schools are also planned, each associated with an international sports 'brand'. There will be a Butch Harmon golf school, a David Lloyd tennis academy and a Manchester

United football academy. The International Cricket Council also intends
to open its first global academy on the site.

(Smith, 2010)

The fact that Dubai is building a 'city within a city' is illustrative of its
ambition to grow its reputation through the exploitation of a sport event tourism
strategy. In event policy terms, while most cities in the major liberal
democracies (e.g. US, UK, Europe and Australia) have to justify investment
on the basis of the logic of urban renewal and regeneration (Gold and Gold,
2008), in Dubai (and, to that end, Qatar and Abu Dhabi), the model is
unashamedly urban entrepreneurial – incentives for private investment are
made available to ensure the biggest and the best sport events are attracted to
the region, without the need for a wider set of beneficiaries to be identified
and, crucially, involved as decision makers or recipients. Scale (size, reach,
media value) and impact (economic, reputational) are the principal drivers,
enhancing the confidence of these small states as they seek to play at the top
table of international economics and, increasingly, politics. That said, there
are signs that wider sport development policies are emerging in the Gulf Region
to ensure that facilities are used after major events depart and to comply with
the expectations of the event owners for equity in participation (e.g. in Qatar,
local girls were allowed to participate in sport only as a result of the 2006
Asian Games).

That the sport event strategy is aimed at attracting outside investment is
illustrated by Smith's (2010) view that 'the developments are mainly aimed
at affluent foreigners and may do little to address social cohesion' (p. 405).
As suggested in Chapter 2, increasingly events are detached from their original
meaning or purpose and now float fluidly across cultural boundaries, fusing
hybrid cultures in a manner that is accepted as an outcome of globalisation
processes (Bryman, 2004). In Dubai, Arab cultures (including a passion for
sport) are fused with Western and capitalist interests to create a space attractive
for global corporate sponsors and the sports industry to promote their sport
as 'entertainment' and 'experience' ambitions.

Dubai: event policy and strategy dilemmas

Bull and Weed (1999) suggest that government has three key roles to play in
terms of developing and sustaining sports event tourism. First, it is responsible
for key infrastructural requirements such as the quality of transport facilities
and provision of adequate water supply. Second, through its environmental
planning policies it can influence both the quality of the physical environment
– and thus the attractiveness of the places in which sports tourism operates –
and also, through its development control mechanisms, the extent to which
sports facilities are permitted to develop. Third, through both its sports and
tourism policies it can specifically encourage sports tourism development, and
through its relevant agencies can promote its assets abroad. Looking at the

case study of Dubai within this context, it clearly provides an exemplar of how to diversify an economic base from a reliance on depleting raw materials. Beyond this, it also provides an interesting counterpoint in our discussion of the key features of event policy around the world. In the final part of this chapter the principal lessons that can be learned from the Dubai case will be elucidated.

To start, it is worth noting the similarities that can be drawn from the approach to event policy prosecuted in Dubai to other examples discussed in this text. First, as Henderson (2006) and Amara (2005, 2008) have indicated, in the Dubai context, success in tourism and sport event terms is premised on a supportive government and a peaceful and stable environment. While there are specific geo-political reasons why this status is particularly important for reassuring a range of stakeholders in the Middle East (i.e. visitors, sponsors, event owners), the key point here is that the Dubai authorities are following an entrepreneurial governance strategy common to many cities and nations across the globe. Focused on market-led coalitions, the interests of commerce are explicitly promoted as the logic of economic exchange is the dominant steering mechanism. This is very clear in Dubai (but also increasingly in Western democracies bidding for major events) as the power and influence of the ruling family is directed at the protection of commerce, the shielding of the market mechanism, and the removal of obstacles to facilitate economic growth. As discussed in Chapter 4, it is about providing the foundations upon which consumerism can flourish. While Glasgow (Chapter 9), New Orleans (Chapter 11) and, to a lesser extent, Singapore (Chapter 12) have to balance the interests of private capital with the rights of citizens, in Dubai, the policy environment is more clearly concerned with promoting conspicuous consumption, affluent lifestyles and tourism, narrowly focused on free market economics. As Bagaeen (2007: 175) indicates, Dubai is 'an emerging dreamworld of conspicuous consumption and what locals dub "supreme life-styles"'. The sport event policies followed in Dubai and in the wider Gulf region comply fully with the aspirational lifestyles of its diverse international population, especially with regard to high-value commercial sport events (e.g. golf, horse racing, tennis and motorsport). However, while this has been successful, in the main, there are some unforeseen consequences that create tension within the region. For example, controls over the purchase and consumption of alcohol and restrictions on the public display of affection have generated global media coverage – highlighting that Dubai is more restrictive than most major sport event tourism destinations in its attitude towards some elements of consumption.

Another key similarity between the Dubai case study and the trajectory of event policy in this text is the establishment of a series of agencies to facilitate the operationalisation of the ruling family's vision into a coherent set of strategies and implementations. While the development of destination marketing organisations (DMOs), or equivalent, is commonplace in the UK and the US as a means of creating coherent narratives of place, the structures of power and authority in Dubai make this approach more problematic. Yet Dubai's tourism marketing vehicle, the DTCM, is remarkably similar in intent and in activity to its Western counterparts. In terms of sports tourism and sports events, the Dubai Municipality, through departments such as Planning, Transportation and General Projects, is responsible for the infrastructural requirements of sports tourism and events and also for the granting of permission and licensing requirements for such events. Furthermore, the DTCM exists 'to position Dubai as the leading tourism destination and commercial hub in the world' (www.dubaitourism.ae, accessed 30 August 2010). The DTCM has been very successful at creating the 'hype' that Henderson (2006) talked about earlier, and its selling of place is in keeping with the increasingly generalised place marketing strategies that were discussed in Chapters 5 and 6.

While the case of Dubai illustrates coalescence around some event policy issues common to much of the global community, there are also crucial differences in the operations of an Arab state that attention needs to be drawn to. The first of these is the atypical governance arrangements with single-party states and monarchical regimes operating in the Gulf region. This affects the rationale for, formation of, and implementation of event policy in a number of unique ways, some of which provide this Emirate with a competitive advantage over its competitors. For example, it is clear that the government policy on sporting events remains one of patronage by the ruling family. Dubai is a caring dictatorship – a power structure that allows the ruling family to operate Dubai as a business with very little separation between government agencies and ruling family control. It also means that the country's direction is influenced by the values of their ruling family, which centrally involves sport (Barclay, 2001). In event policy terms, this political structure has benefited Dubai as the will of the ruling family to procure major sporting events is easily transformed into actions with so little separation between those conceiving the policy and those implementing it. In liberal democracies, there is often a tension evident between those 'experts' with responsibility for designing event policy and the governing political leaders who face numerous competing claims for resources. Take the example of an Olympic bid as a case in point. Carrying the support of the host population through each and every stage of the bid is a challenging task, especially when electoral popularity may be jeopardised in the process. Securing the mandate of the population is much easier in a political environment where the power and influence of the ruling family take precedence. In many respects, the situation in Dubai can be likened to what Roche (2000) has called the irrational decision-making of political leaders that defined the early history of mega-events, before the outcomes of these events were placed under closer scrutiny.

Another significant difference evident in the case of Dubai, though not restricted to this state, is its model for populating the events calendar (mainly sport events). Although most events in Dubai have evolved as a result of the Dubai Municipality's development of the infrastructure required to host major global sporting events (Henderson, 2006; Rein and Shields, 2007) and as a result of the DTCM marketing and promoting Dubai (and indeed the events that it hosts), the Dubai government is not itself responsible for creating and developing events. While city authorities around the world are engaged in bidding for global sporting events such as the Olympic and Commonwealth Games and, on a smaller scale, developing their own events, Dubai has developed a policy of encouraging sporting associations to organise and host events in the Emirate, such as the IRB Rugby Sevens, sponsored by Emirate Airlines. The approach is clearly driven by a concern to 'facilitate', through infrastructural improvement, tax breaks and proactive marketing support, the growth of events supported by global corporate sponsors (e.g. Emirate Airlines, Dubai Duty Free) so that the sport brand is used as a means of attracting tourists, investors and buyers to Dubai.

Dubai has certainly looked to exploit the visibility of sports and sports events as a means of procuring wider media coverage and sponsor involvement. In essence, Dubai is seeking to secure 'emotional heat' (Rein and Shields, 2007: 74) with its sport event place promotion strategy, creating a distinctive range of attractions and facilities that symbolise its 'energy, vigour and strength' in a manner difficult to achieve for a nation trying to reposition itself within the Gulf Region and in the competitive global marketplace. Because sport is unique in its global appeal and attractiveness to the media industries, hosting sport events is currently viewed as one of the most effective mechanisms for increasing visibility, promoting the nation's assets and repositioning the brand. Allied to the effective exploitation of an event platform, this is attractive because of the free publicity gained and the ability to leverage investment in infrastructural improvements, which go towards embedding a sports culture in the destination. It is the holistic nature of this sport (event) brand strategy that differentiates Dubai at the current time. Unsurpassed sporting facilities, state of the art infrastructure, awe-inspiring attractions and the will of the governing authorities make Dubai the leading light as an emerging dream-world of conspicuous consumption.

Summary

Dubai provides an interesting case study context for this book because it is located in a region of the world that is politically, economically and culturally different from many of the other examples used to illustrate event policy rationales, formations and implementations. Yet it is also striking just how similar the event policy rationale is in Dubai, despite clear variations in the way policy is formulated and implemented. Dubai has invested in sport events predominantly because they bring visibility to the Emirate and attract global corporate sponsors and tourism. As a rationale for event policy, there is little difference to the civic boosterism or urban entrepreneurial model followed in many UK or US cities. However, whereas in the liberal democracies of the West, policy formation can be labourious, subject to consultation and debate, responsible for consensus building and accountable to citizens (in theory, at least), in Dubai, the processes are much more streamlined and driven by the singular interests of the all-powerful monarchical rulers. Policy implementation is also rather different in Dubai to that experienced in Glasgow or New Orleans, for example. Free market liberalism reigns supreme and the state only intervenes to create the conditions for the private sector to flourish. Most of Dubai's growing inventory of iconic sports events are resourced by major corporate sponsors and covered by the global media industries, securing valuable attention for the Emirate. The Dubai Sports City development takes this to a different level, with a mix of state funding, private investment and the star appeal of global sport franchises. This planned strategy is designed to place Dubai at the top table of world cities bidding for mega sporting events – with the Olympics the main target. Citizen involvement in policy formulation and implementation is minimal, part of a social contract that trades citizen rights for affluence. While in recent times the global economic downturn has focused greater attention on the sustainability of an economy dependent on real estate and tourism inflows, the Dubai model is certainly one that generates envy among onlookers in the UK and US.

Critical review questions

• What differences exist between event policy in the developed Western European economies and in the Emirate of Dubai, and why?
• What similarities exist between the sports event tourism policies evident in Dubai and those of other nations, and why?
• Why might Dubai's lack of developed policies on issues of equality and human rights affect their chances of being awarded one of the top tier sport events?

Recommended reading

Amara, M. (2005) '2006 Qatar Asian Games: a "modernisation" project from above?', *Sport in Society*, 8 (3): 493–514.
Henderson, J.C. (2006) 'Tourism in Dubai: overcoming barriers to destination development', *International Journal of Tourism Research*, 8: 87–99.
Smith, A. (2001) 'Sporting a new image? Sport based regeneration strategies as a means of enhancing the image of the city tourist destination', in Gratton, C. and Henry, I.P. (eds) *Sport in the city*, London: Routledge.

11 Mardi Gras, New Orleans

Policy intervention in an historical event

Introduction

This chapter focuses on the implementation of event policy in the US around an event that is ambiguous, amorphous and 'owned' by stakeholders outside of the official public policy domain discussed in other chapters. Mardi Gras is an historical 'hallmark' event on which the city of New Orleans, Louisiana, is heavily dependent economically, culturally and socially, especially in the wake of the devastation wrought by Hurricane Katrina in 2005. As the local state attempts to manage Mardi Gras to achieve wider social and public policy outcomes, they face resistance from a powerful lobby of social organisations, the Krewes, who effectively run the Mardi Gras celebrations. As the premodern meets the modern, contestation is created that provides some valuable insights into the dilemmas of event policy implementation associated with an historical event. This chapter draws on primary research, in the form of observation and interviews conducted by the authors, into the 2008 Mardi Gras festivities. These experiences will be used to illuminate the context, where possible.

Mardi Gras: a potted history

In the space of one chapter it is impossible to do justice to the traditions of Mardi Gras, New Orleans. To deepen your knowledge of the event's history, the work of Gill (1997) and Gotham (2005a, 2005b and 2005c) will provide you with the necessary depth of detail, which it is not possible to cover here. Instead, in this chapter, an overview of the event will be provided, before moving to analyse the significance of the policy interventions that have been undertaken in the city and the challenges facing a range of stakeholders in sustaining the economic, cultural and social successes of the Mardi Gras celebrations.

Mardi Gras, from the French, meaning 'Fat Tuesday', is a product of the observance of religious tradition (primarily Roman Catholic) and a festival to welcome Spring. It is thought that the celebration came to North America from France in 1699, representing the faithful's last opportunity for indulgence prior to fasting for Lent (www.mardigrasguide.com, accessed 15 September

2010). New Orleans was the centre of French Louisiana and was predominantly French and some Spanish, until the American immigration began in the second half of the 1800s. Because New Orleans was a Catholic city, Mardi Gras was part of the landscape, and very much part of the celebration of the pre-Lent festivities. Mardi Gras day (also known as Fat Tuesday) actually represents the culmination of the much longer Carnival season. In New Orleans, as in parts of Europe, Carnival is a 'period' rather than a one-off event. It also has a long-standing religious connection, with the word 'carnival' itself loosely translated from Latin as 'farewell to flesh'. Carnival celebrations actually commence on 6 January, the Twelfth Night feast of the Epiphany in the Roman Catholic liturgical calendar. Mardi Gras day is the climax of the season, which ends on the day before the penitential season of Lent begins (Ash Wednesday).

Annually, Mardi Gras falls forty-six days prior to Easter and can be as early as 3 February or as late as 9 March. The changing date is in itself an interesting feature of Mardi Gras as most comparable hallmark events are fixed in space and time to enable visitors to plan their visit and to permit other competing events to schedule alternative dates. The customs associated with Mardi Gras are the topic of much debate, but most commentators accept that the donning of bright costumes and masking is related to the continuation of French traditions. The story goes that returning travellers paraded through the narrow streets of the French Quarter, catching the attention of onlookers. As the New Orleans ladies watched the brightly dressed and disguised young men from their balconies, they threw chocolate and kisses in their direction. From that time on Mardi Gras became a well-established celebration in the New Orleans calendar and masked walking parades became fashionable in Springtime.

In contrast to the very public displays that are now evident on the public thoroughfares of New Orleans, the early Mardi Gras celebrations were predominantly held in private, in the form of balls and parties. Public parades began with the Krewe of Comus in the 1850s, but at this time its organic and amorphous form defined the rest of the celebration. The fragmented nature of the event led the civic leadership to consider having restrictions on Mardi Gras festivities in the post-civil-war years because it was too rowdy and uncontrolled. The response was for the founders of Rex, one of the most famous Krewes, to intervene to give the daytime spectacle some order. The Rex organisation created the idea of a parade and the notion of the King of Carnival (Rex). They started the tradition commanding the Mayor to turn over the keys of the city and inviting 'subjects' to join in the great parade. In the first parade, Rex rode a horse, as did the attendants. There were already a lot of bands and free-form paraders and maskers on the street, but they all fell in line behind Rex and that was the first Rex parade, in 1872. It was a great success, and these gentlemen and others got together and added tradition and lustre to that over the years. Rex became the centrepiece of Carnival and became an enormous tourist draw.

The early history of the event was, then, of disorder being replaced with order, through the formation of Krewes. The Krewes (this term translates as 'social organisations') created floats with the 'King' Krewe member at the head of the parade. This started the tradition of presenting a parade with decorated floats, which was then followed by a grand ball for the Krewe members and 'invited' guests. Indeed, this became such a popular event in Louisiana that in 1875 Mardi Gras was declared a public holiday. Other Krewes were formed later that century, the most notable being Proteus, one of the 'old-line' Krewes that continue parading today. As with many events and festivals, Mardi Gras abounds with rites, rituals and symbolism, and this has generated an abundance of myths and traditions that continue to govern the context and content of the event today. For example, a tradition that stands even now is that of 'throws', where the float riders throw trinkets such as beads, cups, doubloons and stuffed animals to the crowds as the parade travels through the public highways of the city and its environs. As discussed later, these symbolic elements of 'historical Mardi Gras' have become increasingly valuable as the festival is opened up to the vagaries of commerce and commodification.

Moving into the twentieth century, many Krewes began to operate as social aid and pleasure organisations with payment of membership fees governing eligibility for a place on the parade float. The motto of the Rex Organisation, for example, is *pro bono publico* – for the public good. These organisations are the fulcrum of their communities, helping people restore their homes and providing other charitable contributions. In the main, Krewes remained not-for-profit organisations (although this is subject to some change as a result of the pressures of commercialisation) and many were named after mythological entities, such as Eros, Hermes, Pegasus and Orpheus. Driven by the interests and influences of their members, the Krewes worked with complete freedom from governmental interference. Part of the mystique of Mardi Gras is created around the secrecy of the Krewes' activities. For example, each Krewe creates is own annual theme, which remains concealed until parade day, and the identity of the King and Queen of the eagerly awaited Rex Parade is not usually revealed until the night before the event. Interference is discouraged, which provides its own challenges for policy makers within the city, as discussed later in the chapter.

A key feature of many large- and small-scale events alike is their role in identity formation and display. Mardi Gras, New Orleans is no different. Despite being trailed as a very open and accessible celebration, defined in the public's imagination by its public displays of revelry, below the surface, Mardi Gras is a rather less inclusive space for identities to be expressed and tolerated. First, Mardi Gras has been a clearly gendered event throughout its history. Women were actively excluded from the male-dominated social scene and social clubs until 1941 when the Krewe of Venus presented its first ladies' Mardi Gras parade. Women are much more visible in Mardi Gras now, but their visibility often continues to be in stereotypical gendered roles – for example, as Queens held in esteem for their beauty and servitude. They are not heavily involved in the old-line Krewes and their ubiquity as sexual objects in the French Quarter (especially on Bourbon Street) is legendary.

Gill (1997) also argues that Mardi Gras, New Orleans is overshadowed by the politics of race. He contends that Mardi Gras traditions and rituals were largely established by a white male elite at the time of the Civil War. Gill infers that the Krewes are secret societies, which have been involved in the white supremacist movement, and only under pressure from the city government have some of the old-line organisations opened their membership up to blacks and those from other minority ethnic groups. As commercial imperatives broke down 'traditional' value codes, so a plethora of new Carnival organisations were created and they permitted and, sometimes encouraged, blacks, women and all socio-economic groups to join. However, Gill argues that in New Orleans, where 70 per cent of the population is black, the segregated traditions of Mardi Gras continue to be denounced as an affront and an anachronism. When the reproduction of class relations is also added into the mix, then it is possible to suggest that this globally recognised event, which attracts spectators from the world over, is a little less inclusive than it would first appear.

The number of parades gradually increased from the 1930s onwards, and there was a dramatic rise in the 1970s with the establishment of the so-called 'Super Krewes' such as Bacchus and Endymion. Some commentators have argued that the establishment of these Krewes has helped democratise the festivities and there are now Krewes that have mixed gender, race and familial memberships. However, as the large parades have been subject to processes of commercialisation, the nature of the festivity has altered. In recent years, celebrity riders, including Hulk Hogan, Kevin Costner and Salt-n-Pepa, have been the Kings on Super Krewe parades. With the expansion of large parades out of the French Quarter in 1972 and into other areas of the city, Mardi Gras began to have a significant impact on New Orleans' economic, social and cultural life. This can be perceived not only in social and political terms but also in terms of economic return. These are aspects of the festival that will be examined in the next section.

Mardi Gras and destination branding

A growing market for leisure and amusement was a prominent feature of the New Orleans economy by the early 1900s. By the second half of the twentieth century the economy was divided into three sectors – chemicals and petroleum, shipping and tourism (Gotham, 2002). Over the last century and into the present, tourism has now become the dominant asset of the Louisiana state economy and, more particularly, in New Orleans. This has been achieved through levering media exposure, with the city featuring regularly on the CNN network, infotainment network Playboy channel, the BBC and in worldwide publications such as *Condé Nast Traveller*.

Gotham (2005b: 310) describes the Mardi Gras celebrations as 'an interconnection of global and local actions' that, in turn, allow for the growth of tourism. Indeed, it could be said that Mardi Gras is the global 'shop' for

New Orleans and its other festivals, cultural events and attractions. The city is dependent on the heightened global profile of Mardi Gras as its signature event to support the otherwise faltering economy – especially in the aftermath of the Hurricane Katrina tragedy of 2005. Tourism has long been important to New Orleans and this was formally recognised in the 1960s when the Greater New Orleans Tourist and Convention Bureau (GNOTC) was established. Its twenty-first-century successor, the New Orleans Convention and Visitor Bureau (NOCVB) now describes itself as the driving force behind New Orleans' most important industry, tourism. The NOCVB estimates that tourism generates around $5 billion annually in visitor spending for the city (New Orleans Convention and Visitor Bureau, 2008). A study carried out by the University of New Orleans estimated that in 2006 New Orleans welcomed 3.7 million visitors and that this figure rose to 6 million in 2007.

Mardi Gras is clearly of fundamental importance to the tourism product in New Orleans, with one of its ex-Mayors stating it was 'bigger that the Super Bowl' (*New York Times*, 1999). Alongside its other globally recognisable tourism 'assets' – music (jazz), food (gumbo), river (Mississippi) and architecture (French Quarter) – Mardi Gras helps New Orleans in its place-making project. As discussed in Chapter 2, hallmark events (Hall, 1992) provide the host with significant recognition due to their tradition, attractiveness, quality or publicity. For locals and visitors alike, Mardi Gras, New Orleans carries the appeal of its hallmark contemporaries, including Calgary Stampede and Rio Carnival. As Spindt and Weiss (2009: 6) suggest:

> Mardi Gras is unique compared with other festivals in New Orleans, and others around the world, in the way that the event and the city are so closely linked in people's perception. This linkage is particularly pronounced among people outside of New Orleans. If a restaurant in, say, Colorado, is going to have a New Orleans theme it likely will be decorated in purple, green and gold – the colors of Mardi Gras. If a tourist is thinking of some place fun to travel, he or she will be reminded of Mardi Gras even if it is June, as can be evidenced by the sight of tourists wearing Mardi Gras beads in the French Quarter during even the summer months.

But the impact of Mardi Gras goes beyond the perceptual dimension and the brand recognition that it attracts. Since the devastation of Hurricane Katrina, much of the city's economic base has been washed away, with the tides of water breaking through its levees. However, because most of its famous landmarks and historic districts remained largely untouched, the city was quick to extend a welcome back to visitors, evidenced by the controversial decision to go ahead with a scaled-down Mardi Gras event only months after the devastation of Hurricane Katrina. Annually, the event bolsters the city's population in the early months of each year (Mardi Gras is always before Easter), and the most recent economic impact study suggests that it produces a net fiscal benefit to the city in the region of $6,278,888 and a return on investment of \$4.48 for every dollar spent by the city (Spindt and Weiss, 2009). Crucially, in forecasting an economic impact from the event, Spindt and Weiss differentiate between spending *during* Mardi Gras (visitors, locals, Krewe expenses, Krewe members and government) and spending *outside* the Mardi Gras season (merchandise and services, business fixed investment and incremental tourism and brand value). The direct expenditure during the event is important in and of itself to the city's levels of economic activity, but it is the 'franchise value' of Mardi Gras that makes it unique and deemed worthy of significant public (and private) investment.

Because of its economic importance, a variety of public and private organisations now take an active interest in marketing the place and 'motif' of Mardi Gras. Indeed, international corporations have successfully exploited the festival name to promote products that are sold globally. Gotham (2005a) argues that the Mardi Gras name is a versatile and ubiquitous commodity, used as a marketing slogan or banner by a variety of organisations to stimulate consumer demand for their products. This is where the destination branding challenges for the city begin. In terms of controlling direct expenditure during the event itself, the city authorities can ensure that the heightened levels of economic activity benefit 'local' stakeholders (bars, restaurants, hotels, shops, city revenue), but there is a much more significant challenge in retaining the revenues generated from Mardi Gras-related activity within the city boundaries.

Prior to the 1970s, Mardi Gras was a discreetly marketed tourist attraction, generally self-contained and celebrated largely by local, regional and national visitors. However, as the tourism industry offered a panacea to US urban policy makers' vision of civic boosterism in the early 1980s (see Chapter 5), Mardi Gras grew into an all-pervasive industry with many local people employed in the production of floats, souvenirs, books and museums. The business of Mardi Gras has, in recent years, extended into the production of bracelets, trinkets, beads, 'throws', hats, banners and soft toys. Many of these are produced with the traditional Mardi Gras purple, green and gold colours. This commodification of Mardi Gras symbols, artifacts and rituals has gathered pace over the last two decades. King Cakes, one of the key 'symbols' of Mardi Gras, are now decorated with the Mardi Gras colours, which are a potent signal of the whole Mardi Gras cultural system (Gotham, 2005b). Millions of these cakes are now produced for consumption around the US and further afield to observe Mardi Gras celebrations. Yet as Gotham (2005b) suggests, the consumption of these symbols is completely detached from the context in which they generate their meaning. At the same time as commodification processes have intensified, so other traditions have been eliminated from the festivity. Torchlight processions (*flambeaux*) used to accompany parades, and although some continue to be found along the official parade routes, the numbers have decreased significantly. The city of New Orleans has also presided over a long-standing prohibition of advertising on parade floats, which is perceived by some as a defence or breakwater against commodification processes. However, more subtle advertising techniques have been emerging in the last ten years.

The city administration has itself tentatively indicated a desire to attract a headline sponsor for the event as a means of reducing the financial burden that falls upon city authorities with respect to sanitation, policing, clean-up costs and the erecting of barriers:

> The city began giving careful consideration to the idea of soliciting a sponsor to pay for the cost of staging Mardi Gras in 2005 after Hurricane Katrina destroyed the city's finances. Sanitation, police and fire services during Carnival season can run the city $3 million to $5 million a year.
>
> (Spindt and Weiss, 2009)

Spindt and Weiss (2009) indicate that the city authorities spend $3,330,202 in Mardi Gras-related expenditure each year to support the hosting of the event. This figure includes a bill for $2,407,073 on overtime payments to police to ensure public safety and traffic control during the celebrations. Herein lies the principal dilemma facing the city government in managing the invaluable Mardi Gras brand while balancing the local state budget. Mardi Gras is marketed as the 'Greatest Free Show on Earth'. As discussed above, the city permits no advertising or sponsorship along the official parade routes and this tradition continues to be upheld despite the financial pressures being placed upon the city as a result of Hurricane Katrina. The City Council is trapped in a vicious circle over the issue of Mardi Gras resources. Attracting a headline corporate sponsor would reduce the financial burden that currently rests predominantly on its shoulders. However, the city administration, led by the Mayor, is anxious not to be associated with 'selling out' Mardi Gras to a headline corporate sponsor and diminishing the event's uniqueness (and brand value) in the process. Essentially, the city wants to retain Mardi Gras in its current state without incurring the costs associated with hosting it.

However, a further complication in the city's use of Mardi Gras as a destination branding vehicle is that the public authorities (who bear the main costs of the event) are unable to exert full control over the brand message that the watching global audience receives. It has little control over media exposure, and while the event has an informal strategic group, the Mayor's Mardi Gras Advisory Council, the reality is that it has little power and influence over the Krewes and entrepreneurs within the city. In contrast to the over-production of other event genres around the world, Mardi Gras remains fluid, spontaneous and uncertain. In fact, when corporate sponsors were sounded out as to their interest in supporting the event, the feedback was lukewarm mainly due to the lack of control over the Mardi Gras 'brand' – and the potentially negative publicity that could result from an association with the 'Bourbon Street Mardi Gras' experience. There are at least two distinct Mardi Gras events occurring at the same time – one is the 'girls gone wild' Mardi Gras that takes place in the tourist haven of the French Quarter and the other is a family-oriented, wholesome community event that is participatory in nature and occupies an important place in a neighbourhood's activities all year round. Bourbon Street

Mardi Gras is filled with raucous, wild behaviour. During Mardi Gras, the historical street has a constant stench of alcohol, food and trash. Populated by hordes of frat boys and overseas visitors, it attracts the tourist tribes with little care or knowledge of the Mardi Gras traditions. Balconies are adorned with purple, gold and green and 'sold' to those who wish to offer their services to the watching masses below. Jam-packed full with bars, food outlets and tacky souvenir shops, Bourbon Street is everything that the New Orleans authorities want (globally recognisable, party-city status and an anything-goes attitude) and want to avoid (exhibitionism, libidinous behaviour, severe intoxication, debauchery). It attracts a crowd of spectators who are interested in voyeurism, in watching others exhibit themselves to a salacious audience.

While 'this' Mardi Gras secures worldwide exposure to the city, it is the 'other' event that makes Mardi Gras sustainable. In Gotham's terms, the Bourbon Street Mardi Gras is an example of tourism from above, while the family Mardi Gras represents tourism from below. So, for the host community, Mardi Gras is ultimately a participatory family event, not the passive spectacle associated with some events (Roche, 2000). Carnivals have always provided opportunities for an inversion of the world, of the social order of the day, and they occupy spaces of transgression. If only for a few days or a few weeks, they provide the opportunity to invert hierarchies, create temporary utopian spaces and the opportunity for (relative) freedom and recuperation. In New Orleans, post-Katrina, Mardi Gras has been posited as a salvation, as the time to reinvigorate the city, to get it back on its feet. While the commercial imperative is important economically in the recovery, in many respects for New Orleans residents, reclaiming ownership of Mardi Gras is more important. In the long term, opposing the spectacle may, ironically, represent the best opportunity for securing a sustainable future. Family Mardi Gras creates and reproduces tradition as a key facet of social capital building, whereas Bourbon Street Mardi Gras takes 'tradition' and 'heritage' and sells it for commercial gain. It could be argued that the city needs both but that they are at times working towards different ends.

Mardi Gras, New Orleans: event policy and strategy dilemmas

From the preceding discussion, it is clear that the case of Mardi Gras, New Orleans is a challenging one for the formal policy process. As the festival has attracted increased global media attention and has become synonymous with Destination New Orleans, it has become the target of the city's place marketers as the post-Katrina panacea. At one and the same time, the tradition and heritage of the event has been contested by the host population and there has been a reassertion of more long-lasting and rooted values on behalf of the Krewes and the membership that permits these social organisations to put on the Greatest Free Show on Earth. The local state has been forced to act as an enabler or facilitator for the festival, unable to introduce direct control (other than through the permit system) but instead left to regulate the nature of Mardi

Gras celebrations in keeping with the liberal values of the early twenty-first century. The state has little control over the all-powerful Krewes, and yet these organisations are of fundamental importance to the 'product' that the quasi-autonomous state organisations (e.g. the New Orleans Convention Bureau) are charged with the responsibility to promote. The economic returns are potentially lucrative in terms of visitor expenditure and tax revenues, but again, the local state has limited powers to enter agreements with major sponsors or to prevent others riding on the back of the event to promote their own products. An overly determined event risks the wrath of the powerful Krewes and of the watching public, yet at the same time, the dangers associated with an amorphous, free-flowing event parading through the streets of a large (and increasingly crime-ridden) city are also significant – both in terms of public safety and reputational damage. The approach taken by the local government in New Orleans can be viewed as creeping regulation. It has, slowly but surely, attempted to grasp some control over the event by developing a tighter permit system through which each and every parade must be processed. This approach allows the local state to 'guide' and 'frame' the sort of parades it judges as acceptable and, conversely, the ones it views as inappropriate in a liberal and tolerant city (e.g. those with closed memberships). The city has introduced some measures to support, shape and enhance Mardi Gras, but these have been restricted to forcing Krewes to open up their memberships and eradicate discrimination. However, even here the policy and regulatory levers were relatively ineffective, because as private organisations, the Krewes were not bound to change their rules and several simply stopped parading on those 'public' routes where the legislation applied.

Drawing back from the specific state intervention approaches found in New Orleans, it is worth briefly referring to other, similar, historical events that have faced the pressure for destination branding of their cultural assets. A good example is the San Fermin fiesta held annually in Pamplona, Spain. This event, most commonly referred to as the Pamplona Bull Run, has become popularised in media and tourism discourses for its uniqueness and, apparent, authenticity. However, like New Orleans Mardi Gras, this event is reliant upon visitors, who legitimate the introduction of new and revised social values in the city (Ravenscroft and Matteucci, 2002) as residents 'perform' for tourism. The deviant behaviour associated with festivals (and carnivals) is managed to the extent that liminality is packaged as a symbol of differentiation for the destination, while social control over behaviour is increased in a similar vein to that experienced in New Orleans. Similar issues can be said of the famous Palio horse race that takes place annually in Siena, Italy. This event is more than 600 years old and is sustained by the traditions of the Contradas of Siena, districts with their own government, coat of arms, titles, emblems, colours and population. These institutions race in the Palio in July and August each year, attracting a significant level of tourism visitation and media coverage. Berruti (2008) argues that the Palio plays a crucial role in city imaging, while also representing a hugely significant 'local' cultural tradition that sustains community life through song, costume, rituals and even violence. However, as its authenticity has become attractive to media narratives (which have often focused on the risks inherent in the races around the Campo square), so the host has sought to challenge representations and reclaim the event from its media representation. Now the use of 'coats, flags, costumes, colours and their reproduction on objects or publications must be authorized by the *Consorzio*' (Berruti, 2008: 19), a contrada consortium set up to defend the historical traditions of the Palio against tourism exploitation. Commercial rights for the public ceremony are also now controlled. While this control is not the sole preserve of state-sponsored bodies, nonetheless, quasi-governmental agencies are involved in protecting the Siena Palio in a way that is more difficult in New Orleans and Pamplona. The three examples do, however, illustrate the presence of a policy pull towards the increasing regulation of historical events and their promotion through media and tourism discourses. This process is neither seamless nor uncontested, but the direction of travel is clear and this pull is symptomatic of an increasingly globalised policy drive.

Summary

The case of Mardi Gras, New Orleans is illuminating for event policy on a number of levels. First, it illustrates the limits of state intervention in the promotion and delivery of major events. In governing Mardi Gras, the local state and its commercial partners are left relatively impotent in the face of a powerful lobby group from the third sector who are the ultimate event owners of the Carnival celebrations. Following the destination branding logic discussed in Chapter 6, the New Orleans authorities want to utilise Mardi Gras as a means of representing the 'personality' of the city. However, as they attempt to intervene to ensure safety, security and sustainability, the city government threatens to dilute the appeal of the event to its loyal audience. In navigating a minefield of risks and rewards, the authorities are left to adopt a fine balancing act between 'freedom' – a laissez faire governance – and 'regulation' – the desire for a more interventionist, micro management of the Mardi Gras celebrations. Navigating these (often) competing agendas is increasingly common for destinations heavily reliant on their hallmark events. The San Fermin Fiesta in Pamplona and the Palio in Siena are excellent examples of free events with mass popularity now facing increased pressure towards commercial exploitation, media intrusion and (potential) loss of historical value. How destinations successfully ameliorate these tensions, while retaining the uniqueness of their offering, will determine their future position in the global events marketplace.

Critical review questions

- Mardi Gras, New Orleans is dubbed the 'greatest free show on earth'. Taking into consideration the policy issues identified in this chapter,

what challenges does the free nature of this event bring to its various stakeholders?
- As a public policy maker in New Orleans, how would you ameliorate the tensions between the needs of the local population and incoming visitors in their experience of the Mardi Gras celebrations?
- What does the case study of Mardi Gras tell us about the effectiveness of state intervention in events and festivals?

Recommended reading

Gilmore, D.D. (1998) *Carnival and culture*, London: Yale University Press.

Gotham, K.F. (2005b) 'Tourism from above and below: globalisation, localisation and New Orleans's Mardi Gras', *International Journal of Urban and Regional Research*, 39 (2): 309–326.

Sexton, R.L. (1999) 'Cajun Mardi Gras: cultural objectification and symbolic appropriation in a French tradition', *Ethnology*, 38 (4): 297–313.

12 Singapore
A mixed economy of events

Introduction

This chapter addresses the mixed economy of events implementation, which is evidenced by the situation in the city-state of Singapore, South East Asia. This city-state has followed an approach to the delivery of its events that relies heavily on commercial events, but which is also supported by significant public investment (e.g. the Singapore Grand Prix) and, due to its ethnic mix, is also identifiable with an array of multi-ethnic 'indigenous' festivals, which reflect the essence of more organic, community-focused events. Unlike the policy environment within which Mardi Gras, New Orleans operates, the Singapore example is of a much more interventionist state apparatus in which planning for positive externalities is very much part of the culture of this city-state. As a result, significant state and quasi-state resources have been invested in upscaling the event product of Singapore. Policy makers have worked to position this small city-state as the 'Entertainment and Events Capital of Asia' or, in 2010, 'A Uniquely Eventful City'. By attracting a range of cultural (e.g. MTV Awards, 2005) and sporting events (the 2008 F1 Grand Prix and the 2010 Youth Olympics), Singapore is clearly striving to impress the major event owners so that it can become a key player in the global events circuit. These experiences will be used to reveal how Singapore has progressed from its reliance on tightly planned and state-controlled economic, political, social and cultural development to a position where private enterprise makes an increasingly important contribution to its mixed economy of events. That said, it continues to focus on governed events (as opposed to consumed) and with the pretence of openness (for citizens) as opposed to planned.

This chapter draws on primary research, in the form of observation and interviews, conducted by the authors at a range of Singaporean festivals and events over the last decade. These experiences will be used to illuminate the context, where possible.

Singapore: new nation, contested freedoms and international opportunities

Singapore is a relatively new nation-state that has risen rapidly since its independence from Britain in 1965. Geographically positioned at the centre of the Asia-Pacific region, it is strategically placed to become a 'total business centre' for the Asian region. Although a young nation, Singapore's development trajectory from industrialism to post-industrialism (and beyond) appears impressive when compared with economies of nations with greater history. In the space of four decades, Singapore has reached a situation in which it promotes itself as the 'bridge between the West and the East'. While much of the impetus for this transformation can be attributed to the historical legacy of British colonialism (Kong, 1999), such rapid growth is also directly attributable to the unique developmental circumstances of Singapore.

Much of Singapore's progress can be traced to the governing People's Action Party (PAP). Although evoking a representative democracy and with official United Nations' recognition as a parliamentary republic, the PAP has been the dominant, and relatively uncontested, political force within the country for half a century. From the point of independence, the PAP pursued a strategy of restructuring the economic, political, social and cultural content of the nation and its people. Small in physical size, spanning only two miles by sixteen miles, Singapore has a high population density of 4.5 million people, drawn from a multi-ethnic mix of Chinese (76.8 per cent), Malay (13.9 per cent), Indian (7.9 per cent) and others (1.4 per cent) (www.singstat.com, accessed 9 November 2010). The PAP pursued, in the first three decades at least, an authoritarian policy regime (Tamney, 1996) in order to build an industrialised nation. Such authoritarianism stems, in part, from the historical development of Singapore as a nation-state that gained independence in 1965. Prior to this, it was subject to Dutch and British colonialism and Japanese occupation, and was part of an independent Malaysian Federation. Upon gaining independence, not only did Singapore have to contend with a legacy of colonialism, occupation and expulsion from Malaysia, it also had to deal with huge social and economic problems. In 1965, unemployment and population growth were high, while public health and housing conditions were poor. The developments along the river, the infrastructure change and inward investment in the city-state over the ensuing forty-year period is unrivalled by any other country. In juxtaposing the necessary Asian values of work ethic, discipline and self-sacrifice against those of the perceived decadent West, the PAP sought to project a unique Singaporean identity within the global village. However, this policy of 'protection' alongside the cultivation of shared national values changed with the economic climate during the 1990s.

In the 1990s, the PAP moved to embrace a post-industrial strategy of inward investment and entrepreneurial growth, with cultural events (e.g. Chingay Parade) seen as keystone activities to continue economic development and a vehicle to promote a unique Singaporean identity. The Ministry of Trade and Industry and the Singaporean Tourism Board (STB) represent the institutional state vehicles used to ensure direction and coordination of the PAP's strategic model for development. This strategic shift in direction was vindicated in the late 1990s and early twenty-first century, with Singapore the most economically successful nation in South East Asia (Ooi, 2002).

This has also been matched by a socio-cultural shift whereby Singapore and its citizens now reflect the transition from work-based to consumption-based economies (Rojek, 1995). Tourism is already one of its largest industries (9.7 million visits in 2006) and is targeted to rise to 17 million visits by 2015. As Foley *et al.* (2008) have suggested, Singapore now increasingly invests in its creative and cultural offering out of necessity. The nature of its topography and lack of natural resources meant that Singapore decided to pursue 'an ambitious strategy to attract global tourism spending by rebranding Singapore as more than a business travel destination' (Foley *et al.*, 2008: 58).

The STB vision for tourism 2015 states clearly the aim to use events as part of a strategy for brand diversification and to attract the attention of global audiences (Foley *et al.*, 2008). The arts have benefited as the focus of policy makers has shifted from securing economic stability and the development of a public education system towards a greater commitment to cultural development, involving both importing and exporting cultural products. The development of the Esplanade, the new National Sports facilities, the Integrated Resorts and the International Cruise Terminal are all part of a long-term strategy that puts culture and sport at the heart of Singapore's urban planning processes. One outcome of the 'governed' nature of events (sporting and cultural) is that the Singapore Masters, the Singapore Marathon, Chingay Parade, Thaipusam Festival and the National Day Parade have become significant tourism attractions, as well as fulfilling important political, social and cultural roles internally. Add these developments together and you are left with a clear perception of a destination looking to diversify its offer to incoming visitors and residents alike. Since 2002, in simultaneously exploiting its urban landscape and its ethnic mix (unique to Singapore), festivals and events have been used as a key strategic goal to attract visitors and to retain them for longer 'dwell-times'. The STB Chairman highlights that in 2008, visitors stayed longer and spent more despite the economic slowdown globally (Singapore Tourism Board, 2008). Winning the rights to host a round of the F1 Grand Prix circuit in 2008 (the first night-time Grand Prix) further embedded Singapore as the main destination and consumer hub with the Asia-Pacific region. With Singapore now labelled a 'global arts city', 'Uniquely Singapore' or the 'Events and Entertainment Capital of Asia' (Foley *et al.*, 2008), the strategy of the PAP appears to have been a success story in rebranding. However, there remains a tension between the local and citizen and the global and consumer that can be illustrated by looking at the way some of the main events are planned and organised. It is to this tension that discussion in the chapter now turns.

Singapore: local (citizen) and global (consumer)

Singapore's post-industrial economic strategy of using sporting and cultural events to generate visibility and inward investment is shared by many of the major cities of the developed, and developing, world (see Chapter 6). From the traditional heritage of London, Paris or Rome, to the modern, or as some might argue, postmodern creations of Sydney and Las Vegas, all cities with global pretensions have strategies that incorporate a progressive calendar of events to help project an attractive vision of the destination to would-be visitors, investors and residents (Richards and Palmer, 2010). In essence, the production of major cultural and sporting events has become a means to capture the gaze of the world's travelling consumers and major investors – while at the same time helping to cement a range of localised and national identities at home (see Chapter 10 on Dubai's rise to prominence). Singapore has a particularly strong desire to talk to the local and the global at one and the same time. As a relatively new nation it has felt the need to create togetherness and a shared sense of identity to manage possible internal ethnic tensions. Moreover, as a major economic player in the region it wants to diversify its attractions to encourage high-spending consumers that are central to its changing economic base.

The event policy rationales, formations and implementations specific to Singapore provide a good illustration of the complexities involved in achieving planned externalities or outcomes. Singapore is both a post-colonial city and a nation-state and it attempts to foster a strong national cultural identity while simultaneously reasserting the rights of its multi-ethnic population by preserving their indigenous cultural heritage and identity – albeit one that is rigorously controlled and regulated by the neo-authoritarian state. As an exemplar, Singapore sits well within global-local (Robertson, 1992) debates, having successfully projected itself on a global scale through the West-meets-East agenda, moving beyond the fears that Western culture would infiltrate Singaporean culture (Kong and Yeoh, 2003). The state has played a significant role in navigating this difficult path achieved mainly through its institutional tourism and economic development vehicles.

A primary example of Singapore using events and festivals to address its internal audience while at the same time contributing to its international success is the National Day Parade (NDP) celebrations, which take place annually in August. Created by the PAP as a means of enshrining the notion of the nation within the context of a multi-ethnic population, this event complies with Hobsbawm's (1983a) notion of invented traditions – ceremonies, parades and gatherings – that played a crucial role in the nineteenth and twentieth centuries, especially in Europe. The NDP is politically motivated (as opposed to events organised by social groups), organised and promoted by the state apparatus to engage the public imagination and secure 'popular resonance' (Hobsbawm, 1983b: 264) for its activities. The PAP has consistently used the NDP to secure the consent and co-operation of its subjects – although that has not been overly problematic in a neo-authoritarian state. As a public ceremony, the NDP was crucial in legitimating state political power, built around official and unofficial elements alongside popular festivities celebrating and commemorating the idea of the 'nation' (e.g. military ceremonies, wearing of the national colours, the Sing Singapore Medley).

These celebrations were particularly important in the early days of independence, for the internal promotion of shared values, the maintenance of a
collective national identity and the securing of consent to the authoritarian
regime of the early PAP leaders. However, the NDP continues to be extremely
popular with the population of Singapore as it represents the culmination of
a yearlong set of activities embedded within its neighbourhoods.

Other cultural festivities have also played a crucial role in Singapore's
internal and (increasingly) external relations. The Chingay Parade at Chinese
New Year and the Thaipusam Festival (see Chapter 2) address the religious
and cultural traditions of some of the largest constituencies of Singapore's
multi-ethnic population. More than three-quarters of the population of Singapore is Chinese, and so Chingay Parade plays an important symbolic role for
the city-state. As a globally celebrated event, Chinese New Year also acts as
a useful showcase for Singapore, attracting significant numbers of participants
and viewers, animating the cityscape and bringing in tourism revenue. The
Chingay Parade has been used to 'position' and 'market' Singapore as an attractive international destination.

In contrast, the Thaipusam Festival plays a more important role in cementing
the place of the smaller Hindu population in the nation. Thaipusam is a one-
day festival involving a thanksgiving procession undertaken by Hindu
devotees. By remaining relatively 'invisible' to the global circuit of tourism,
the Thaipusam Festival provides an example of 'home' and 'locality' being
protected from global influences. However, like Chingay Parade, the rich
symbolism and ritualistic dimensions of Thaipusam are attractive to those
responsible for the prosecution and delivery of policies for tourism in
Singapore. In other words, while Thaipusam's principal *meaning* resides with
the relatively small population of Hindu devotees in Singapore, its future shape
and 'success' may be dependent on the city-state's use of events and festivals
as forms of external promotion. As a very distinctive festival (devotees are
often pierced with two spears, one through the tongue and one through the
cheeks), Thaipusam has great potential for a watching audience and could
contribute to the 'uniqueness' that Singapore is trying to cultivate. Focusing
on external promotion is certainly a strategy that has emerged over recent years,
most clearly expressed by the ambitious move to attract an F1 Grand Prix to
Singapore in 2008.

Global spectacular: the F1 Singapore Grand Prix

While cultural products (including festivals and events) have been imported
to Singapore in recent years to help diversify the tourism product, the city-
state has an excellent track record in hosting major sporting events for the last
two decades. The Singapore Open (golf) is a successful event, and the
Singapore Sports Hub, a significant infrastructural development for the city-
state, secured investment to proceed in 2010. The Sports Hub provides
Singapore with an integrated sporting venue for world-class sport events. The

similarities with Dubai's Sports City are clear, apart from the fact that Singapore has a more embedded sport participation culture. However, compared with the regional and world reach of previous sporting events, the Singapore F1 Grand Prix represented a much more ambitious strategy from its tourism and economic development agencies. As the first night-time Grand Prix, it was designed as a 'high-revving economic engine' that would see Singapore challenge the other 'exotic locations' of F1 'from Bahrain and Budapest to Melbourne to Montreal' (McMullen, 2008). With '1600 light projectors along a circuit that winds through the business district' (Reuters, 2008), the event, run over three days and with the 5,067-kilometre Marina Park circuit, 'served up a kaleidoscope of entertainment . . . in order to maximize the sport's commercial potential' (Guardian Sport Blog, 2008). With over 40,000 spectators from overseas and viewers projected at over 100 million people, the public relations and media value was worth US$300 million to Singapore, placing it firmly in the global spotlight (Youngblood, 2008).

The decision to host the first night-time F1 Grand Prix was taken on the basis that the operational risks were outweighed by the lucrative commercial rewards on offer through place marketing and promotion. Singapore used the night-time spectacle to showcase its iconic cityscape, effectively 'lighting' its signature buildings and other attractions for the tourist gaze. This strategy was designed to demonstrate Singapore's capability in delivering on its promises in a uniquely Asian way. In other words, the organisational efficiency and professionalism demonstrated by the host further emphasised the competence of Singapore as a 'safe' pair of hands for large-scale (sporting and cultural) events. Other event owners were encouraged to consider Singapore as a venue for their events in the future. Furthermore, Singapore also invested in infrastructural developments to 'sustain' the hosting of F1 for the future, building on the numerous other developments (the Esplanade, Marina Park, Integrated Resorts and Sports Hub) that have taken place over the last decade. This approach is in line with the city-state's long-term goals of competing on a global level and presenting itself as safe Asia (Foley *et al.*, 2007; Foley *et al.*, 2008), offering sanitised Asian experiences alongside dominant Western ideologies of consumption. Events and festivals have become a key plank of the city's global strategy to communicate, or present, an alternative Singaporean identity to the rest of the world.

While the Singapore F1 Grand Prix was fundamentally a 'spectacle' targeted overseas, for most Singaporean residents it was disruptive to daily life and represented, at best, a detached, mediated experience. Road closures and disruptions to malls, markets and even the weekly '20,000 churchgoers' in Suntec City caused 'upset' for locals, businesses and office workers (Xinyi, 2008). In being run against the backdrop of the city at night, with its glittering skyscrapers and top landmarks shown off to a global audience (*The Straits Times*, 2008), this event was one 'aimed at turning the city-state into the 'Monaco of Asia,' enticing the super-wealthy who come to the race to consider setting up homes' (Youngblood, 2008). As a result, in the hierarchy of fans and consumers – global tourist or local resident – the Singaporean F1 Grand Prix was an exclusive experience. Given the unique aesthetic of the event and the centrality of beaming its mediatised representation to global audiences, local Singaporeans were on the margins of the marketing strategy. With Singaporeans given the 'call to duty', evoking the work ethic, servile efficiency and exploitation of the shared values instilled by the authoritarian regime, the role of the local at the F1 Grand Prix was to clean up, marshal the event and ensure safety (Xinyi, 2008). However, in imprinting the F1 brand, with its 'lavish yacht parties . . . gala night festivals . . . adding to the carnival atmosphere' (Youngblood, 2008), the identity and values exhibited by Singaporean 'clockwork organization' (Reuters, 2008) could be threatened with the self-same Western decadence that Singapore and the PAP has, in the past at least, eschewed.

Of course, the F1 brand yields exceptional promotional power. The Chief Executive of the STB has stated that securing the F1 night race, which will run annually for five years, presented Singapore in a new light to more than 110 million viewers worldwide. It attracted 40,000 overseas visitors and generated S$168 million in tourism receipts (Singapore Tourism Board, 2008). A key message being delivered here is that Singapore saw the F1 Grand Prix as an opportunity to develop its brand equity and add depth to the wider Singapore Experience. This is being achieved by working with more private enterprise partners (airlines, attractions, hotels) to secure image and profile and take market share away from others in the region. The strategy is aggressively entrepreneurial. It also reflects a subtle change in policy preoccupation for the PAP and its state-supported agencies. Instead of being 'governed' and state-led, the Singapore F1 Grand Prix was much more about consumption and free enterprise, facilitated by the state but not for the reasons of shared values or the maintenance of national identity *per se*. It is as if Singapore has come to realise that its overly interventionist or governed approach to events and festivals potentially limits the possibilities of reaching an increasingly knowledgeable global event audience. Having now added the global F1 spectacular to an already impressive portfolio of festivals and events, Singapore can generate much desired international profile, while continuing to utilise its 'unique' cultural events to maintain shared values, engage its diverse ethnic population and develop its reputation in the creative and cultural arenas. The final part of this chapter will now consider the event policy and strategy dilemmas created in the furtherance of the afore-mentioned approach.

Singapore: event policy and strategy dilemmas

Over the last decade in particular, Singapore has made it clear that it strives to become a 'must-visit destination' through an adoption of an holistic visitor experience. The Singaporean authorities believe that the more attractive they are as a destination, the more the discerning visitor will be attracted to

Singapore within the Asian market rather than only targeting the global traveller on stop-over visits. While the F1 night race had a global appeal, they are all too aware that their policy has to 'remain relevant and competitive' (STB Annual Report 2009) if it is to be sustainable in the longer term – especially when their close neighbours in the Asia-Pacific region are upping the stakes with their own major sporting and cultural events. Singapore does, however have an advantage over some of its competitors who have (and continue to) bid for large-scale events for political, rather than for sporting or cultural, reasons. Singapore has taken a more strategic view in developing its events portfolio. It has simultaneously developed its built infrastructure and attracted major events to populate it. So, for example, Singapore has developed large areas of its urban and waterfront landscape in order to be capable of hosting the sorts of events it is targeting (e.g. the Marina Park area was used for the F1 Grand Prix). This approach can be compared with Glasgow's transformation over the last two decades. Glasgow used its European Capital of Culture success in 1990 to propel the development of associated infrastructure to enable it to bid for, and win, other sporting and cultural events. Singapore has, similarly, created a series of leisure spaces that can be adapted to suit different events, whether sporting or cultural. The development of its Sports Hub only advances the capabilities of the small city-state to compete with larger rivals in the future. Having successfully won and delivered the Youth Olympics in 2010, Singapore has demonstrated its competence to influential event owners (i.e. the IOC) and this can only be of benefit to the city-state if (or when) it decides to bid for other major events. Its list of successes is already impressive. Hosting the MTV Asia Awards in 2005, the F1 Grand Prix since 2008 and the aforementioned Youth Olympics in 2010 reinforces Singapore's credentials.

However, while there is much to applaud in terms of Singapore's recent successes in attracting events with a global reach, there are also tensions for policy makers that flow from this approach. In implementing a more pronounced commerce- (or enterprise-)facing event strategy, questions of economic, social and cultural sustainability are generated. Over recent years, a number of scholars have queried whether an events-led strategy based on the logic of consumption alone will be productive in the longer term. For example, elsewhere (Foley *et al.*, 2008) the authors have identified some problems with the singular drive towards overly commercial event strategies and these apply to Singapore too. Singapore has been described as a neo-authoritarian state with tight control exercised over the behaviour of citizens and freedom of speech in return for relative economic prosperity. However, as it seeks to attract a wider range of visiting audiences, the city-state has to strike a careful balance between openness and governance in implementing its event-led strategies. They have to be careful not to produce, 'intensely regulated, or gated, communities' or the impression of 'a public culture controlled and contained, managed and directed' (Foley *et al.*, 2008: 56). In the case of the Singapore F1 Grand Prix, the authorities ensured that the tourist tribes were well catered for. Local populations were expected to give their consent for their everyday lives to be disrupted in the name of commercial return – for the greater good of economic civic boosterism. However, there are long-term dangers inherent in the approach that seeks to animate its existing attractions and landscapes to communicate positive, cosmopolitan credentials to regional and international audiences:

> Should the balance of power shift too far towards a reliance on dis-connected and de-territorialized media events, then Singapore may be relying on an aspirational Event and Entertainment Capital of Asia brand built more on the pursuance of symbolic identity than on material logic.
> (Foley *et al.*, 2008: 63)

Furthermore, Ooi (2002) and Chang and Huang (2005) also caution that Singapore is in danger of ignoring its past, which they argue should be acknowledged and remembered. There is some evidence that the Singaporean authorities are matching their drive for entrepreneurial spirit with an awareness of their host community. For example, the case of Thaipusam reflects the delicate balance between observing the traditions of an indigenous culture and the commodification of heritage. To date, the authorities have avoided the explicit touristic promotion of this event. It remains firmly anchored within the Hindu community in Singapore, with its core 'meaning' currently prevailing over the 'money' that could be generated with enhanced marketing and promotion. Given its insistence on the creation of a coherent and strong national identity, Singapore has to manage a difficult dilemma, internally and externally. If it continues to focus its attention on attracting events with little innate connection to its historical or cultural assets, there is the risk that national identities become background props with local communities often displaced and marginalised in the name of global capital.

Summary

Singapore provides an interesting case study context for this book because it is a city-state that espouses its representative democracy and has official United Nations' recognition as a parliamentary republic and yet, in practice, it has operated as a one-party state for nearly fifty years. That puts it in the unique position of having a well-developed language of 'citizenship' within which its event policy rationales, formations and implementations are framed but which also permits its leaders fairly free reign to shape strategy and policy. There are clear similarities with Dubai here. As argued in Chapter 10, whereas in the world's liberal democracies (e.g. the US, UK and Australia) policy rationales, formations and implementations can be labourious, subject to consultation, debate and consensus building and accountable to citizens, in Singapore (like Dubai) the processes are much more streamlined and driven by the singular interests of the all-powerful PAP. As in Dubai where the citizens are governed by monarchical rulers, for Singapore residents many of the citizen rights taken for granted in parliamentary democracies are essentially conceded in return for economic prosperity. In Singapore, the PAP's particular brand of economic, political and social planning has generated prosperity, albeit with curtailed freedoms in the civic realm. In Singapore, the state actively intervenes to create the conditions for the private sector to flourish, including in the terrain of events (sporting and cultural) and festivals. This state intervention has been, until recently, more important in defining the events product of Singapore than that of corporate sponsorship. However, there are signs that, bearing in mind the dual factors of economic recession and intensified global competition for events, Singapore's leaders are loosening their grip on centralised planning to facilitate greater corporate involvement in major events. The Singapore F1 Grand Prix provides an ideal example of this shift. Although subsidised heavily by the state apparatus, entry to the global corporate party that F1 represents was just as important for Singapore's visibility and reputation as a global player. It is clear from the examples provided in this chapter that citizen involvement, other than through populating the crowd, was minimal. Singapore does, however, have some impressive cultural festivals that are much more embedded in the neighbourhoods and ethnic groupings that make up this city-state, and these are also now increasingly promoted as part of the events and festivals product that Singapore possesses. In summation, then, Singapore can be placed somewhere between the liberal democracies of the US (Mardi Gras, New Orleans) and the UK (Glasgow 2014 Commonwealth Games) and the monarchical regime of Dubai. In event policy terms Singapore espouses a commitment to the concept of citizenship (translated through the National Day celebrations) and its state intervenes to secure planned externalities from its various events (e.g. subsidy, state-sponsored tourism agencies). However, in its authoritarian approach to the management of its population's civil society, Singapore's approach to event policy mirrors that of Dubai. It does not countenance dissent and uses its cultural events as a means to inculcate shared values that tie this relatively new nation together.

Critical review questions

- For what reasons can Singapore's approach to the governance of its festivals and events be considered similar to Dubai's?
- Identify four reasons why Singapore sought to attract the F1 Grand Prix.
- What dangers face the Singaporean authorities in pursuing an entrepreneurial event-led strategy?

Recommended reading

Foley, M., McGillivray, D. and McPherson, G. (2008) 'Establishing Singapore as the events and entertainment capital of Asia: strategic brand diversification', in Ali-Knight, J., Robertson, M., Fyall, A. and Ladkin, A. (eds) *International perspectives of festivals and events: paradigms of analysis*, London: Elsevier.

Foley, M., McPherson, G. and Matheson, C. (2007) 'Cultural identity and festivity: generating Singapore through citizenship and enterprise in events activity', in Aitchison, C. and Pritchard, A. (eds) *Festivals and events: culture and identity in leisure, sport and tourism*, LSA Publication No 94, Brighton.

Henderson, J.C., Foo, K., Lim, H. and Yip, S. (2010) 'Sports events and tourism: the Singapore Formula One Grand Prix', *International Journal of Event and Festival Management*, 1 (1): 60–73.

13 Conclusions

Introduction

This book was conceived to address a gap in the event management literature. In the introduction we argued that, while there were many texts addressing Stage 1 (Event Management) and some recent contributions to Stage 3 (Event Studies), Stage 2 (Event Policy and Strategy) was poorly catered for. We argued that this stage was concerned with the contextualisation of macro-level ideas, though considered through the lens of policy and strategy and evaluated in the context of the social, cultural and economic effects (or impacts) of events upon various stakeholders in a global setting. This text deliberately sought to be differentiated from existing texts by its specific focus on policy, its coherence (i.e. not an edited collection), its depth (i.e. not a 'how to do it' manual), its scope (i.e. by placing events in a global and local context beyond the confines of hospitality or leisure management) and its approach (i.e. by locating the phenomena of events and festivity within a wider theoretical and strategic framework). A series of guiding research questions were derived for this text, and this conclusion will commence with a reappraisal of how these were addressed. It will then conclude with an appraisal of the future policy directions and dimensions likely to guide the early part of the twenty-first century and the implications of these for policy makers, practitioners and graduates alike.

Addressing the research questions

What is the rationale for events and festivals being 'used' as a mechanism for the achievement of wider social outcomes, and how does this differ in different geographical territories?

Across a number of chapters it has been demonstrated that events and festivals are increasingly used for the achievement of planned externalities – outcomes that are often unrelated to the original meanings associated with events. It is now generally accepted that support (and consent) for events requires these outcomes to be made explicit. For example, in Chapter 2, we emphasised the generalised adoption of the language of regeneration as a rationale for bidding for and delivering events and the implication of this policy for the nature of events now part of the destination portfolio. Events can be changed, temporally and spatially, in the pursuit of economic, political and social outcomes, and this has become a global trend. In early understandings of the purpose of events, they were invariably 'unplanned', or at least they were not as clearly 'created' for a specific purpose (with the exception of the World Fairs and Expos from 1851 onwards) – to the point where they are now frequently planned by 'experts' with intended outcomes in mind. These outcomes (or new functions) are so powerful that they can alter the very fabric of the event as originally conceived. During the nineteenth century, many events were banished from the calendar in the name of 'civilisation' and new ones were 'invented' to fulfil a more meaningful social function and to civilise the masses. This practice is even more pronounced in the contemporary period as ritualistic practice is threatened by the logic of regeneration. In Chapter 10 we showed the extremes of event flexibility, with new events being created to 'fix' a 'new' destination (Dubai) in the minds of potential investors, residents and visitors. While it is more difficult to de-contextualise events from their original purpose in the liberal democracies of the West – because of the established tenets of democracy – we argue that there remains a trend towards an instrumentalist logic, which is relatively common as the global circuit of events gains a foothold.

Which ideologies and discourses underpin the rationale for, and subsequent formation of, policy with respect to events and festivals across alternative geographical territories?

In addressing the specifics of this research question, it is our contention that the neoliberalised order, with its associated urban entrepreneurial local state, is the dominant discourse, whether that be for the Olympic Games (see Sydney 2000 as an example) or for the ongoing sustainability of even the smallest events. In the early twenty-first century, neoliberalism is a powerful 'framework' structuring the parameters for the governance of urban development as it effectively defines the nature of appropriate policy choices, the extent of democratic participation (restricted) and the means of evaluating success. When thinking about the specific context of event policy, neoliberalism, as a modality of governance, provides the parameters for appropriate choices around what the function of events is in the early twenty-first century. While this book has drawn upon examples of event destinations where you might expect that the political and economic system would reject aspects of neoliberalism (e.g. China, Singapore and Dubai), the reality of our investigations is the remarkably similar discourses adopted across the globe. Clearly, within a structuring framework that naturalises market relations, events are deemed valuable only insofar as they contribute to economic restructuring or growth (the Singapore

F1 Grand Prix is a good example). Of course, this economic imperative is easily measured and it continues to dominate thinking around the purpose of events. What is also relatively consistent is that the institutional arrangements flowing from a neoliberal framework must also enable growth coalitions to form and public–private partnerships to flourish in the name of place making and promotion. Events are re-envisaged as boosterist strategies designed to assuage the problems associated with de-industrialisation, or with a lack of global visibility. In those nations with alternative governance systems in place – the Singapore and Dubai case study chapters represent these in this book – the means of achieving the outcomes desired are different but the underlying rationale for event policy remains very similar. The achievement of economic imperatives is the primary rationale for creating new events, bidding for peripatetic sporting and cultural events or growing existing events. And increasingly, the emerging BRIC nations (Brazil, Russia, India and China) and those in the Middle East (e.g. Qatar, Dubai, Bahrain) are succeeding over their Western counterparts in bidding for and winning events.

What role do events play in new forms of urban governance and inter-urban competition, and what effect does this have on local and central government strategies across the world?

There is little doubt that the intensification in the use of events as a key facet of the capital accumulation process is marked, and this affects the strategies of local and central state entities across the world. For example, throughout the book we have argued that local actors are largely peripheral to the power play and decision-making processes that legitimate event policy objectives. Events are now so closely aligned with neoliberal market logic that there appears to be only limited space for alternative discourses to find a place. Cities have certainly become sites of intense consumption across the globe. Previously reliant on an industrial economic base that required the exploitation of land and labour, cities now sell their softer, less tangible assets to the visitor, investor or potential resident. Cities have become 'destination brands' and identities are drawn up around 'places' representing saleable material and symbolic goods. Events and festivals bring these brands to life by animating static attractions. Local and central governments now create destination-marketing organisations to exploit the branding potential of the city, developing major event strategies that contribute to the aggregate brand narrative of an urban area. In order to remain competitive the local state is under pressure to purchase profile in the form of major events. But there are weaknesses to this approach as the creation and manufacture of saleable events with little connectedness to the host community can produce unequal distribution of beneficiaries in the consuming events city. Moreover, there are surely diminishing returns as more events (cities) compete for a finite population of event tourists. We envisage that cities will become more adept at repackaging their existing festivals and events to ensure that the host population and incoming visitors spend locally, contributing to economic additionality, but securing greater ROI in existing events will not, in the longer term, address the threat of intense global competition.

While we have suggested that events increasingly align with consumption logic (economic), it is important to acknowledge that they also act as a means of enhancing the social and cultural fabric of communities (social). Inevitably, in the liberal democracies of the West, investment in events must be accountable and transparent (although that might be increasingly tokenistic), and they also more frequently have to 'involve' citizens and other stakeholders (businesses) in decision-making and delivery. This is not necessarily the case elsewhere (e.g. Singapore) where the need for local legitimation is much less pronounced.

How are ideas of consumption, commerce and entrepreneurialism accommodated alongside notions of citizenship, community and culture with respect to the intention and outcomes of event policy?

As discussed above, the ideas of consumption, commerce and entrepreneurialism are now inseparable from a discussion of event policy, whatever the particular political system adopted by nations or cities across the world, from Melbourne to Munich, Qatar to Quebec. This is becoming the key influence upon event policy rationales in particular and, to an extent, on the sort of policy formations that are evident. However, just because economic narratives have taken on additional importance in post-industrial economies, that does not mean that citizenship, community and culture are invisible in event policy debates and discussions. It is a matter of degree – for the undemocratic nations of the world these concepts may be less important because of the absence of citizen rights (or at least a different social contract).

In the neoliberalised order there is a need to rework conceptions of citizenship, community and everyday life. As the dominant ideology, neoliberalism requires the reconceptualisation of the relationship between citizens and cities, between the central and local state and between events and the economy. The local political system facilitates (even subsidises) entrepreneurial activity in place of welfare and secures the consent of the electorate (legitimation) on the promise of progress and growth – based on the notion that benefits will 'trickle down' to the majority of citizens. This analysis suggests that market relations have been naturalised in local government as cities vie to attract the right sort of capital, people and images, yet in the process the private sector's needs are given precedence over other (often competing) claims upon public resources. This policy environment values interventions that incentivise incoming visitation over investment in the social welfare of the host population, making the ideas of citizenship and community mere afterthoughts to assuage fears over the overly 'hard' outcomes of neoliberalism.

Who gets to be counted as a stakeholder and what roles do stakeholders play in influencing policy decisions, and what power relations are in operation that act to include and exclude some interests over others?

It has been argued above that those actors counted as stakeholders are increasingly restricted to the likely beneficiaries of event policy formations and implementations. In the liberal democracies of the West, stakeholders are potentially more multiple, but their relative power may be constrained by the planned externalities being sought by the policy implementation. For example, in Chapters 5 and 6, it was argued that, as the neoliberalised order predominates in many parts of the world (whether the political system acknowledges this or not, e.g. China), the main beneficiaries of events are determined by the market, facilitated by the entrepreneurially focused local state. The language of economic regeneration and the market increasingly determine the shape of institutions, limiting the policy levers available to the local state and excluding some of the likely stakeholders for events. A good example of the mobilisation of state power to support free market activity is the development of public–private or quasi-autonomous organisations that can act relatively independently of local government to compete with other cities (inter-urban competition) for business in the realm of tourism and major events. In democratic and undemocratic nations alike, institutions are established to compete (the language of the market is evident here) for the privilege of hosting events – citizen support is required, albeit often instrumentally, to demonstrate 'public support', but the main audience being addressed is of investors, brand managers and the like. Informal networks of local business leaders and elected officials assemble to provide the catalyst for a series of policy interventions. It is argued that this approach overcomes the inertia inherent within the disjointed power relations of (democratically elected) local government, producing a level playing field on which cities can compete. It has been argued here that citizens of those cities that have followed a boosterist urban strategy suffer from the narrowly defined nature of the officially endorsed approach to urban development. Progressive ideas around citizen 'participation', 'ownership' or 'voice' are silenced as those who deploy power condition and constrain the strategic direction of urban policy.

However, the argument in this text is not simply that the neoliberalised order has succeeded without evidence of contestation or of resistance. On the contrary, across a number of chapters the argument has been made that the power of the existing order is fragile, at best, and an alternative mode of governance and thinking is possible and, perhaps, preferable. For example, in Chapter 5, the argument was posited that the language of regeneration, from which events are inseparable, could anaesthetise our critical understanding of the social polarisation wrought by these policies. If the involvement of non-business stakeholders in event policy remains 'tokenistic' and without meaningful legitimation, then the patience of other 'potential' stakeholders for their ROI from events and festivals may be stretched. Think of the growing expressions of discontent associated with the Olympic Games as an example. Here, a plethora of alternative stakeholders come together (many with little in common outside of their contempt for the 'corporate Olympics') to protest the unequal distribution of benefits arising from this event. Claims that major events can exacerbate the notion of the divided city of 'haves' and 'have-nots' persist. It is argued that cities are more inequitable – in terms of power, cultural and economic differences – than they have been previously. While the Olympics and other mega-events will continue apace whether subject to criticism or not, there is certainly a sense that sanctioning bodies are having to consider the views of the host population more seriously than they have previously when awarding the right to host their events. The social and cultural value of events and festivals as policy vehicles (Chapters 7 and 8) is also gaining in interest and influence. Historically, events played an important social role for communities, whether urban or rural – though the form of these celebrations was often less managed than is evident today. In this book it has been demonstrated that the value of events as a form of social release or social glue is being recognised by policy makers. While a critical perspective might associate events with social control (the invented traditions of the nineteenth century were often about this), there is a growing body of literature that suggests that events can make a contribution to dismantling power differentials between groups, increasing intergenerational and inter-faith dialogue and building social capital in the post-industrial city. The evidence for such lofty claims remains largely untested, but suffice it to say that debates over ownership, empowerment, equity, fair distribution of benefits and the social sustainability of events now frequently receive attention.

How do we know whether policy interventions in the realm of events are effective in achieving the desired outcomes?

In Chapters 3 and 4 a critique of the methods and measures used to assess the success or otherwise of event policy interventions was developed. Over recent years it has become clear that the monitoring and evaluation function is closely linked with policy development. The planned outcomes associated with sporting, cultural, corporate and other events are increasingly influenced by wider political aims, and the choice of what is evaluated and judgements on success or failure cannot be detached from the overarching political (and economic) environment of the time. In that sense, the role of monitoring and evaluation can be viewed as a means of legitimising event policy objectives. In Chapter 4, the work of Habermas was used to unmask the 'interests' at work in employing specific techniques to validate narrowly defined market-led outcomes accruable from an investment in events. Clearly events are no longer simply defensible on the basis of their intrinsic cultural value alone (especially if in receipt of public monies). Instead, they must be objectified, turned into quantifiable assets and measured according to the logic of advanced capitalist economic systems. As political actors (in coalition with private capital) set the agenda as to the policy objectives of the central or local state, their decisions have then to be legitimated by a system of appraisal that is often narrowly channelled to ensure that the desired outcomes are forthcoming. If evaluation is conceived of as a method of judging whether there is a rationale for policy interventions, and to monitor progress in achieving these, then the selection and use of particular evaluation techniques is an important battleground for the question of legitimating event policy. Principally, this is because the appropriateness of evaluation techniques (e.g. economic impact studies) can become self-fulfilling if they demonstrate the achievement of (set) objectives. It is certainly the case that the evaluation techniques employed in both public and private sector event contexts are now ever more connected to the managerialist language of KPIs. Here, policy objectives are broken down into a set of measurable indicators that are easily quantified and manipulated using statistical techniques. In the democratic nations of the world at least (legitimation is very different in the Middle East, for example), the important political (and economic) issue is whether public sector investment and support 'leverages' additional benefits and provides a healthy ROI for public and private stakeholders, or whether the beneficiaries are restricted to private capital and political elites – as some commentators have suggested.

While there has been a fairly significant degree of criticism directed towards the politics of evaluation in this book, there are signs of change evident in the thinking of policy makers and those undertaking the evaluation of events. For example, alternative concepts of value – the social, the cultural and the environmental – are now supplementing economic measurements. This does not mean that the economic rationale is now defunct. Instead, a wider understanding of social, cultural and environmental impacts is augmenting it and there is attention being paid to measuring the 'softer' outcomes of events. These alternative measurements of value will continue to develop as long as major event owners request a wider evaluation of impact in their bidding processes and post-event analysis. This will also bring non-democratic nations into the realm of accountability and transparency both within their own borders and to an external audience.

Event policy directions

In Part 3 of this text, the focus of attention shifted to consideration of real-life policy implementations in four destinations worldwide – Glasgow, Dubai, New Orleans and Singapore. These four destinations were chosen deliberately as they represent a useful typology for thinking about the status of event policy as we enter the second decade of the twenty-first century. Across the book we have proposed that state intervention in events takes a number of forms, ranging from almost no involvement to state-created and implemented celebrations. On another level, this text has also illustrated that events can be described, variously, as either 'open' and focused on 'citizens' (Mardi Gras,

New Orleans would be a good example) or 'planned' and 'governed' (Glasgow's Commonwealth Games is an exemplar). Taking the case study exemplars developed in Part 3 of the book, Figure 13.1 illustrates the policy positioning of the four destinations (and key events) at present.

However, while this illustration may reflect the current situation in these destinations, it does not provide enough detail on the *direction* of policy in these destinations and in others like them. Figure 13.2 provides an illustration of the policy *pull* towards much more planned and governed events that seek to achieve planned externalities (e.g. economic impact, place promotion, social regeneration, national identity). In order to minimise the risk of failing to secure these externalities, the policy pull is towards more explicit (and interventionist) governance of the events, although these arrangements involve a plethora of state, private and third sector stakeholders.

While Figure 13.2 illustrates a policy pull towards many events being more planned and governed, there is a further level of complexity to the policy

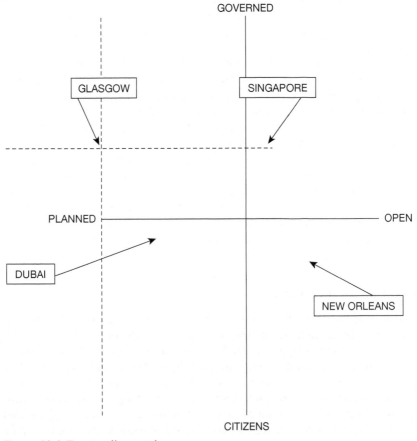

Figure 13.1 Event policy typology.

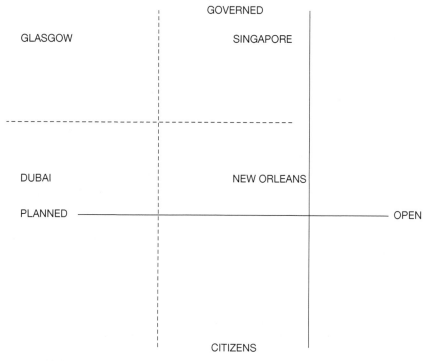

GOVERNED

GLASGOW   SINGAPORE

DUBAI   NEW ORLEANS

PLANNED ───────────────┼───────────────────── OPEN

CITIZENS

Figure 13.2 Event policy 'pull'.

equation that needs explanation. Whereas the actions of state-sponsored or public–private growth coalitions are to plan and govern key events to ensure positive externalities are secured, the means of achieving these outcomes are, at times, contradictory to the self-same governance and planning tendencies. As events become overly planned and governed, the attractiveness of greater openness and citizen involvement increases. Events such as Mardi Gras must be promoted as epitomising freedom, escape and an anything-goes attitude, while more subtly the authorities in the city attempt to minimise negative coverage of the less salubrious elements of this traditional festivity in the name of economic ROI. Similarly, as major sporting events are subject to increasing levels of criticism over their detachment from the interests of host residents and inequity in the distribution of benefits, organisers are responding with enhanced forms of citizen engagement and greater opportunities for open and collective celebration (e.g. fan festivals). In policy terms, there is a difficult balance to be struck between justifying state intervention in events on the basis of greater planning and tighter governance and maintaining the attractiveness of the contemporary 'circuses' to consumers with unique and accessible celebrations. For those involved in making these difficult policy choices, developing a balanced portfolio of events including those at different ends of the freedom continuum is one strategic solution – and one that is increasingly popular. So, in Barcelona, the La Merce Festival is organic, free flowing, accessible and community-oriented, making it an ideal vehicle for promoting the city as a vibrant culturally rich destination. Selecting which events to support, whether financially or in-kind, depends on the policy makers' understanding of alternative event *dimensions* and what each means in terms of audience, support and outcomes. The final part of this conclusion will address this quandary.

Event policy dimensions

To conclude the book, it is necessary to provide a final critique of existing policy perspectives and then draw together the main theoretical and policy issues into an agenda for professional, institutional and organisational reflection among those studying, working and researching in the sector. To do this, we will first provide a description of the prevailing event dimensions of our time and then propose what these will mean for the stakeholders identified above. First, to the event dimensions.

To summarise the three dimensions depicted in Table 13.1, events can be delineated by those that *happen to happen* (first dimension) – events that appear unplanned although are often intentional (take Mardi Gras, New Orleans as an example); those that are *made to happen* (second dimension) – conceived, planned and managed to achieve clearly identified goals (take major sports events as exemplars); and those that *happen as a result of other happenings* (third dimension), such as resistance to-made-to-happen events.

The three dimensions do not operate in isolation from each other; on the contrary, the second dimension events could not exist without their first dimension counterparts, nor would you have resistance events without mainstream events to protest about. Moreover, while it is tempting to imply 'progress' or 'improvement' as each of the dimensions develops, this is not the intention of the framework. For those organising the second dimension events (e.g. Local Organising Committees) there is certainly a sense that they are making progress and improvement on the more organic or traditional events found in the first dimension (including their global responsibilities for the environment and human rights), but several chapters in this book have sought to critique whether overly planned and governed events are as effective as proposed. Similarly, those behind their conception and delivery will perceive many of the third dimension events as progressive and an improvement on the overly instrumental events found in the second dimension. For example, those groups critical of the way in which the Olympic Games has become entwined with the interests of big business and political elites hold a number of resistance events each year. While it remains unlikely that these events will become second dimension events (or would want to), another feature of the event dimensions in Table 13.1 is that there can be movement between them – especially from first to second and, perhaps, from third to first. For example,

Table 13.1 Event dimensions

Dimension	Characteristics	Examples
First	*Apparently uncontrolled but intended occurrences* Control more apparent than 'real'? Raises issues of authenticity, expression and heritage Consistent with desires to seek 'freedom' Market segmentation Managed risk a recent development Some evidence of planning, though emphasis on embodied experience Time bound/time imprisoned Perpetual and continuing Popular Audience and participants delineated but close proximity	The Ba' Game Local gala days Camino de Santiago de Compostela Pilgrimage Palio di Siena Pamplona Bull Run La Merce Festival Up Helly Aa
Second	*Mobilisation of prevailing orthodoxies* Reflect the values of their time and place of origin Issues of identity – reinforcing and challenging State involvement/intervention key Media involvement/management Market segmentation and brand building Managed risk central to appeal Sophisticated planning – spatial, social, economic Rational approach to legacy Competition to 'host'/between venues Populist Audience and participants/exhibits spatially distant	The Great Exhibition The Olympic Games The Commonwealth Games Edinburgh International Festival Festival of Britain F1 Grand Prix Circuit Soccer World Cup Celtic Connections Glastonbury Festival The Asian Games
Third	*Eventualities, unintended 'policy'* The 'post'-event Conceived and constructed around instrumental market possibilities Driven by lifestyles, elites, 'neo tribes' Increasingly 'virtual' Perceived as central to success/identity/visibility of a community Exclusive Risk apparent, if not 'real' Audience self-aware as participants within the spectacle State-regulation	Hogmanay events Burning Man Rave events, resistance events (e.g. G20) 'Orange', 'Apple'-owned events 01SJ Biennial, San Jose

as discussed in Parts 1 and 2 of the text, events whose origins were religious or tied to a form of industry are increasingly de-contextualised and de-territorialised in order to contribute to contemporary externalities (e.g. regeneration). Good examples of events that face pressure to move from the first to the second dimension (or at least towards this) are the Palio, Siena and the Pamplona Bull Run. While both events are attractive because of the opportunity to seek freedom and authenticity, they are also time-bound and time-imprisoned, popular, perpetual and continuing and have their audience and participants delineated but in close proximity. They are increasingly managed (in terms of risk, brand activation and media promotion) and the distance between audience and participants is widening. Like the second dimension examples, these events are being *made to happen* in the name of instrumental means–end, 'global' outcomes, when their original purpose was intentionally symbolic and 'local'.

Another important trend to consider is towards events conceived and constructed around instrumental market possibilities that take the second dimension to another level. Since the 1984 Los Angeles Olympics, major sponsors have helped revitalise the Olympic Games and other major sporting events. Corporate sponsorship is now big business for all major sporting (and some cultural) events. However, some corporations view significant investment in sport or cultural events as too risky for their carefully constructed brand narratives and, instead, create their own events as a platform for the achievement of their goals. Here, carefully managed events operate as brand vehicles for their creators, eliminating the unknown pitfalls associated with major sports events (e.g. terrorism or bad publicity). These events can be described as those that *happen as a result of other happenings* because their creation is a response to concerns over the effectiveness of traditional event sponsorship approaches. The UK supermarket chain Morrisons has, for example, threatened to sue FIFA over the so-called failure to adhere to its own bidding guidelines in awarding the 2018 and 2022 World Cup Finals to Russia and Qatar, respectively. The company, which invested £1 million into the England bid for the 2018 event, argue that it was an unfair process because FIFA was clearly determined to award the event to 'new lands' no matter how impressive the technical bid of competing nations was. This sort of conflict will certainly alter the relationship that major sponsors have to major sport event bids and draws further attention to the politics inherent within the global events circuit.

Implications for the events profession

There is little doubt that the field of second dimension events has fuelled the exponential growth of event management as a field of study over the last two decades. This is mainly because these events are *made to happen* and, by definition, need to be professionally managed to secure the planned externalities (economic, political, social, cultural and environmental) associated with them. However, while the implications flowing from second dimension events are significant for policy makers, practitioners and those studying in the events field, the first and third dimension events also generate opportunities and threats that the field needs to be aware of and respond to.

First, those events that reside in the first dimension (we might associate these with the more 'open' and 'citizen-focused' events depicted in Figures 13.1 and 13.2) often work to sustain communities in some form or other – whether a community of interest, e.g. the Camino de Santiago de Compostela Pilgrimage, or a geographical community, e.g. the Ba' Game in Orkney, Scotland. These events are built on localised connections and are, therefore, invaluable to the economic and social circumstances of their locale. They are often sustained by a relatively small number of committed enthusiasts, and to ensure their ongoing viability these events need the support of expertise from the local state, educational establishments and local events practitioners. Of course, as some of these first dimension events begin to take on the characteristics of the second dimension, the need to engage with the fields of logistics, health and safety, marketing, PR and communication intensifies. Policy makers tend to be involved in supporting or enabling these events to be self-sustaining so that they generate a net benefit to the local economy rather than a net cost. As social and community assets, the major challenge facing these first dimension events is that, because they happen to happen, there is a danger that they are not subject to investment in the way that second dimension events are – yet their loss would threaten the social and cultural fabric of countless locales around the world. A good example of events that occupy a position between the first and second dimensions is the US state fair. These are enormous events that run for weeks and contribute significantly to the social and cultural fabric of the community (first dimension) as well as offering a touristic dimension. Yet there is also a substantial level of state support for these events in terms of planning and health and safety that takes them into the second dimension.

With respect to the second dimension (what we also view as the planned and governed events depicted in Figures 13.1 and 13.2), there is clearly a policy pull towards these events. As discussed at length in Parts 1 and 2 of this book, the growth of urban entrepreneurial governance arrangements across much of the globe has intensified the need for events and festivals to be utilised as attractive vehicles for the achievement of positive economic, social and cultural outcomes. Bidding for and delivering peripatetic sporting and cultural events now requires a professional cadre of policy makers, practitioners and graduates, with the necessary range of expertise to ensure that the ambitious policy outcomes can be achieved. The development of a discrete 'events profession' has been promoted, practitioners armed with a set of creative and managerial skills alongside a knowledge base to utilise in the pursuit of socially valued impacts. As discussed in earlier chapters, however, the absence of a set of agreed-upon professional standards, barriers to entry into the field and an explicit code of practice act as impediments to the creation of a recognised professional domain – although the growing interest in the academy in researching mega-events and their impacts alongside the effectiveness of rural and urban policies and strategies for events does indicate an opportunity for events and festivals to be established fully as an area of both government interest and academic endeavour. There are, however, a few notes of caution that should accompany the second dimension of events. First, these events cannot be viewed as the panacea for economic, social and cultural policy as there are too many examples of overestimated benefits and underestimated costs to be complacent of their (positive) outcomes. Second, many of the organisers of second dimension events have allowed their events to move too far away from the interests of their audiences (read 'citizens') and their ongoing sustainability is compromised in the process. Third, policy makers need to make the case for second dimension events more effectively to ensure their legitimacy is maintained and enhanced. Making the case should also involve greater attention to the meaningful involvement of a wider group of stakeholders in making these events a success – even if this leads to less economically successful outcomes. While state institutions and investment continue to support major sporting and cultural events, citizens have the right to expect greater standards of accountability and transparency – at least in those parts of the world where the social contract between the state and citizens offers rights in return for consent to act on their behalf.

Perhaps most interestingly of all are the implications of the third dimension of events for policy makers, practitioners and educational establishments. While the most significant issues facing second dimension events surround the professed economic, social and cultural benefits, for third dimension events, the challenges are very different. For those resistant events that were born as a result of the perceived inequities of second dimension events, there is a need to hold politicians and growth coalitions to account through raising awareness of alternative discourses and narratives about the potential contribution of events to economic, social and cultural life. As a specific example, there is a need for the academy to help develop graduates with the critical insights to recognise the potential for legitimacy deficit in major sporting and cultural events and to arm them with the tools to mobilise citizen and community action (e.g. around the citizen media). An example of this approach in practice is the emergence of a critical media movement around the Olympic Games (#media2012 is a Twitter hashtag for searching on this topic) that seeks to develop citizen media skills to ensure more open, egalitarian and accessible media coverage of the London 2012 Olympics. In addition, in order for third dimension events to offer alternative readings of the world around us, there is a need for the academy and policy makers to facilitate the creative development of new events that might better contribute to the outcomes being sought by policy makers and practitioners alike.

Not all third dimension events are concerned with reluctance, refusal or resistance. These 'post'-events may be more driven by lifestyles, neo-tribes and youth cultures and may be as likely to occur virtually, at least in part, than in the places and spaces of major urban areas. These events pose even greater challenges for policy makers, practitioners and the academy because of their inseparability from (often) notions of identity (formation, reinforcement and reproduction). They are invariably successful at engaging their communities, though the exclusivity and need to be 'in the know' makes their utilisation as policy vehicle much more difficult and, some would say, undesirable. Yet there are lessons to be learned from these events in terms of their success at engaging audiences and communicating their messages effectively. Adherents would shun the possibility of being considered as a second dimension event, but the creativity of their participants and success of ensuring close proximity between participants and audience (in fact these may not even exist as separate categories) is the envy of many other events.

Concluding comments

When we started this book our intention was to explore how and why governments were utilising events in one of two ways – events *as* policy and event policy. Two years ago, we felt that separating events into these categories was a useful explanatory device. Now, after engaging critically with government policy and strategy documents, in-depth case studies and the prevailing academic literature, we can conclude that the event policy world is too complex to be easily reduced to two principal classifications. Rather, the event policy field, globally, is multi-faceted and tied to political, economic, social and cultural agendas in a way that few other policy environments can equal. We have illustrated the principal policy dimensions and directions as we move into a period of intense global competition to attract, deliver and secure positive impacts from events. At the heart of our arguments about the events sphere, globally, has been a call to assign greater value to the underlying social and cultural meanings attributable to events as a means of challenging the supremacy of the economic hegemony.

We have also presented a 'policy pull' event typology that forecasts the direction of travel for event policy in the first half of the twenty-first century. Events are now, undoubtedly, a public policy tool and not just in the liberal democracies of the West. Events (especially peripatetic sporting ones) offer access to the planned externalities that neoliberal policy makers are seeking. The 'policy pull' typology shows that available policy levers are being used in a substantive form to govern and plan events (and their outcomes) in a manner unheard of even a decade ago. Events (the circuses) represent a good news story in times of political, economic and social uncertainty, but to undermine the open, citizen-involved and fluid function of festivity threatens the very basis of the policy outcomes being sought. Can sporting and cultural events be revaluated as a force for good in the world whereby event owners contribute positively to a growing global consciousness, or will they remain tarnished by the association with commodification, consumption and corruption? It is unlikely that the answer(s) to this conundrum will be found in a single publication. This book should only be the starting point on a journey towards creating a more critical engagement on the future of events as a credible policy vehicle – a debate that needs to take place in the academy, in the industry and with event participants.

Bibliography

Adorno, T. (2001) (J.M. Bernstein, ed.) *The culture industry: selected essays on mass culture*, London: Routledge.

Ali, S. (2005) 'The UAE is the sporting capital of the Middle East', *Gulf News*, 30 November 2005.

Ali-Knight, J. and Robertson, M. (2004) 'Introduction to arts, culture and leisure', in Yeoman, I., Robertson, M., Ali-Knight, J., Drummond, S. and McMahon-Beattie, U. (eds) *Festivals and events management: an international arts and culture perspective*, Oxford: Elsevier.

Ali-Knight, J., Robertson, M., Fyall, A. and Larkin, A. (2008) *International perspectives of festivals and events: paradigms of analysis*, Oxford: Elsevier.

Amara, M. (2005) '2006 Qatar Asian Games: a 'modernisation' project from above?' *Sport in Society*, 8 (3): 493–514.

—— (2008) 'The Muslim world in the global sporting arena', *Brown Journal of World Affairs*, 14: 67–76.

Amin, A. and Graham, S. (1997) 'The ordinary city', *Transactions of the Institute of British Geographers*, 22 (4): 411–429.

Arai, S. and Pedlar, A. (2003) 'Moving beyond individualism in leisure theory: a critical analysis of concepts of community and social engagement', *Leisure Studies*, 22: 185–202.

Auckland Plus (2008) *Positioning Auckland as a major event destination*, a business unit of Auckland Regional Council, New Zealand, May.

Auge, M. (1995) *Non-places: introductions to an anthropology of supermodernity*, London: Verso.

Baade, R., Baumann, R. and Matheson, V. (2008) 'Selling the game: estimating the economic impact of professional sports through taxable sales', *Southern Economic Journal*, 74 (3): 794–810.

Baade, R. and Matheson, V. (2004) 'The quest for the cup: assessing the economic impact of the World Cup', *Regional Studies*, 38 (4): 343–354.

Bagaeen, S. (2007) 'Brand Dubai: the instant city or the instantly recognizable city?', *International Planning Studies*, 12 (2): 173–197.

Bailey, P. (1979) *Leisure and class in Victorian England*, London: Routledge.

Balakrishnan, M.S. (2008) 'Dubai – a star in the East: a case study in strategic destination branding', *Journal of Place Management and Development*, 1 (1): 62–91.

Barclay, S. (2001) *Sport in Dubai: creating a brand identity in the global sports network*, MPhil Dissertation, Glasgow Caledonian University.

Bauman, Z. (1994) 'Desert spectacular', in Tester, K. (ed.) *The flaneur*, London: Routledge.

Berridge, G. (2006) *Event design*, Oxford: Butterworth Heinemann.

Berruti, G. (2008) 'Urban public spaces in the Augmented City', in Eckardt, F. (ed.) *Media and urban space: understanding, investigating and approaching mediacity*, Leipzig: Frank & Timme.

Bianchini, F. and Schwengel, H. (1991) 'Re-imagining the city', in Corner, J. and Harvey, S. (eds) *Enterprise and heritage: crosscurrents of national culture*, London: Routledge.

Black, D. (2007) 'The symbolic politics of sport mega-events: 2010, in comparative perspective', *Politikon*, 34 (3): 261–276.

Bid Brochure presented in Melbourne 2006, available at: www.glasgow2014.com/NR/rdonlyres/F40B0597-EBD9-4703-8CE0-3563D018639C/28041/A352602014 Brochure.pdf (accessed 23 June 2010).

Blake, A. (2005) *The economic impact of the London 2012 Olympics*, Christel Dehaan Tourism and Travel Institute, Nottingham University Business School.

Bob, U. and Swart, K. (2009) 'Resident perceptions of the 2010 FIFA Soccer World Cup stadia development in Cape Town', *Urban Forum*, 20 (1): 47–59.

Boissevain, J. (ed.) (1996) *Coping with tourists: European reactions to mass tourism*. Oxford: Berghahn Books.

Bourdieu, P. (1983) 'The forms of capital', trans. R. Nice, in Kreckel, R. (ed.) *Ungleichheiten (Soziale Welt, Sonderheft 2)*, Goettingen: Otto Schartz & Co.

—— (1984) *Distinction: a social critique of the judgement of taste*. London: Routledge.

—— (1985) 'The social space and the genesis of groups', *Social Science Information*, 24 (2): 195–220.

—— (1990) *The logic of practice*, Stanford, CA: Stanford University Press.

—— (1992) *Outline of a theory of practice*, Cambridge: Cambridge University Press.

Bowdin, G., Allen, J., O'Toole, W., Harris, R. and McDonnell, I. (1999) *Events management* (1st edn), Oxford: Elsevier.

Boyer, C.M. (2005) *CyberCities: visual perception in the age of electronic communication*, New York: Princeton Architectural Press.

Brenner, N. and Theodore, N. (2005) 'Neoliberalism and the urban condition', *City*, 9 (1): 101–107.

Brighenti, O., Clivaz, C., Deletroz, N., Favre, N. and Chappelat, J. (eds) (2005) *From initial idea to success: a guide to bidding for sports events for politicians and administrators*, Sentelaps Consortium, Chavannes-Lausanne, Switzerland.

Brown, A. and Massey, J. (2001) *The sports development impact of the Manchester 2002 Commonwealth Games: initial baseline research*, UK Sport.

Bryman, A. (2004) *The Disneyization of society*, London: Sage.

Bull, C. (2003) *An introduction to leisure studies*, Harlow: Pearson Education.

Bull, C. and Weed, M. (1999) 'Niche markets and small island tourism: the development of sports tourism in Malta', *Managing Leisure*, 4: 142–155.

Bunce, D. (1995) *Major sports events and local authorities: who benefits?* MSc Strategy and Resource Management Dissertation, University of Northumbria.

Burbank, M.J., Andranovich, G. and Heying, C.H. (2002) 'Mega-events, urban development and public policy', *Review of Policy Research*, 19 (3): 179–202.

Burnham, L.F. and Durland, S. (2007) *Help wanted! Communities reach out*, CAN Publication, available: at www.communityarts.net/readingroom/archivefiles/2007/02help_wanted_com.php (accessed 21 February 2007).

Burr, A. (2006) 'The "freedom of the slaves to walk the streets": celebration, spontaneity and revelry versus logistics at the Notting Hill Carnival', in Picard, M. and Robinson, M. (eds) *Festivals, tourism and social change: remaking worlds*, Clevedon: Channel View Publications.

Caillois, R. (2001) *Man and the sacred*. Urbana: University of Illinois Press.

Cambridge Policy Consultants (2003) *Commonwealth Games 2002: an independent cost and benefit analysis*, Revised Executive Summary.

Campbell, C. (1987) *The romantic ethic and the spirit of modern consumerism*, Oxford: Basil Blackwell.

Candidate City File Summary Document, available at: www.thecgf.com/media/games/2014/G2014_Summary.pdf (accessed 8 September 2007).

Candidate City Operational Review, available at: www.glasgow2014.com/NR/rdonlyres/53D29C88-DBC8-4807-96D2-AC8B76F3A972/0/FINALG2014_Operational_Review.pdf (accessed 30 June 2007).

Carlsen, J. (2004) 'The economics and evaluation of festivals and events', in Yeoman, I., Robertson, M., Ali-Knight, J., Drummond, S. and McMahon-Beattie, U. (eds) *Festivals and events management: an international arts and culture perspective*, Oxford: Elsevier.

Carlsen, J., Getz, D. and Soutar, G. (2000) 'Event evaluation research', *Event Management*, 6 (4): 247–257.

Carlsen, J. and Taylor, A. (2003) 'Mega events and urban renewal: the case of the Manchester 2002 Commonwealth Games', *Event Management*, 8 (1): 15–22.

Casey, D. 'The impact of mega-events', Presentation at Glasgow Caledonian University Masterclass, April 2008.

Chalip, L. (2006) 'Towards social leverage of sport events', *Journal of Sport and Tourism*, 11 (2): 109–127.

Chalip, L. and Costa, C.A. (2005) 'Sport event tourism and the destination brand: towards a general theory', *Sport in Society*, 8 (2): 218–237.

Chang, T.C. and Huang, S. (2005) 'Recreating place, replacing memory: creative destruction at the Singapore River', *Asia Pacific Viewpoint*, 46 (3): 267–280.

Clark, G. (2008) *Local development benefits from staging global events*, OECD.

Coalter, F. (1990) 'Analysing leisure policy', in Henry, I.P. (ed.) *Management and planning in the leisure industries*, Basingstoke: Macmillan.

Cohen, S. and Taylor, L. (1976) *Escape attempts: the theory and practice of resistance to everyday life*, London: Routledge.

Coleman, J. (1988) 'Social capital in the creation of human capital', *American Journal of Sociology*, 94, Supplement S95–S120.

Connell, J. and Page, J.S. (2005) 'Evaluating the economic and spatial effects of an event: the case of the World Medical and Health Games', *Tourism Geographies*, 7 (1): 63–85.

Cornelissen, S. (2004) 'Sport mega-events in Africa: processes, impacts and prospects', *Tourism and Hospitality Policy and Development*, 1 (1): 39–55.

Crespi-Vallbona, M. and Richards, G. (2007) 'The meaning of cultural festivals', *International Journal of Cultural Policy*, 13 (1): 103–122.

Crompton, J.L. (1995) 'Economic impact analysis of sports facilities and events: eleven sources of misapplication', *Journal of Sport Management*, 9: 14–35.

—— (2001) 'Public subsidies to professional team sport facilities in the USA', in Gratton, C. and Henry, I.P. (eds) *Sport in the city: the role of sport in economic and social regeneration*, London: Routledge.

Crompton, J.L. and McKay, S. (1994) 'Measuring the economic impact of festivals and events: some myths, misapplications and ethical dilemmas', *Festival Management and Event Tourism*, 2 (1): 33–43.

Crossley, N. (2003) 'Even newer social movements? Anti-corporate protests, capitalist crises and the remoralization of society', *Organization*, 10 (2): 287–305.

Cunningham, H. (1980) *Leisure in the industrial revolution*, London: Croom Helm.

Cutler, M. (2008) 'Taking on the tiger', *SportBusiness International*, 4: 15.

Dandaneau, S.P. (2008) 'Critical theory, legitimation crisis and the deindustrialization of Flint, Michigan', in Kivisto, P. (ed.) *Illuminating social life: classical and contemporary theory revisited* (4th edn), Thousand Oaks, CA: Pine Forge.

Daniels, M.J., Backman, K.F. and Backman, S.J. (2003) 'Supplementing event economic impact results with perspectives from host community business and opinion leaders', *Event Management*, 6 (3): 175–189.

Debord, G. (1973) *The society of the spectacle*, New York: Zone Books.

De Bres, K. and Davis, J. (2001) 'Celebrating group and place identity: a case study of a new regional festival', *Tourism Geographies*, 3 (3): 326–337.

De Certeau, M. (1988) *The practice of everyday life*, trans. S. Rendall, New York: University of New York Press.

Derrett, R. (2003) 'Making sense of how festivals demonstrate a community's sense of place', *Event Management*, 8: 49–58.

Dimanche, F. (1996) 'Special events legacy: The 1984 Louisiana World Fair in New Orleans', *Festival Management & Event Tourism*, 4 (1): 49–54.

Du Gay, P. and Pryke, M. (2000) *Cultural economy: cultural analysis and commercial life*, London: Sage.

Durkheim, E. (1912) *The elementary forms of religious life*, trans. K.E. Fields, New York: Free Press, 1995.

Edensor, T. (1998) 'The culture of the Indian street', in Fyfe, N. (ed.) *Images of the street: planning, identity and control in public space*, London: Routledge.

Elkington, J. (1998) *Cannibals with forks: the triple bottom line of the 21st century business*, Stony Creek, CT: New Society Publishers.

Elsheshtawy, Y. (2004) 'Redrawing boundaries: Dubai, an emerging global city', in Elsheshtawy, E. (ed.) *Planning Middle Eastern cities: an urban kaleidoscope in a globalizing world*, London: Routledge.

Emery, P.R. (2002) 'Bidding to host a major sports event: the local organising committee perspective', *The International Journal of Public Sector Management*, 15 (4/5): 316–335.

Emirates Airline (2005) *Dubai Rugby Sevens official programme*, Dubai, Emirates Airline.

Evans, G. (2001) *Cultural planning: an urban renaissance*, London: Routledge.

Flinn, J. and McPherson, G. (2007) 'Culture matters? the role of art and culture in the development of social capital', in Collins, M., Holmes, K. and Slater, A. (eds) *Sport, leisure, culture and social capital: discourse and practice*, Eastbourne: Leisure Studies Association.

Flyvbjerg, B. (2005) 'Design by deception: the politics of megaproject approval', *Harvard Design Magazine*, Spring/Summer: 50–59.

Foley, M. and McPherson, G. (2007) 'Glasgow's Winter Festival: can cultural leadership serve the common good?', *Managing Leisure*, 12 (2–3): 143–156.

Foley, M., McPherson, G. and Matheson, C. (2006) Glocalisation and Singaporean festivals, *International Journal of Event Management Research*, 1 (2): 1–16.

Foley, M., McPherson, G. and Matheson, C. (2007) 'Cultural identity and festivity: generating Singapore through citizenship and enterprise in events activity', in Aitchison, C. and Pritchard, A. (eds) *Festivals and events: culture and identity in leisure, sport and tourism*, LSA Publication No 94, Brighton.

Foley, M., McGillivray, D. and McPherson, G. (2008) 'Establishing Singapore as the events and entertainment capital of Asia: strategic brand diversification', in Ali-Knight, J., Robertson, M., Fyall, A. and Ladkin, A. (eds) *International perspectives of festivals and events: paradigms of analysis*, London: Elsevier.

Foley, M., McGillivray, D. and McPherson, G. (2009) 'Policy, politics and events: a match made in heaven?', in Musgrave, J. and Raj, R. (eds) *Event management and sustainability*, London: CABI.

Fredline, E. and Faulkner, B. (2002) 'Variations in residents' reactions to major motorsport events: why residents perceive the impacts of events differently', *Event Management*, 7: 115–125.

Frew, M. and McGillivray, D. (2008) 'Exploring hyper-experiences: performing the fan at Germany 2006', *Journal of Sport Tourism*, 13 (3): 181–198.

Frost, W., Wheeler, F. and Harvey, M. (2008) 'Commemorative events: sacrifice, identity and dissonance', in Ali-Knight, J., Robertson, M., Fyall, A. and Ladkin, A. (eds) *International perspectives of festivals and events: paradigms of analysis*, Oxford: Butterworth Heinemann.

Furedi, F. (2006) *Culture of fear revisited: risk-taking and the morality of low expectation*, London: Continuum.

Gabr, H.S. (2004) 'The Dubai Shopping Festival as a catalyst for tourist development and urban transformation', in Robinson, M. (ed.) (2004) *Festivals and tourism marketing and management evaluation*, London: Business Education Publishers.

Garcia, B. (2004) 'Urban regeneration, arts programming and major events', *International Journal of Cultural Policy*, 10 (1): 103–118.

—— (2007) 'Can policy be artist-led? Perspectives from a policy analyst/researcher', Know your place seminar series, Midwest, Birmingham (7 March 2007).

Garcia, B. and Miah, A. (2007) 'Ever decreasing circles? The profile of culture at the Olympics', *Culture @ the Olympics: issues, trends and perspectives*, 9 (2): 10–13.

GCMB (2007) 'Glasgow's Tourism Strategy to 2016', Glasgow City Marketing Bureau.

Geertz, C. (1957) 'Ethos, world-view and the analysis of sacred symbols', *The Antioch Review*, 17 (4): 421–437.

Getz, D. (1997) *Event management and event tourism* (1st edn), New York: Cognizant Commnications Corp.

—— (2007) *Event studies: theory, research and policy for planned events*, Oxford: Elsevier.

Ghilardi, L. (2001) 'Cultural planning and cultural diversity', in Bennett, T. (ed.) *Differing diversities: cultural policy and cultural diversity*, Council of Europe Publications.

Gibson, L. and Stevenson, D. (2004) 'Urban space and the uses of culture', *International Journal of Cultural Policy*, 10 (1): 1–4.

Gill, J. (1997) *Lords of misrule: Mardi Gras and the politics of race in New Orleans*, Jackson: University Press of Mississippi.

Gilmore, D.D. (1998) *Carnival and culture*, London: Yale University Press.

Gilmore, J.H. and Pine, J.P. (1999) 'Customer experience places: the new offering frontier', *Strategy and Leadership*, 30 (1): 4–11.

Glasgow 2014, films about Glasgow's bid, available at: www.glasgow2014.com/The
Bid/MediaArchive/DVDs/ (accessed 30 September 2010).

Glasgow City Council (2006) 'Glasgow's cultural strategy: Glasgow, the place, the
people, the potential – be part of it', Glasgow City Council, March.

Gleick, J. (1999) *Faster: the acceleration of just about everything*, New York:
Pantheon.

Goetzmann, W.N. (2005) *Dubailand*, New Haven, CT: Yale School of Management.

Gold, J.R. and Gold, M.M. (2005) *Cities of culture: staging international festivals
and the urban agenda 1851–2000*, Aldershot: Ashgate.

—— (2008) 'Olympic cities: regeneration, city rebranding and changing urban
agendas', *Geography Compass*, 2 (1): 300–318.

Goldblatt, J. (2004) *Special events: events leadership for a new world*. New York:
Wiley.

Goodwin, J. (2003) *Price of honor: Muslim women lift the veil of silence on the Islamic
world*, New York: Plume.

Gorman, E. (2009) 'Virgin could buy Formula One team', TimesOnline, available at:
www.timesonline.co.uk/tol/sport/formula_1/article5762402.ece (accessed 1 August
2009).

Gotham, K.F. (2002) 'Marketing Mardi Gras: commodification, spectacle and the
political economy of tourism in New Orleans', *Urban Studies*, 39 (10): 1735–1756.

—— (2005a) 'Tourism gentrification: the case of New Orleans' Vieux Carre (French
Quarter)', *Urban Studies*, 42 (7): 1099–1121.

—— (2005b) 'Tourism from above and below: globalisation, localisation and New
Orleans's Mardi Gras', *International Journal of Urban and Regional Research*,
29 (2): 309–326.

—— (2005c) 'Theorizing urban spectacles', *City*, 9 (2): 225–246.

Gould, H. (2001) 'Culture and social capital', in Matarasso, F. (ed.) *Recognising
culture: a series of briefing papers on culture and development*, Stroud: Comedia
in partnership with the Department of Canadian Heritage and UNESCO.

Graham, S., Goldblatt, J. and Delpy, L. (1995) *The ultimate guide to sport event
management and marketing*, Chicago, IL: Irwin.

Gratton, C., Shibli, S. and Coleman, S. (2006) 'The economic impact of major sports
events: a review of ten events in the UK', *Sociological Review*, 54 (2): 41–58.

Gray, C. (2007) 'Commodification and instrumentality in cultural policy', *International
Journal of Cultural Policy*, 13 (2): 203–215.

Guardian Sport Blog (2008) 'Gripping and wildly unpredictable, Singapore shines in
the lights', available at: http://guardian.co.uk/sport/blog/2008/sep/29/formulaone.
motorsports/print (accessed 29 September 2008).

Habermas, J. (1976) *Legitimation crisis*, trans T. McCarthy, London: Heinemann.

—— (1988) *From theory to practice*, Boston, MA: Beacon Press.

Haider, D. (1992) 'Place wars: new realities of the 1990s', *Economic Development
Quarterly*, 6 (2): 127–134.

Hall, C.M. (1992) *Hallmark tourist events: impacts, management and planning*,
London: Belhaven.

—— (2006) 'Urban entrepreneurship, corporate interests, and sports mega-events:
the thin policies of competitiveness within the hard outcomes of neo-liberalism',
The Sociological Review, 54 (2): 59–70.

Hall, C.M. and Rusher, K. (2004) 'Politics, public policy and the destination', in
Yeoman, I., Robertson, M., Ali-Knight, J., Drummond, S. and McMahon-Beattie, U.

(eds) (2004) *Festivals and events management: an international arts and culture perspective*, Oxford: Elsevier.

Hall, P.A. (1999) 'Social capital in Britain', *British Journal of Political Science*, 29: 417–461.

Hannigan, J. (1998) *Fantasy city: pleasure and profit in the postmodern metropolis*, London: Routledge.

Harvey, D. (1989) *The condition of postmodernity*, Oxford: Blackwell.

Hassan, G., Mean, M. and Tims, C. (2007) *The dreaming city and the power of mass imagination*, Demos Report.

Heard-Bey, F. (1982) *From trucial states to United Arab Emirates: a society in transition*, London: Longman.

Henderson, J.C. (2006) 'Tourism in Dubai: overcoming barriers to destination development', *International Journal of Tourism Research*, 8 (2): 87–99.

Henderson, J.C., Foo, K., Lim, H. and Yip, S. (2010) 'Sports events and tourism: the Singapore Formula One Grand Prix', *International Journal of Event and Festival Management*, 1 (1): 60–73.

Henry, I.P. (1990) (ed.) *Management and planning in the leisure industries*, Basingstoke: Macmillan.

—— (1997) 'Sports policy in Lyon', *Managing Leisure*, 2 (2): 65–81.

Higham, J. (1999) 'Commentary – sport as an avenue of tourism development: an analysis of the positive and negative impacts of sport tourism', *Current Issues in Tourism*, 2 (1): 82–90.

Hiller, H.H. (1998) 'Assessing the impact of mega-events: a linkage model', *Current Issues in Tourism*, 1 (1): 47–57.

—— (2000) 'Mega-events, urban boosterism and growth strategies: an analysis of the objectives and legitimations of the Cape Town 2004 Olympic bid', *International Journal of Urban and Regional Research*, 24 (2): 449–458.

Hitters, E. (2000) 'The social and political construction of a European Cultural Capital: Rotterdam 2001', *International Journal of Cultural Policy*, 6 (2): 183–199.

Hobsbawm, E. (1983a) 'Introduction: inventing traditions', in Hobsbawm, E. and Ranger, T. (eds) *The invention of tradition*, New York: Cambridge University Press.

—— (1983b) 'Mass producing traditions: Europe, 1870–1914', in Hobsbawm, E. and Ranger, T. (eds) *The invention of tradition*, New York: Cambridge University Press.

Horne, J. and Manzenreiter, W. (2004) 'Accounting for mega events: forecast and actual impacts of the 2002 football World Cup finals on the host countries Japan/ Korea', *International Review for the Sociology of Sport*, 39 (2): 187–203.

—— (eds) (2006) *Sports mega events: social scientific analyses of a global phenomenon*, Oxford: Blackwell.

Hubbard, P. and Hall, T. (1998) 'The entrepreneurial city and the "new urban politics"', in Hall, T. and Hubbard, P. (eds) *The entrepreneurial city*, New York: John Wiley & Sons.

Hunter, C. and Shaw, J. (2007) 'The ecological footprint as a key indicator of sustainable tourism', *Tourism Management*, 28 (1): 46–57.

Impacts 08, Creating an impact: Liverpool's experience as European Capital of Culture (2010), available at: www.liv.ac.uk/impacts08/Publications/publications.htm (accessed 15 January 2011).

Ingham, A.G. and McDonald, M.G. (2003) 'Sport and community/*communitas*', in Wilcox, R., Andrews, D.L., Pitter, R. and Irwin, R.L. (eds) *Sporting dystopias: the making and meaning of urban sport cultures*, Albany: State University of New York.

Insight Economics (2006) *Triple bottom line evaluation of the Commonwealth Games*, Report to the Office of Commonwealth Games Coordination.

Jackson, P. (1999) 'Commodity cultures: the traffic in things', *Transactions of the Institute of British Geographers*, 24 (1): 95–108.

Jones, C. (2000) 'Mega-events and host-region impacts: determining the true worth of the 1999 Rugby World Cup', *International Journal of Tourism Research*, 3 (3): 241–251.

Kavaratzis, M. (2004) From city marketing to city branding: towards a theoretical framework for developing city brands, *Place Branding*, 1 (1): 58–73.

Kellner, D. (2003) *Media spectacle*, London: Routledge.

Khalaf, R. and Wallis, W. (2006) ' "Adolescent" Dubai shifts focus of its energy inland', *Financial Times*, 22 May, Lexis Nexis.

Klein, N. (2001) *No logo*, London: Flamingo.

Kong, L. (1999) 'The invention of heritage: popular music in Singapore', *Asian Studies Review*, 23 (1): 1–24.

Kong, L. and Yeoh, B. (2003) *The politics of landscapes in Singapore: constructions of 'nation'*, Syracuse, NY: Syracuse University Press.

Law, C. (2002) *Urban tourism*, London: Continuum.

Lee, M.J. (1993) *Consumer culture reborn: the cultural politics of consumption*, London: Routledge.

Lim, L. (2008) 'Beyond expectations', *The Straits Times*, available at: www.straits times.com (accessed 13 September 2010).

Long, J. and Sanderson, I. (2001) 'The social benefits of sport: where's the proof?', in Gratton, C. and Henry, I.P. (eds) *Sport in the economic and social regeneration*, London: Routledge.

Lowes, M.D. (2002) *Indy dreams and urban nightmares: speed merchants, spectacle, and the struggle over public space in the world-class city*, Toronto: University of Toronto.

McCarthy, J. (1998) *Dublin's Temple Bar: a case study of culture-led regeneration*, Centre for Planning Research, School of Town and Regional Planning, University of Dundee.

—— (2006) 'Regeneration of cultural quarters: public art for place image or place identity?', Journal of Urban Design, 11 (2): 243–262.

McCartney, G., Thomas, S., Thomson, H., Scott, J., Hamilton, V., Hanlon, P., Morrison, D. and Bond, L. (2009) *A systematic review of the impact of major sports events on host populations* (Interim findings report to key stakeholders), Glasgow: MRC Social and Public Health Sciences Unit.

MacDonald, P. (2001) 'Tourism in the Gulf: Dubai shows the way', Arab British Companies Directory.

McDonnell, I., Allen, J., O'Toole, W. and Harris, R. (1999) *Festival and special event management*, Brisbane: John Wiley & Sons.

McGuigan, J. (2005) 'Neo-liberalism, culture and policy', *International Journal of Cultural Policy*, 11 (3): 229–241.

McLain, J.J. (1999) 'The economic impact of Mardi Gras, 1998', *Louisiana Business Review*, 30 (1): 10–12.

—— (2000) 'Mardi Gras: its economic impact', *Louisiana Business Review*, 31 (2): 2–4.

MacLeod, G. (2002) 'From urban entrepreneurialism to a "Revanchist City"? on the spatial injustices of Glasgow's renaissance', *Antipode*, 34 (3): 602–624.

McMullen, E. (2008) 'Night racing in Singapore: Grand Prix tour de force', *Seattle Post-Intelligencer*.

Malcolmson, R.W. (1973) *Popular recreations in English society, 1700–1850*, Cambridge: Cambridge University Press.

Marcuse, P. and Kempen, R. van (2000) 'Conclusion: a changed spatial order', in Marcuse, P. and van Kempen, R. (eds) *Globalizing cities: a new spatial order?*, Oxford: Blackwell Publishing.

Mellor, R. (1997) 'Cool times for a changing city', in Jewson, N. and MacGregor, S. (eds) *Transforming cities: contested governance and new spatial divisions*, London: Routledge.

Miles, S. and Miles, M. (2004) *Consuming cities*, New York: Palgrave Macmillan.

Miller, T. and Yudice, G. (2002) *Cultural policy*, London: Sage.

Mintz, J.R. (1997) *Carnival song and society*, Oxford: Berg.

Misener, L. and Mason, D. (2006) 'Creating community networks: can sporting events offer meaningful sources of social capital?', Managing Leisure, 11 (1): 39–56.

—— (2008) 'Towards a community centred approach to corporate community involvement in the sporting events agenda', *Journal of Management and Organisation*, 16 (4): 495–514.

Mitchell, D. (1995) 'The end of public space? People's Park, definitions of the public and democracy', *Annals of the Association of American Geographers*, 85 (1): 108–133.

Mitchell, R.K., Agle, B.R. and Wood, D.J. (1997) 'Toward a theory of stakeholder identification and salience: defining the principle of who and what really counts', *Academy of Management Review*, 22 (4): 853–866.

Mooney, G. (2004) 'Cultural policy as urban transformation? Critical reflections on Glasgow, European City of Culture 1990', *Local Economy*, 19 (4): 327–340.

Mooney, G. and Johnstone, C. (2000) 'Scotland divided: poverty, inequality and the Scottish Parliament', *Critical Social Policy*, 20 (2): 155–182.

Moore, B. and Sykes, R. (2000) 'Monitoring and evaluation', in Roberts, P. and Sykes, H. (eds) *Urban regeneration: a handbook*, London: Sage.

Mossberg, L. (ed.) (2000) *Evaluation of events: Scandinavian experiences*, New York: Cognizant Communication Corp.

Mules, T. and Faulkner, B. (1996) 'An economic perspective on special events', *Tourism Economics: The Business and Finance of Tourism and Recreation*, 2 (2): 107–118.

Muniz, A.M. and O'Guinn, T.C. (2001) 'Brand community', *Journal of Consumer Research*, 27 (4): 412–432.

Munoz, F. (2006) 'Olympic urbanism and the Olympic villages: planning strategies in Olympic host cities, London, 1908–2012', *The Sociological Review*, 52 (s2): 175–187.

Musgrave, J. and Raj, R. (eds) (2009) *Event management and sustainability*, Wallingford: CABI.

National Statistics (2007) 'Life expectancy at birth and age 65 by local area in the UK, 2004–06', *Health Statistics Quarterly* (Winter 2007).

Nauright, J. (2004) 'Global games: culture, political economy and sport in the globalized world of the 21st century', *Third World Quarterly*, 25 (7): 1325–1336.

Ndlovu, S.M. (2010) 'Sports as cultural diplomacy: the 2010 FIFA World Cup in South Africa's foreign policy', *Soccer & Society*, 11 (1 and 2): 144–153.

New Orleans Convention and Visitor Bureau (2008) Tourism/Hospitality Industry Update, August.

New Orleans Picayune (January 1995) 'Revelers made 1994 a carnival to bank on'.

New Orleans Tourism Marketing Corporation (2007) Press Release, May.

New York Times (February 1999) 'For New Orleans, Mardi Gras is becoming an all-year cash cow', Section 3.6.

Nye, J.S. (2004) *Soft power: the means to success in world politics*, New York: Public Affairs.

O'Brien, D. and Chalip, L. (2007) 'Executive training exercise in sport event leverage', *International Journal of Culture, Tourism and Hospitality Research*, 1 (4): 296–304.

Ooi, C.-S. (2002) *Cultural tourism and tourism cultures*, Copenhagen: Copenhagen Business School Press.

Pacione, M. (2004) 'Environments of disadvantage: geographies of persistent poverty in Glasgow', *Scottish Geographical Journal*, 120 (1–2): 117–132.

Paddison, R. (1993) 'City marketing, image reconstruction and urban regeneration', *Urban Studies*, 30 (2): 339–349.

Peterson, J.E. (2003) 'The United Arab Emirates: economic vibrancy and US interests', *Asian Affairs*, 34 (2): 137–142.

Philo, C. and Kearns, G. (1993) 'Culture, history, capital: a critical introduction to the selling of places', in Kearns, G. (ed.) *Selling places: the city as cultural capital, past and present*, London: Pergamon Press.

Pine, J.P. and Gilmore, J.H. (1999) *The experience economy*, Boston, MA: Harvard Business School Press.

—— (2007) *Authenticity: what consumers really want*, New York: Harvard Business School Press.

PMP Legacy (2005) Feasibility study on Glasgow 2014 Commonwealth Games Bid, London.

Portes, A. (1998) 'Social capital: its origins and applications in modern sociology', *Annual Review of Sociology*, 24: 1–24.

Pratt, A.C. (2005) 'Cultural policy and the cultural industries: an oxymoron?' *International Journal of Cultural Policy*, 11 (1): 31–44.

Preuss, H. (2004) *The economics of staging the Olympics: a comparison of the Games 1972–2008*, Cheltenham: Edward Elgar.

Putnam, R. (1993) 'The prosperous community: social capital and public life', *The American Prospect*, 13: 35–42.

—— (2000) *Bowling alone: the collapse and revival of American community*, New York: Simon & Schuster.

QAA (2008) Hospitality, Tourism, Leisure and Sport Revised Subject Benchmarks, June.

Quinn, B. (2005) 'Arts festivals and the city', *Urban Studies*, 42 (5/6): 927–943.

Ravenscroft, N. and Mateucci, X. (2002) 'The festival as carnivalesque: social governance and control at Pamplona's San Fermin fiesta', *Tourism Culture & Communication*, 4 (1): 1–15.

Reed, R. and Hao, W. (2005) *The Melbourne 2006 Commonwealth Games: implications for the local housing market*, Abstract for the 11th Annual Pacific Rim Real Estate Conference.

Rein, I. and Shields, B. (2007) 'Place branding sports: strategies for differentiating emerging, transitional, negatively viewed and newly industrialized nations', *Place Branding and Public Diplomacy*, 3 (1): 73–85.

Reuters (2008) 'F1 fever grips Singapore', *Reuters Press*, available at: www.times ofmalta.com/articles/view/2008/09/motoring/f1-fever-grips-singapore.229574 (accessed 1 August 2009).

Richards, G. and Palmer, R. (2010) *Eventful cities: cultural management and urban revitalisation*, Oxford: Butterworth-Heinemann.

Richards, G. and Wilson, J. (2004) 'The impact of cultural events on city image: Rotterdam, Cultural Capital of Europe 2001', *Urban Studies*, 41 (10): 1931–1951.

Robertson, R. (1992) *Globalization: social theory and global culture*, London: Sage.

Roche, M. (2000) *Mega-events and modernity: olympics and expos in the growth of global culture*, London: Routledge.

Rojek, C. (1995) *Decentring leisure*, London: Sage.

Sampler, J. and Saeb, E. (2003) *Sand to silicon, achieving rapid growth: lessons from Dubai*, London: Profile Books.

Schimmel, K. (2006) 'Deep play: sports mega events and urban social conditions in the USA', *Sociological Review*, 54 (2): 160–174.

Scottish Government (2009) 'A games legacy for Scotland'.

Sennett, R. (1994) *Flesh and stone*, London: Faber.

Sexton, R.L. (1999) 'Cajun Mardi Gras: cultural objectification and symbolic appropriation in a French tradition', *Ethnology*, 38 (4): 297–313.

Shaw, C.A. (2008) *Five ring circus: myths and realities of the Olympic Games*, Gabriola Island, BC: New Society Publishers.

Shone, A. and Parry, B. (2001) *Successful event management*, London: Continuum.

Short, J.H. and Kim, Y.-H. (1999) *Globalization and the city*, Harlow: Pearson Prentice Hall.

Shoval, N. (2002) 'A new phase in the competition for the Olympic Gold: the London and New York bids for the 2012 Games', *Journal of Urban Affairs*, 24 (5): 583–599.

Silk, M. and Amis, J. (2005) 'Sport tourism, cityscapes and cultural politics', *Sport in Society*, 8 (2): 280–301.

Silvers, J., Bowdin, G., O'Toole, W. and Nelson, K. (2006) 'Towards an international event management body of knowledge (EMBOK)', *Event Management*, 9 (4): 185–198.

Singapore Tourism Board (2008) 'Building your future: building our future', Annual Report 08/09.

Smith, A. (2001) 'Sporting a new image? Sport based regeneration strategies as a means of enhancing the image of the city tourist destination', in Gratton, C. and Henry, I.P. (eds) *Sport in the city*, London: Routledge.

—— (2010) 'The development of "Sport City" zones and their potential value as tourism resources for urban areas', *European Planning Studies*, 18 (3): 385–410.

Smith, A. and Fox, T. (2007) 'From "event-led" to "event themed" regeneration: the 2002 Commonwealth Games legacy programme', *Urban Studies*, 44 (5/6): 1125–1143.

Smith, N. (2002) 'New globalism, new urbanism: gentrification as global urban strategy', *Antipode*, 34 (3): 427–450.

Spindt, P. and Weiss, T. (2009) *The economic impact of Mardi Gras season on the New Orleans economy and the net fiscal benefit of staging Mardi Gras for the City of New Orleans*, Report for the Carnival Krewe Civic Fund, New Orleans.

Sport England (2007) *The economic importance of sport in England, 1985–2005*, Sport Industry Research Centre, Sheffield Hallam University.

Stevenson, D. (2003) *Cities and urban cultures*, Maidenhead: Open University Press.

Stokowski, P. (2004) *Leisure in society: a network structural perspective*, London: Mansell.

Tamney, J.B. (1996) *The struggle over Singapore's soul*, Berlin: Walter de Gruyter.

Tibbot, R. (2002) 'Urban regeneration and sports stadia', *European Planning Studies*, 10 (7): 71–73.

Tönnies, F. (2001) (J. Harris, ed.) *Community and civil society*, Cambridge: Cambridge University Press.

Tourism 2020 Vision (2009), available at: http://unwto.org/facts/eng/vision.htm (accessed 5 July 2011).

Tribe, J. (2004) 'Knowing about tourism: epistemological issues', in Goodson, L. and Phillimore, J. (eds) *Qualitative research in tourism: ontologies, epistemologies and methodologies*, London: Routledge.

Tucker, M. (2008) 'The cultural production of cities: rhetoric or reality? Lessons from Glasgow', *Journal of Retail and Leisure Property*, 7 (1): 21–33.

Turner, V. (ed.) (1982) *Celebration: studies in festivity and ritual*, Washington, DC: Smithsonian Institution Press.

—— (1995) *The ritual process: structure and anti-structure*, Hawthorne, NY: Aldine de Gruyter.

UN World Tourism Organization (2009) 'World tourism barometer', 7 (2).

Van der Wagen, L. (2002) *Event management for tourism: cultural, business and sporting events* (1st edn), Frenchs Forest, NSW: Pearson.

Veblen, T. (1899) *The theory of the leisure class*, Chicago, IL: University of Chicago.

Veyne, P. (1990) *Bread and circuses: historical sociology and political pluralism*, trans. B. Pearce, London: Penguin.

Virilio, P. (2000) *Polar inertia*, London: Routledge.

Vrettos, A. (2006) 'The economic value of arts and culture festivals: a comparison of four European economic impact studies', Masters Thesis, University of Maastricht.

Waitt, G. (2001) 'The Olympic spirit and civic boosterism: the Sydney 2000 Olympics', *Tourism Geographies*, 3 (3): 249–278.

—— (2004) 'A critical examination of Sydney's 2000 Olympic Games', in Yeoman, I., Robertson, M., Ali-Knight, J., Drummond, S. and McMahon-Beattie, U. (eds) *Festivals and events management: an international arts and culture perspective*, Oxford: Elsevier.

—— (2008) 'Urban festivals: geographies of hype, helplessness and hope', *Geography Compass*, 2 (2): 513–537.

Walters, G. (2008) 'Bidding for major sporting events: key issues and challenges faced by sports governing bodies in the UK', Birkbeck Sport Business Centre Research Paper series, 1 (1).

Waterman, S. (1998) 'Carnivals for elites? The cultural politics of arts festivals', *Progress in Human Geography*, 22 (1): 54–74.

Webb, J., Schirato, T. and Danaher, G. (2002) *Understanding Bourdieu*, London: Sage.

Weed, M., Coren, E., Fiore, J., Mansfield, L., Wellard, I., Chatziefstathiou, D. and Dowse, S. (2009) *A systematic review of the evidence base for developing a physical activity and health legacy from the London 2012 Olympic and Paralympic Games*, UK Department of Health.

Whitford, M. (2004) 'Regional development through domestic and tourist event policies: Gold Coast and Brisbane, 1974–2003', *UNLV Journal of Hospitality, Tourism and Leisure Science*, 1: 1–24.

Whitson, D. and Horne, J. (2006) 'Underestimated costs and overestimated benefits? Comparing the outcomes of sports mega-events in Canada and Japan', *Sociological Review*, 54 (2): 71–89.

Whitson, D. and Macintosh, D. (1993) 'Becoming a world-class city: hallmark events and sport franchises in the growth strategies of Western Canadian cities', *Sociology of Sport Journal*, 10 (3): 221–240.

Wilson, E. (2003) *Bohemians: the glamorous outcasts*, London: Tauris Parke Paperbacks.

Xinyi, L. (2008) 'S'pore F1 a roaring success', *The Straits Times*, available at: www.blogs.straitstimes.com/2008/9/28/s-pore-f1-a-roaring-success (accessed 10 August 2009).

Yeoman, I., Robertson, M., Ali-Knight, J., Drummond, S. and McMahon-Beattie, U. (eds) (2004) *Festivals and events management: an international arts and culture perspective*, Oxford: Elsevier.

Youngblood, R. (2008) 'Singapore Grand Prix next weekend will be first Formula 1 night race', in *Bangkok Post*, available at: www.asiathisweek.com/index.php?module=articles&func=display&ptid=9&aid=3713 (accessed 10 August 2009).

Zukin, S. (1995) *The cultures of cities*, Oxford: Blackwell.

Index

Pages containing relevant figures and tables are given in *italic* type.

Abu Dhabi, UAE 42–43
additionality, impact analysis 34, 36, 55
advanced capitalism 50, 52
AEME *see* Association for Event Management Education
Africa: tourist arrivals *38, 40*; 2010 World Cup 3–4, 46, 47
alcohol sponsorship 84
ambulant events *see* peripatetic events
Americanisation 110
Americas: 2016 Rio Olympics 46, 47; tourist arrivals *38, 40*; *see also* United States
Asian Games 43, *43, 44*
Asia-Pacific region: 2008 Beijing Olympics 2–3, 44; India 23, 45; 1998 Kuala Lumpur CWG 121; tourist arrivals 38, 39, 40, *40*, 44–45, *44*; *see also* Singapore
Association for Event Management Education (AEME) 12
attribution, impact analysis 55
Auckland, New Zealand 82–83, 118–119
Australia: Melbourne 84, 85–86, 120; Sydney 69, 71, 105, 127

'Back the Bid' campaign, 2014 Glasgow CWG 126–128
Bahrain F1 Grand Prix *43*
balanced scorecard approach, evaluation 57, *57*
Barcelona, Spain 108, 119, 172

Beijing, China, 2008 Olympics 2–3, *44*
benchmarks, HE events curriculum 11–12
Berlin Olympic Stadium 25
bidding 33, 34, 35, 53–54, 78; Commonwealth Games 118–121; 2014 Commonwealth Games, Glasgow 90, 117, 122–128; European Cities of Culture 5; Olympic Games 46, 72
Black, David 124
Blair, Tony 46
boosterism 29, 33, 45, 50, 52, 67, 160, 165, 167
Bourdieu, Pierre 92, 106–107
brand communities 83–84
branding, destinations 69–71, 78–79, 81–87, 103, 104, 105, 149–150, 165; Dubai 134; Glasgow rebranding 121–122; image/image promotion 58, 69, 71, 77–81; and Mardi Gras, New Orleans 144–148
Brazil, 2016 Rio Olympics 46, 47
bread and circuses 79–80
Bread Not Circuses, Toronto 91
Brenner, Neil 66, 67
budget over-runs 36
Burbank, Matthew 69, 72
Burr, Angela 111

Canada 91, 118; Molson Indy Vancouver 95, 96
candidate cities: European Cities of Culture 5; Olympic Games 2

capital accumulation 71
capitalism 28–29; advanced 50, 52; industrial 23–24; legitimation of 51–54, 54–55
carnivals 26, 79; Notting Hill Carnival, London 111; and public space 23–24; *see also* Mardi Gras, New Orleans
Casey, Derek 126
Chalip, Laurence 81–82
China 2–3, *44*, 45
Chinese New Year 156
Chingay Parade, Singapore 27, 156
cities *see* consuming cities; destinations
'citizen-focused' events 169–172, *170–171*, 175–176
citizen participation 50–51
city boosterism *see* boosterism
city branding *see* branding, destinations
city imaging *see* image/image promotion
civic pride, and European Cities of Culture 5–6
'closed' cities 30
coalitions *see* growth coalitions
Coleman, Richard 57
commodification 30, 78, 81, 108, 109, 146
Commonwealth Games (CWG) 98, 117–118; 2014 Glasgow 90, 117, 122–128; 2002 Manchester 97, 119–120; 2006 Melbourne 120; need for bidding 118–121
communities: brand communities 83–84; and social capital 91–94
Community Benefits Clauses, bidding 90
computable general equilibrium modelling 56
construction company interests 73
consuming cities 76–79, 110; and branding 81–87; figured/disfigured cities 86; selling places 79–81
consumption 29–30, 68, 137, 165, 166
Cornelissen, Scarlett 47
cosmopolitan ethic 106
cosmopolitanism, narratives 124, 126

Costa, Carla 81–82
cost–benefit analysis 56
cultural capital 102; contested ownership 106–111
cultural consumption 84
cultural democracy 5
cultural economy 102–103
Cultural Olympiad, 2012 London 93, 107–108
cultural outcomes 98–99
cultural planning 105
cultural policy 104–106
cultural quarters, cities 105, 110
culture: commodification of 78, 81, 108, 109; 'culture' concept 103–104; and regeneration 104–105, 108, 110; Singapore 154; *see also* European Capitals of Culture (ECoC)
CWG *see* Commonwealth Games

'dead' spaces 29–30
de Certeau, Michel 74
democracy: cultural 5; and legitimation 54–55
demographics, visitors 40
Department of Tourism and Commerce Marketing (DTCM), Dubai 132, 138
destination marketing 39, 70, 79–81, 103, 139, 165–166
destination marketing organisations (DMOs) 70, 137–138
destinations: candidate cities 2, 5; 'closed' cities 30; cultural quarters 105, 110; global recognition 25; and history of events 21–25, 26; holistic 82; 'new divided city' 72; 'soft' attributes 77, 80, 87; sports cities 135; *see also* branding, destinations; consuming cities
'disciplined spontaneity' 24
displacement of residents 51, 94, 98
distinctiveness, loss of 29
divided cities 72
DMOs *see* destination marketing organisations
Doha, Qatar, 2006 Asian Games 43, *43*

DTCM *see* Department of Tourism and
    Commerce Marketing, Dubai
Dubai, UAE 43, 130, 131, *170–171*;
    growth as tourist destination
    131–133; sports event tourism
    133–136; strategy dilemmas 136–139
Durkheim, Émile 22

economic impact assessment/analysis
    32–33, 89–90
economic models, evaluation 55–58, *57*
economic proposition, Olympic Framing
    123, 124, 125
economics: capitalism 23–24, 28–29,
    50; capitalist system legitimation
    51–54, 54–55; cultural economy
    102–103; and impact analysis 35; and
    neoliberalism 66; and tourist arrivals
    37–38
Edensor, Tim 23–24
Edinburgh, UK, Hogmanay 108
education, events 11–13
EMBOK (Event Management Body of
    Knowledge) 12
entrepreneurial event policy 65, 67–71,
    102–103, 136, 166;
    advantages/disadvantages 71–73
equilibrium, economic 56
Europe: state intervention, leisure 24;
    tourist arrivals/expenditure *38, 40,
    41–42, 41–42*; *see also* Germany;
    Italy; Spain; United Kingdom
European Capitals of Culture (ECoC)
    98–99, 122; Liverpool 5–6, 99
Europeanisation 110
evaluation process 49, 168–169;
    economic models 55–58, *57*; and
    legitimation crises 51–54, 54–55;
    measurement 55, 169; and 'official
    future' 50–51; and public
    opinion/protest 58–60
'eventful city' approach 91, 105, 111
EventImpacts 99
event management 7–8, *7*, 11–13,
    174
Event Management Body of Knowledge
    (EMBOK) 12
event policy *7*, 8–10; dimensions,
    trends and implications 172–177, *173*;

need for 10–13; typology and 'pull'
    169–172, *170–171*
event studies *7*, 9–10
events: form and function 25–27;
    growing significance of 1–6; politics
    of 27–30; spatial dimensions 23–25,
    26, 29–30, 73–75, 108, 110–111;
    temporal 21–23, 26, 29; *see also*
    tourism impacts
event analysis 6–13, *7*
event education 11–13
event-led urban strategies 49–51
event profession 175–176
Event Studies (Getz) 10–11
event-themed strategies 87, 108
externalities 34, 36, 163–164

F1 *see* Grand Prix
Fan Parks, Germany 74–75
festivals 106; 'manufacturing' new
    festivals 110; Palio horse race, Siena
    149–150, 174; Pamplona Bull Run
    149, 174; rural 22; Singapore 27, 106,
    155–156, 160; winter/New Year 108,
    156
FIFA *see* World Cup football
figured/disfigured cities 86
flexible space 23
Foley, Malcolm 27
football *see* World Cup football
footloose events *see* peripatetic
    events
Formula 1 *see* Grand Prix

GCMB *see* Glasgow City Marketing
    Bureau
GDP (Gross Domestic Product) 34
gentrification 72
'geographies of helplessness' 86
geographies of 'hope' 82
Germany: Berlin Olympic Stadium 25;
    2006 World Cup 4, 42, *42*, 74–75
'Getting Involved' scheme, Melbourne
    120
Getz, Donald *7*, 10–11
Glasgow City Marketing Bureau
    (GCMB) 70
Glasgow, UK 78, *170–171*; 2014
    Commonwealth Games 90, 117,

122–128; 'Govan Wave of Change' project 93; rebranding campaigns 121–122

global events *see* Olympic Games; World Cup football

global recognition, cities 25

'Govan Wave of Change' project, Glasgow 93

governance *see* neoliberal urban governance

'governed' events 169–172, *170–171*, 175–176

government roles, sports event tourism 136

Grands Prix *43*, *44*; Singapore 156–158

Gratton, Chris 57

Gross Domestic Product (GDP) 34

growth coalitions 50, 53, 59, 65, 67, 68, 78, 81, 137, 165, 171, 176; Melbourne 85–86

growth politics 68–69

Habermas, Jürgen 51–54

Hall, C. Michael 68, 72–73

'hallmark' events 25, 76–77; Notting Hill Carnival, London 111; *see also* Mardi Gras, New Orleans

health agenda 90

Higher Education benchmarks 11–12

historical events 79, 106, 111, 149–150; *see also* Mardi Gras, New Orleans

history of events 21–25, 26

Hobsbawm, Eric 23

Hogmanay, Edinburgh 108

holistic destinations 82

homogeneity, cities/events 80, 109

Horne, John 73, 90

Hospitality, Tourism, Leisure and Sport benchmarks 11–12

idealistic proposition, Olympic Framing 123, 124

identity: Germany and 2006 World Cup 4; and Mardi Gras, New Orleans 143–144; place identity 77; Singapore 155

image/image promotion 58, 69, 71, 77–81; *see also* branding, destinations

impact assessment/analysis 32–33, 35, 55–56; *see also* evaluation process

Impacts 08 programme, Liverpool 5–6, 99

impacts of events: learning from 120–121; negative impacts 97–98

India 23, 45

industrial capitalism 23–24

Industrial Revolution 22–23

input–output model 56

instrumental rationality 52–53

International Olympic Committee (IOC) 46

international tourist arrivals 34, 37–45, *38*, *40–44*

invented traditions 23, 26, 30, 155, 164

Italy: Palio horse race, Siena 149–150, 174; 2006 Winter Olympics, Torino 60

Japan, 2002 World Cup *44*, 45

Kavaratzis, Mihalis 70

Kearns, Gerry 80

Kent, UK, and 2012 Olympics 93

Keynesian multiplier 34–35, 56

Key Performance Indicators (KPIs) 55, 169

Krewes, New Orleans 142–144, 148

Kuala Lumpur, Malaysia 121

La Merce Festival, Barcelona 108, 172

legitimation 51–54, 54–55, 59, 67, 68, 127

leisure: creation of leisure institutions 24; networks 91–92; state intervention 22–23, 24–25, 28–29

leisure management 8

Leisure Studies 9

leveraging 38, 59, 169; social benefits 94–99

lifeworlds 51, 52

Liverpool, UK, ECoC 5–6, 99

London, UK: 2012 Cultural Olympiad 93, 107–108; Notting Hill Carnival 111; 2012 Olympics 46, 93

Lowes, Mark 95, 96

McPherson, Gayle 27
Maktoum family, Dubai 131, 132, 133, 138
Manchester, UK 78–79; 2002 Commonwealth Games 97, 119–120
Mardi Gras, New Orleans 26, 141–144, *170–171*; and destination branding 144–148; strategy dilemmas 148–151
marketability 26, 27
marketing campaigns, bidding 53
marketing, destinations 39, 70, 79–81, 103, 137–138, 139, 165–166; *see also* branding, destinations
market-led coalitions *see* growth coalitions
market-led economics 28–29
market logic 28–29, 58, 66, 69, 70, 159–160, 165
market shares, international tourism 40–41
Martin, Louise 126
Mason, Daniel 85–86
Matheson, Cathy 27
measurement: KPIs, event outcomes 55, 169; tourist impacts 33–37
media coverage 2–3, 4, 147
mega-events 25, 26, 39, 69, 71, 78; importance of 1–6; and political rationale 45–46, 47; *see also* Commonwealth Games (CWG); Olympic Games; World Cup football
Mega-events and Modernity (Roche) 9
Melbourne, Australia 84, 85–86, 120
Mellor, Rose 78
Middle East: tourist arrivals *38*, *40*, 42–44, *43*; *see also* United Arab Emirates (UAE)
Misener, Laura 85–86
Molson Indy Vancouver (MIV) 95, 96
Morrisons, and World Cup bid 174
multiculturalism 106
multiplier analysis 34–35
multiplier effect 56
Mumford, Lewis 77

narratives 74, 124, 126
National Day Parade (NDP), Singapore 155–156

national events *see* European Capitals of Culture (ECoC)
national holidays 24–25
negative impacts 97–98; learning from 120–121
neoliberal urban governance 65, 65–67, 164–165, 166; and event outcomes 71–73; and event policy 67–71; and public spaces 73–75
networks, leisure 91–92
'new divided city' 72
New Orleans Convention and Visitor Bureau (NOCVB) 145
New Orleans, USA *see* Mardi Gras, New Orleans
New Year celebrations 108, 156
New Zealand 82–83, 118–119
Notting Hill Carnival, London 111

'official future' 50–51
'Olympic Framing' 123–125
Olympic Games 26–27, 39, 46, 47, 135, 168; 1992 Barcelona 119; 2008 Beijing 2–3, *44*; benefits of 2–3; and cultural capital 107–108; 2012 London 46, 93; negative impacts 98; and private interests 72–73; 2000 Sydney 69, 71, 127; 2006 Winter Olympics, Torino 60
Olympic Stadium, Berlin 25
'open' events 169–172, *170–171*, 175–176
opening ceremonies 107

Pacific region *see* Asia-Pacific region
Palio horse race, Siena 149–150, 174
Pamplona Bull Run, Spain 149, 174
patriotic proposition, Olympic Framing 123, 124, 125
People's Action Party (PAP), Singapore 153, 155–156
peripatetic events 2, 29, 33; *see also* Commonwealth Games (CWG); Olympic Games; World Cup football
Philo, Chris 80
place marketing *see* destination marketing
'place platform' strategy, Dubai 134

place(s) *see* destinations; space(s)/
  spatial dimensions
'planned' events 169–172, *170–171*,
  175–176
planning, cultural 105
planning, urban 29–30
political interests, bidding 35
politics: of events 27–30; 'growth
  politics' 68–69; and impact
  assessment 33; and rise of mega-
  events 45–46, 47; *see also* evaluation
  process
post-industrial period 26, 76, 79, 86, 92,
  97–98, 110, 122; Singapore 153,
  154–155
power relations 74, 167–168
pre-industrial period 22, 26, 29
private interests 72–73
privatisation, public space 108, 110–111
'profane' versus 'sacred' 22
propaganda exercises 71
public opinion/protest 58–60; 'tactical
  resistance' 74–75
public relations (PR): and 2008 Beijing
  Olympics 2–3; bidding campaigns
  53–54, 126–128
public space(s): and carnivals 23–24;
  creation of 24; privatisation of 108,
  110–111; reclamation of 73–75
public–private coalitions/partnerships
  50, 53, 65, 67, 68, 71, 78, 108, 167,
  171; Melbourne 85–86

Qatar, UAE 39, 43, *43*

race, and Mardi Gras, New Orleans 144
Rational Recreation movement 24
recreational welfare 28
regeneration 6, 26, 72, 90, 93; and
  culture 104–105, 108, 110; and
  spaces 29–30
'regeneration games' period, Olympics
  27
religious festivals 22, 23
resistance events 172, 176–177
resistance, 'tactical' 74–75
return on investment (ROI) 57, 169
Rio de Janeiro, 2016 Olympics 46, 47
Roche, Maurice 2, 9

Rugby World Cup, 1999 Wales 121
rural festivals 22

'sacred' versus 'profane' 22
San Fermin fiesta, Pamplona 149, 174
Schimmel, Kimberley 68
Scottish Commonwealth Games
  Association (CGA) 126
selling places 79–81
Shaw, Christopher 123, 124
Shibli, Simon 57
Shoval, Noam 68
Siena, Italy, Palio horse race 149–150,
  174
Singapore 45, 104, 105, 152–156,
  170–171; festivals 27, 106, 155–156,
  160; Grand Prix 156–158; strategy
  dilemmas 158–160
Single Regeneration Budget (SRB) 120
skills agenda 94
Smith, Neil 66, 72
soccer *see* World Cup football
social capital 91–94, 168; leveraging
  benefits 94–99
social impacts 36, 89–91
social inequalities, and cultural capital
  106–107
social protest groups 58–59
social space 73–75
'soft' attributes, cities 77, 80, 87
'soft' outcomes 87, 99
South Africa, 2010 World Cup 3–4, 46,
  47
South America, 2016 Rio Olympics 46,
  47
South Korea, Asian Games/World Cup
  44, 45
space(s)/spatial dimensions 23–25, 26,
  29–30, 73–75, 108, 110–111
Spain: Barcelona 108, 119, 172;
  Pamplona Bull Run 149, 174
spectacle 77, 78, 86, 103
Spindt, Paul 145–146, 147
sponsorship 73, 84, 147
sports cities 135
sports event tourism: Dubai 133–139;
  Singapore 154, 156–160
Sports Hub, Singapore 156–157
SRB *see* Single Regeneration Budget

198   *Index*

stakeholders/stakeholder theory 72, 73, 93, 96, 97, 100, 167–168
state fairs, US 175
state intervention 167, 171; in leisure 22–23, 24–25, 28–29; *see also* Singapore
state subsidy, cultural events 109
Sydney, Australia: 2000 Olympics 69, 71, 127; Opera House 105
symbolic elements, cities 77–78, 80, 82, 103

'tactical resistance' 74–75
temporal dimensions 21–23, 26, 29
Thaipusam Festival, Singapore 27, 106, 156, 160
Theodore, Nik 66, 67
tiger economies 44–45
time *see* temporal dimensions
tobacco sponsorship 84
tokenism 50–51, 53, 97, 100, 166, 167
Torino, Italy, 2006 Winter Olympics 60
Toronto, Canada 91, 118
tourism: Dubai 131–139; and Mardi Gras, New Orleans 144–148; Singapore 154, 156–160
tourism impacts: measurement 33–37; tourist arrivals 34, 37–45, *38, 40–44*
traditions 22–23, 24, 52, 109; invented 23, 26, 30, 155, 164; *see also* Mardi Gras, New Orleans
transcendence, narratives 124, 126

United Arab Emirates (UAE) 39, 42–43, *43*, 130–131; *see also* Dubai
United Kingdom 32, 60, 108; HE benchmarks 11–12; Hogmanay,
Edinburgh 108; Liverpool, ECoC 5–6, 99; Manchester 78–79, 97, 119–120; 1999 Rugby World Cup, Wales 121; state intervention, leisure 24, 28; *see also* Glasgow; London
United States 3, 46, 68, 69, 175; *see also* Mardi Gras, New Orleans
unity, narratives 124
urban governance *see* neoliberal urban governance
urban planning 29–30
urban symbolism 77–78, 77–78, 80, 82, 103

Vancouver, Canada, MIV 95, 96
vertical ties, social capital 97
Victorian Major Events Company (VMEC), Australia 85
visitor demographics 40

Waitt, Gordon 69, 71
Wales, 1999 Rugby World Cup 121
Weiss, Toni 145–146, 147
Welfare State, and recreation 28
Whitson, David 73, 90
winter festivals 108
Winter Olympics, 2006 Torino 60
working classes, Rational Recreation movement 24
World Cup football 174; 2006 Germany 4, 42, *42*, 74–75; 2002 Japan/South Korea *44*, 45; 2010 South Africa 3–4, 46, 47
World Cup rugby, 1999 Wales 121
World Tourism Organisation (WTO), tourist arrival data *38*, 39, *40–44*